India - One Act of Kindness

Brendan McCauley

India - One Act of Kindness
© Brendan McCauley 2004

First edition January 2004 USA

Second edition February 2004

Published by

Heart of the Fathers
PO Box 38
Downpatrick
Northern Ireland
BT30 6YH

List of Contents

Acknowledgements

Special gratitude to super typists
Judy Mc Gookin and Pat Rafferty
of Coleraine, Northern Ireland.
These golden-fingered ladies
who hail from different tribes
in our divided society are
Holy Spirit bridge builders.
They and their husbands have been
our good friends for many years.

Heartfelt thanks also
to those friends and supporters
who have walked part of the journey
with Angela and I over the years.
Your love, prayers and support
have strengthened our hands
and kept us going.
Keep on keeping on.

Especial appreciation
to our dear friend
Aine Mc Carthy
of Abbeyfeale,
Co. Limerick.
You're a Lady.

Dedication

For my beautiful wife Angela
and our fourteen blessed children,
Shann,
Brendan,
Nora,
Aaron,
Mary,
Hannah,
Ruth,
John,
Patrick,
David,
Jacob,
Isaac,
Abraham,
Angela and
My lovely mother Mary.

1

One Act of Kindness

"How many people have you baptized?" I asked the man lying next to me.

"Twenty five, maybe thirty," he yawned. Outside our cheap hotel room the rain had stopped and a few eager bullfrogs were starting their night shift. Earlier, during a break in the monsoon, I'd watched him immerse ten or eleven young people in the hotel swimming pool.

"Twenty-five or thirty? Back in Ireland, one year I baptized about fifty."

"That's a minimum. It could be more. I'm not sure. Maybe forty thousand. I never counted."

He was talking thousands while I was talking units. The difference in our words and worlds surfaced in my blunder. I'd come to India during the rainy season to search out the story of this man and his family. I wanted to know the secrets of their life and power. I began to ask another question only to be silenced by the steady sound of his breathing. He was asleep, exhausted by a virus and his recent trip to America. My quest would have to wait until morning. I quietly switched off the lights and thought of my suitcases lost in Bahrain. I wished I'd had the foresight to pack earplugs in my hand luggage for outside in the darkness the great slimekings were growing louder and louder by the minute. *How many,* I wondered, *did it take to create such an uproar?*

"Veg or non veg?" The elderly waiter inquired at breakfast. Our table looked out onto the hotel garden and the sea beyond through a large cracked windowpane held together by a faded stick-on sign that barely whispered, "We accept Visa."

"Vegetarian," replied Thampy.

"Same here," I smiled, not wanting meat so early in the day.

Outside, a young barefoot woman, sheltering under the hotel's gazebo, scratched the back of her left leg with her right foot, while shaking and folding her umbrella as she laughed with her friend, all the time looking out at the troubled ocean.

"See the boats?" asked Thampy. On the horizon two specks bobbed up and down hardly visible through the rain. "Small wooden craft," he said. "Fishing."

At the next table the waiter served a non-vegetarian breakfast of scrambled eggs and toast with butter and jam. When he brought our *idiappam* and tomato curry, I regretted I hadn't asked exactly what "veg and non veg" meant.

"Good?" asked Thampy.

"Not too bad."

After breakfast Thampy went back to bed. My small talk had only drained him more. I wandered outside to the beach where the downpour had now stopped. *It's a lot like Ireland,* I mused, *with the rain turning on and off to its own rhythms like a shower with a mind of its own.* I thought of the American comedian, Bob Hope's jibe, "If you don't like the weather in Ireland, wait a minute." Back home we can experience all four seasons within the hour. It could also apply to monsoon India. Only here the shower's thermostat was firmly stuck on a very hot setting. I was missing the fresh summer breezes of home. I was also missing my wife Angela and our fourteen children; my quickest prayer for whom is always, *God bless Shann, Brendan, Nora, Aaron, Mary, Hannah, Ruth, John, Patrick, David, Jacob, Isaac, Abraham and Angela.* I often mention I called my fourteenth child after my wife so as to prove I'm not sexist. Bob Hope is not the only comedian in this story.

I thought of Angela. Summertime, with the kids at home can turn stressful. Regularly we'll have a family or some friends staying over - great fun, but occasionally exhausting. Holidays are important to us. We'll normally combine ministry with holidays in Ireland in counties as far apart as beautiful Donegal and the magnificent kingdom of Kerry. Our old fifteen-seater bright yellow minibus is regularly seen parked in glorious disarray on beaches, at fleadh cheoils, outside churches, outside seisiuns, at Gaelic games, and at friend's homes as we swim, sing, drum, dance, preach, pray, prophesy, kick balls and fellowship our way through the long summer months.

As I stood alone on this beach in Goa I wondered if I had missed it somehow. Was I wasting my time in India? Thampy was in no form for conversation. His wife Mariamma, the wisdom keeper of the family's lore, was in far away Australia. I was eager to gather the story of the harvest of souls in India but no one was talking. I leaned on an old wooden boat and perfunctorily watched two lines of shore fishermen hauling in their nets. My thoughts were elsewhere. I remembered that day in Tamil Nadu when it all began for me. Then I was visiting Mariamma's father, Ranjit Singh, while I waited for my wife to join me from Ireland. Ranjit, a small man in his eighties, was talking over afternoon tea. The air had been hot and stifling and I was ready to nod off when Ranjit began to tell a story. His rhetoric and very proper vocabulary evoked images of former days in India when colonial masters and their wives sipped similar tea on similar afternoons on carefully manicured lawns.

"My father was a scoundrel and a debaucher," Ranjit began. "In his youth he was a very amoral and lazy fellow. His energy was given to alcohol and other base pursuits. One day he and other disreputable chaps were sheltering from the sun underneath a large banyan tree. They were imbibing cheap toddy and gambling. In the midst of their cursing and swearing his attention was distracted from the card game. A beautiful white lady appeared, as if by magic, walking towards them. She was bare headed and bare footed in the midday heat. This sight was very curious to him. Her saffron sari showed she was a spiritual person. A sannyasin. One who has renounced the world and all its pleasures. Dad was fascinated. He thought he was seeing a vision. Across a nearby river a naked child had been crying for a long time. Tears mixed with mucus flowed down its grubby face. Earlier the gamblers had thrown stones to chase it away. But it still remained within an annoying ear range."

Ranjit pushed a plate towards me. "More food please?"

"No thanks. Not just at the moment."

"Please Mr. Brendan. This was made especially for you. Do full justice."

I took another *vadais*.

Ranjit continued, "These people who lived across that river were called Untouchables. They were the lowest of the low. Downtrodden people of lesser value than animals. Dogs were allowed to walk on the main roads but these fellows were not. The beautiful lady forded the river. She picked up the dirty urchin and began to comfort it. She carried the child to the river where she washed it. She dried it with her own handkerchief, all the time lulling it's whimpering with soft and gentle words. She was oblivious that her clothes were being soiled. My father was greatly shocked. Never before had he witnessed such kindness to one of these pariahs. As if in a trance he left his friends and followed the lady and child. They walked into the untouchable village hidden beyond the forest of trees. He watched the lady reunite the child with responsible persons. He quietly followed until she came to her own dwelling in the village. Like the rest it was a kennel-like shelter made from mud, sticks and banana leaves. The floor was made of cow dung. *How can such a wonderful lady live in this filthy place?* he thought. Then he shouted, 'Amma, Amma!' She turned, alarmed at the red eyed drunkard. 'No! No! I won't harm you,' he cried. 'One thing only I desire. Tell me please. What kind of a god is it you serve? What god enables you to love these dirty downtroddens? I want to know this god. Can I worship it? What sacrifice does it require?'

"That's how my father met the young English girl from the Salvation Army," beamed Ranjit. "In India we have 333,000,000 gods. Through that *one act of kindness* my father came to know the true and living God. That one event has changed the history of our family forever." With more than a hint of pride he added, "In time, Papa joined the Salvation Army. He became the first Indian Brigadier General in its history. He became the favorite Indian interpreter of Evangeline Booth, the founder's daughter." Noticing my empty plate, he again said, "Please Mr. Brendan. Do full justice!"

As I awakened next morning his story was running through my mind like a broken record, "One act of kindness. One act of kindness - changed forever - our family forever." I thought of his daughter Mariamma and her husband Thampy, founders of New *India Church of God*. When I first met them in 1996 they had just over four hundred churches. Now a few years later the total was around the one thousand mark. How much a part did that *one act of kindness* play in the history and growth of this work? As I lay alone in that warm dawn listening to the sounds of a nation awakening I pondered just how many other simple acts of love performed in obscurity have changed the history of our world for the better. God only knows. Then clear as a bell the Holy Spirit spoke to my spirit, "I want you to write this story." I knew He meant the story from Rangit's father's conversion to the

9

present day. I thought of all the reasons that disqualified me. I believe indigenous people should write their own stories. What do I know about India and its complex histories and cultures? What in my four visits would enable me to write about this mysterious land that holds one sixth of the world's population? *There are stories about Jesus in Ireland I should write first,* I reasoned. One of my pet hates is foreign Christians writing books about Irish Christianity that have no basis whatsoever in reality. Was I to do the same thing in India? God forbid. I firmly oppose all ethnocentric attitudes that refuse to see how God moves as he wishes in particular situations. The McDonaldization of Christianity is not one of my primary life goals. God is a God of startling variety. I have worked with many cross-cultural Christian groups yet I am still constantly amazed at how uninformed one community can be about their brothers and sisters in another country. Too often I've heard visiting Christians dismiss and demonize much that is precious in Irish Christianity simply because it doesn't exist in their own particular experience. Yet it's not all a one-way street and no one has a monopoly on ignorance. We all have our blind spots.

I remember once talking to a Native American singer/songwriter/ educator called Mitch Walking Elk. We were discussing the many issues his people were facing in modern America. We talked about the similarities between Native Americans and the Irish in their culture, history and how they were treated. I felt we were really gelling. I decided to tell Mitch the story of how the Irish monk St. Brendan the Navigator discovered America long before Christopher Columbus. Mitch listened politely. Then he said, "Brendan, no white man discovered America. We were already here." I was dumbfounded. I imagined myself very much against the injustices of imperialism. Yet all the while my conditioned thinking held me locked into a colonial worldview. That which Oscar Wilde said of cynics could so easily be applied to many of us, "They know the price of everything and the value of nothing." *Lord, help me change my mind,* I had prayed. It's a prayer I mouthed again on the beach at Goa as the fishermen dragged their catch onshore.

A crowd of gulls and dogs and colorful women with wicker baskets on their heads suddenly appeared. I later learned these ladies would immediately take public transport to the surrounding countryside where their customers would be eating fresh fish for lunch. What I love about India, is the absolute newness of a place so ancient, so unlike my own. A marvelous adventure into people's lives, if they'd be so open as to let me in. Many of us in the West are stuck. We may never hear or know the stories of our brothers and sisters in this vast country. We have much to learn, so much to give and so much to receive.

I felt inadequate for the task at hand. I prayed for God to open my eyes as I returned to our hotel. The darkened room was full of the pungent aroma of the Tiger balm emollient Thampy was using. Sleepily he handed me a telephone memo from reception. His daughter Beena had rang. She and her husband Martin would be calling soon to take me to their home for lunch and talk. At last some fish were swimming my way. I wondered what they held in their mouths.

2

Visions of Jesus

On the previous day, Sunday, I'd been prophesying at Martin and Beena's church. Pastor Martin said something that reminded me of John Wimber the 'signs and wonders' man who had so impacted my part of the world in the nineteen eighties. Martin said he'd been relating to the church as if it were his own. Its needs and concerns were consuming his thinking. Before the congregation he repented of this attitude. He gave the church back to God. This is exactly the same message John Wimber brought to the church in the West. With signs following he had boldly proclaimed, "God wants his church back." He declared God wanted his church back from the clutches and control of the elders, pastors, deacons, the select vestries, church boards, trustees and all other such agencies. God wanted to lead His church Himself. It is still a prophecy to be fulfilled. The scripture in Hebrews 11:4, "And by faith he still speaks, even though he is dead," is entirely appropriate in John Wimber's case. His word is still current. Martin had never heard of Wimber.

I'd first met Martin and Beena in 1996 on my initial trip to India. They seemed very much in love for a couple about to have an arranged marriage. Our talk had centered on issues concerning courtship like: "Should the engaged parties ever hold hands or ever talk to one another alone?" I remember little about the conversation except the feeling that Martin was not a man to be hemmed in by tradition. I sensed he would hold hands if he wanted to. I only wish courting Christians in the West should struggle with such issues. Thampy and I flew from Cochin to Goa. Martin and his young son Daniel collected us at the airport. As we drove along Martin began to sing and speak in tongues. Immediately I was given the interpretation. From the back seat, I said, *"Brother Martin do you know the meaning of what you are saying?"* Our eyes met in the windscreen mirror. "No, Brother Brendan. Do you know?"

12

"Yes," I said. *"You are declaring, 'The steps of a righteous man are ordered by the Lord'."* His face lit up like a Christmas tree. "Praise the Lord," he beamed. "That is one of my most favorite verses of scripture. I always use it when I'm praying for people. Hallelujah!" We were off to a good start.

Later Martin, Beena and myself were seated around the table in their flat sipping tea. Overhead the creaking fan took the edge off the midday heat. Three months pregnant with her second child Beena shifted into as comfortable a position as the wooden chair would allow and quietly began to talk. She said, "My parents brought me up in godly and spiritual ways and taught me to love Jesus. When I was six years old Mum gathered us - her four children - together and told us about the Baptism in the Holy Spirit. She then prayed for us and I was filled with the Holy Spirit. I began to speak in tongues. From then on as I watched my parents going about the work of the ministry I knew in my heart God had also called me to do His work. It was six years later, when I was in boarding school, that God really spoke to me clearly for the first time. One night I was wakened out of my sleep by a loud voice that said, 'Beena get up and read Luke 8:10.' I was very sleepy and replied, 'Lord I can't get up and read the Bible now. If I do I will waken all these sleeping children.' Nobody else in the dormitory heard the voice except me. They were all fast asleep. 'Beena get up and read Luke 8:10,' the voice kept repeating. I eventually obeyed. I quietly took my Bible outside to the toilets. I turned on the small light and read:

> The knowledge of the secrets of the kingdom of
> God has been given to you, but to others I speak in parables,
> so that,

> 'though seeing, they may not see;
> though hearing, they may not understand.'

"I had no idea of the meaning of this scripture or how it applied to me. Not knowing what else to do I just learned it off by heart before going back to sleep. This was the first time I heard God's voice. When I went home for the holidays I was so excited. I told everybody who would listen to me about this experience. No one offered any interpretation of the verse. They soon forgot all about it but I never forgot it for a moment. It was always in my heart. Often I would repeat it and pray, *Lord what do You mean by this scripture? Please show me.* It was a year later that God started answering my prayer.

"One night I had a dream in which I felt I was being taken out of this world. Throughout this dream there was also another presence with me. They acted like a guide, but whether they were male, female or an angel I don't know. I was never able to actually see them. In the first part of the dream I was taken to a very beautiful place."

The way Beena pronounced beautiful and the expression on her face made me smile. She was every inch her mother's daughter. Just like Mariamma, she half closed her eyes, pouted her lips and accentuated the chosen word so as to emphasize the meaning while at the same time adding an extra syllable, "*beeeuuuuteeeefull.*" Listening to her was a very visual experience. She said, "In the place where I was taken in my dream people moved around as if they were floating. It was then I realized I was not on this earth. It was wonderful to be there. I said to the presence with me, 'I can feel so much love and peace here.' Even when no one was talking I was constantly aware of a marvelous atmosphere of love and tranquility. I was wondering where I was. Then I saw someone walking in front of me. Although His back was toward me I knew it was Jesus. I told the presence beside me, 'I think it is Jesus.' When I said this, the figure turned and looked directly at me. It was Jesus! He tenderly gazed at me the way a mother would look at her small child. Immediately I ran to Him. We embraced. I felt so loved, so secure, yet a part of me was also baffled. I knew I wasn't dead but still very much alive. 'Lord Jesus,' I said, 'do You know how many people there are on the earth that are longing for Your return?' He just smiled and continued to hold me in His arms. I asked him about a Christian friend who had died sometime before, 'Lord where is Shibu?' He replied, 'He is here. He is happy here.' When He said this I saw Shibu's face in front of a big mansion. The wind was blowing through his hair and he had a big smile. Then I turned and saw Jesus in a beautiful garden playing happily with lots of small children. All this time I had a feeling of being soaked in pure love and peace. Then I was taken somewhere else and shown many rooms in a large building. They were of all different shapes and sizes and colors. I couldn't fully grasp what I was seeing because here everything was so different from earth. Then the presence took me to a huge lounge and said, 'In the Father's house are many mansions.' I said, 'I thought each person got their own mansion.' 'There are mansions and there are rooms like this as well,' the presence said. After this I was taken to a place through an entrance like a long dark cave. The atmosphere there was of terrible fear; so much fear. At this point I thought, *Lord I'm dead and I'm going to hell.*

"I have never experienced such fear in my life. It actually came inside and completely paralyzed me. I was totally numb. Other people were also here. They seemed like shadows drifting through the thick smoke. A dreadful heat was everywhere. The presence explained, 'This is how the people come to hell. They pass through here on their way to the fire.' I looked and saw an area where the heat burned hot as a furnace. Then I saw some people rushing towards us. 'These poor people have got their lives back and are returning again to earth,' the presence said. They were running as fast as they could. As they charged past us I could see horror etched on their faces. Then, thank God, I woke up but that terrible fear was still with me. It remained day and night for two weeks. During this time I realized I'd been allowed to experience a little of both heaven and hell. The fear that stayed with me produced a great feeling of numbness. The dread that people experience when they realize that they are going to hell is terrible beyond words. That place is totally empty of all love. This dream had the effect of strongly encouraging me to share the good news of Jesus to all my friends and everyone I met. Each morning at college I'd pray, *Lord, please give me an opportunity to share your gospel today.* I'd tell others what I had seen and heard. I also explained from the Bible about the awful realities of heaven and hell. When I thought about the great love and peace of heaven and the terrible fears in hell I was all the more strengthened to serve my Lord. The fire in me burned brighter and brighter. I knew this was what I wanted to do with my life. I longed so much to bring people to the place of eternal life where the love was. In heaven, even more than the joy, was the wonderful feeling of God's love. I wish everyone could experience that love."

"What did Jesus look like?"

Beena thought for a moment before replying, "I can't exactly remember the details of His face. I only remember it was full of love. I can still see His eyes. I remember His eyes so well. They were eyes beaming with love."

Outside the cawing of crows startled me. I suddenly realized I was very thirsty. I quickly finished my now cool tea. Beena continued, "Once when there were severe persecutions in the church, God gave me another dream. I was fifteen or sixteen at the time. This was a very difficult period for me. The church was growing very quickly and the whole ministry was moving onto a new level. Satan really started to attack us. He stirred up some people to say bad things about my dad. They claimed he was stealing kidneys from people and selling them to countries in the West. This lie became big news in the whole of Kerala. In many churches people were being warned from the pulpit to keep away from my dad. 'Thampy will steal your kidneys,' they said."

Martin explained another man also named Thampy had been arrested for suspected kidney trafficking. Enemies of *New India Church of God* had taken advantage of this to start rumors so as to cause confusion among the people. (I later learned Thampy, which means second son, is a very common name in India) Beena said, "I became scared to go to college. Everyone was talking about these things. On the bus people would be gossiping. They'd say things like, 'Did you hear Pastor Thampy has been arrested at Cochin airport? When the customs opened his suitcase it was packed full of kidneys.' I was too embarrassed to go outside and too ashamed to go to school. All the pupils had heard these bad stories. Dad wasn't troubled at all by these rumors. He was so excited about the good things God was doing in the ministry. He was always singing and rejoicing. One night I was really calling out to God. I asked, 'Lord why is all of this happening to us?' We were just youngsters. It was really very difficult and upsetting. Before I went to sleep I began to sing *'Open My Eyes Lord, I Want To See Jesus.'* I sang with all my heart. Then I had a vision. I saw a small light coming toward me. It grew into a large movie screen. On the screen a mountain appeared. Then I saw a cross on top of the mountain. Jesus was on the cross. I cried out, 'Oh Jesus!' His whole body, from head to toe, was full of blood. His hair was wet with fresh blood that ran down all over His face. Blood was coming from the thorns in His head. From His hands, His feet and His side. No part of His body was free from blood. He looked at me. His eyes were blood red. They were just staring at me. Then a voice told me, 'Beena I am suffering this for you; to redeem you. I am going through all this pain for you.' When I heard this I started to cry.

"Then one by one I was shown the persecutions Jesus went through.

I saw him being pushed from one place to another. They were mocking Him. Then I saw people beating him with a big whip. After each stroke flesh was torn from his body and blood gushed from the wounds. At every single lash He turned and looked at me. The voice said, 'Beena this pain is for you, to redeem you.' Then I saw four or five people gather around Him. They began to scoff. They talked bad words as they jeered and laughed. Each time they said these evil things, He would silently turn and look at me. Throughout all this I kept saying, 'Lord, I don't want to see them do this to You.' Then they spat at Him. On the face. On the nose. On the neck. In His eyes. He closed His eyes and turned His face because of the spittle. Then He looked at me. I could hear the voice softly saying, 'Beena, it's all for you. I'm suffering this humiliation for you.' Then the screen went blank. Afterwards I saw Jesus going up into the sky. He was still looking at me only this time He was smiling and His eyes were full of love. I could plainly see the scars in His hands and feet. They were so fresh. Then another light came and wrote in the Malayalam language beneath the figure of Jesus, *I'll be coming back just like I'm going.* Still in the vision I saw myself sharing all of this with my Hindu friend Maya. She was saying, 'Beena, all you have said is true. Now I understand. This is the truth. I believe.' Then on the screen appeared a large field and beyond it a big city full of lights. I said to Maya, 'Look at that beautiful city. That is where we are going to go when Jesus comes back for us.' That was the vision. When I opened my eyes they were still flowing with tears. I was weeping and weeping and weeping.

"That vision really encouraged and strengthened me. I was able to rejoice after that. I thought of all that Jesus had suffered for me. It put my little troubles concerning the 'kidney rumors' into perspective. Our family and the whole church were strengthened through that vision."

"Did you ever share this vision with your friend Maya?"

"Yes, I shared it with twelve of my school friends. Ten were nominal Christians, one was a Brahmin and the other was Maya. They all received Jesus as their Savior. The Brahmin girl is a very strong Christian although she has remained a secret believer. Unfortunately I couldn't invite the denominational Christian girls to our church because in Kerala Pentecostal believers don't allow the wearing of jewelry. I didn't want to get into these issues. I was just happy I had the opportunity to share my vision with my friends and that they'd accepted Jesus as their Lord and Savior."

17

Beena was now in full flow. Other dreams and visions flooded back to her. She said, "I'd like to share an incident that happened when I was seventeen concerning my examination results for university entrance. In Kerala a lot of importance is attached to education. It is considered a big shame for the parents and the pupil if major exams are failed. The examination numbers of successful candidates are always posted upon a notice board at the college. Biju, my elder brother, went to get my results. When he looked at the pass sheet my number wasn't there. I was so shocked. I couldn't believe I'd failed for I'd worked very hard. That night I cried like I've never cried in my whole life. I wept until my strength was gone. I was exhausted. Then someone came to me and put their arms around me. I could only see the arms and one hand. I can remember that hand so clearly. When it embraced me it didn't feel like a human hand at all. It felt cold like snow. The instant it touched me all my burden and concern about the exams left immediately.

"For ten to fifteen seconds I felt so secure in that embrace. Then the person spoke to me like a friend, saying, 'Don't be afraid. Why are you so worried? I am here with you.' I was so relieved and refreshed. I felt the love and the joy of the Lord. I then had a good night's sleep. When I got up in the morning the local newspaper carried details of my exam results. I had passed with flying colors. The sheet at the college had been in error. All day I kept wondering about the meaning of this experience. I think Jesus had been upset because I was upset. He'd come to comfort me. The next day a prophet came to our home. He prophesied God would speak to me in visions and dreams. He said, 'Even two nights ago I came and embraced you. You are special to me.' This was a confirmation. It really encouraged and strengthened me."

"What did this prophet look like?"

"He was a small fellow around fifty years old."

"Was he called Iype?"

"Yes," she exclaimed. "Do you know him?"

The previous week I'd been sitting in Thampy's house at Chingavanam talking to Pastor T. M. Kuruvilla. He has been with Thampy from the very early days. He is one of Thampy's right hand men. Better known as Rajan, he is currently principal of the Bible School there. He is also an accomplished teacher/preacher/writer and a great interpreter. He has interpreted for me many times. Like all skilled people he makes it seem very easy. Without an interpreter one is lost in India. We were discussing a recent article he had written about various crusades throughout the history of the *New India Church of God* when Iype just wandered into the room unannounced. Rajan talked to him in Malayalam. He then said to me, "This fellow is in the same business as you. He is also a prophet."

"Tell him that," I replied.

When Iype discovered this news he immediately prophesied and prayed for me while Rajan interpreted. I then prophesied and prayed for him, Rajan again interpreting. Then he was gone just as quickly as he'd appeared. I related this information about our common friend to Beena.

"That's the way it is with some prophets," Beena said. "They're like the wind, blown here and there by the Spirit. You never know where or when they'll appear next." I liked her wisdom. She continued, "After the experience with the exam results I got very close to God. I became very strong in the Lord. I started reading and sharing His word more. I also made a decision to pray and fast for three days each month. I'd felt the presence of God and I didn't want to lose it. I prayed, *Lord I want to know You more.* Those were very intimate days for me. Afterwards God began to speak to me clearly through His word. Sometimes, in dreams, I would also see written scriptures. Not chapter and verse but actual scriptures I hadn't known before, written in Malayalam. I'd go to Mum and share these things with her. She'd always take me seriously and encourage me. She'd also know where the verses were in the Bible. One I remember was from Psalm 37:25. It said, 'I have never seen the righteous forsaken or their children begging bread.' Another from Daniel 10:14 said, 'Now I have come to explain to you what will happen to your people in the future, for the vision concerns a time yet to come.' Mum and I were always so blessed and encouraged when this happened.

"Around the time my marriage was arranged I was also finishing my degree in English. This was a very stressful period for me. One day I felt completely overwhelmed. I cried out, 'Lord how can I cope. How can I cope?' That night, I had a vision in which I saw two people coming down from above. They were both female. They had candles in their hands. They were dressed like normal people in saris. One went off to someone else and one came to me. She started talking as if she'd known me all my life. When she approached I felt the closeness of God so strongly. She asked, 'Do you know who I am?' I said, 'I know you're from God because I can feel His presence.' Then I started speaking in tongues. She said, 'Beena why are you so feeling so worried? Do you not know when your heart aches the heart of God also aches? Put your trust in Him. When you have problems, leave them to Him. He is there to carry your burdens.' She was speaking like a friend, mentioning issues concerning our family and giving me advice. She said things like, 'You are going through that because of such and such . . .' She also told me to, 'Take it easy.' When this person started speaking to me immediately my burdens lifted. I responded like a friend. We even started joking together. She commented about Biju. She said, 'Biju is doing an excellent job.' I felt really comfortable speaking with her. Then suddenly she just left. She'd talked about Mum and other family members as if she knew them so well. Biju was in England at Mattersey Bible School in those days. I told my mum about this experience. She was very encouraged especially about the part concerning Biju. From then onwards I don't carry the burden myself when I have problems. I give it to God. I believe when my heart aches then God's heart aches as well. I don't want that to happen. I know God loves and cares for me. I don't want to cause Him any pain by carrying hurt in my heart. The Bible tells us not to let our hearts be troubled. I also remember another dream that I had when I was engaged to Martin."

Martin who is listening to Beena's story pipes up and says, "I was engaged to all these dreams!" We laughed.

"In this dream," said Beena, "I was standing outside my house looking up into the sky at something, which at first, I thought was an airplane. As I continued to watch I realized it was not an airplane but an angel gliding in the sky. She was wearing a white dress. She had long hair. As this angel passed I saw five flags appear in the sky. One was American, one was Australian and one was a white and red color. I tried to look at the other flags but they disappeared before I could recognize them. Still in the same dream, I saw the identical scene repeat itself. As before I couldn't remember the last two flags."

"These are the nations you will travel to while preaching the word and telling your story," I said.

"Maybe?" She mused.

"No. Not maybe. This is typical of God. Some things He will show us clearly. Some things not so clearly while other things may be completely hidden. He talks to us in dark speech, because it is always His intention we

20

keep close to Him for further revelation. It says in Job 33, sometimes God speaks to us in dreams we forget. He seals it up so we may not perceive it. He does this because He wants to keep us from pride. This may be the case here. Three of the flags, representing nations, are not yet fully revealed to you. We must be careful when and to whom we share our revelations. In the scriptures, Joseph got into a lot of trouble with his brothers because he naively shared his dreams with them."

Martin said, "Around this time we were getting married and I was anxiously asking the Lord about His plans for our lives. This dream settled my heart. I realized our marriage would not limit me. Through this dream I knew God would open five nations to us in His time. I forget many of Beena's dreams and visions but I haven't forgotten this one. It continues to encourage and strengthen me."

"Maybe that's why the Lord gave Beena the dream twice; once for her and once for you. Certainly He was underlining his intentions."

Beena said, "After we got married the doors opened for us to go to Australia. I've always had such a hunger and a desire to serve God. In the past I was such an inferior person. A lot of these dreams and visions have made me feel better about myself. I always think my sister and brothers are more intelligent than me. They seem to pick up things so quickly but I'm not that sort of person. But then God started speaking to me through various people. He said He had different plans and purposes for me."

As Beena was speaking I experienced a strong anointing of the Lord upon me. I loudly and slowly proclaimed, "You *are a prophetess! You are a prophetess! You are a prophetess!"* She stared at me and we all fell silent. The noise from the ceiling fan filled the room as it clanked away at its work. Martin touched Beena's hand and spoke quietly in Malayalam. At this point the telephone rang. Beena went to answer it. I stood up and stretched my legs. The lady who helped Beena, for an hour each day, was making chapattis, rolling the dough, sprinkling it with flour and kneading in oil. She was very nimble-fingered. Out the front window I saw four men in a shop playing cards as they waited for customers. There were large puddles all over the street although the rain had stopped. I looked out the back window and among the jackfruit and coconut trees a large pot bellied pig was noisily rooting in the long grass. Further along, four long horned cows were slopping through the watery ground. Down to the right a man was sleeping behind the wheel of his parked car. The driver's door was open. A small lady in a bright green sari waddled past carrying a load of sticks on her head. A ginger cat crossed her path and began to follow her.

Beena returned. She said, "Just now Martin reminded me of something that happened five weeks ago. The previous night I'd prayed, 'Lord what is it You want me to do in Your Kingdom?' At the time I was feeling like I was accomplishing nothing. I wanted to do more. I wanted direction. Early morning, as I lay in bed, I heard a voice. It said to Martin, 'Your wife is a prophetess and a governor for My kingdom.' Martin, sound asleep, didn't hear it. I was so excited. Later that morning at the Ladies Prayer Meeting I shared I'd heard the voice of God and that I was greatly encouraged. I was too embarrassed to mention the part about the, 'prophetess and a governor.' I called my mum and told her about it. Her excitement gave me the confidence to share it with Martin. Unfortunately Mum told my brothers who started to tease me about it. 'Hello, Governor Beena,' they laughed when I talked to them on the telephone. They were only teasing but it made me want to forget all about the whole thing. But just now after you prophesied three times, 'You are a prophetess,' Martin said to me, 'Beena do you remember what the voice said?' Now I am greatly encouraged because you have confirmed part of what the voice spoke. There was no way you could have known about this."

I said, *"One of the most important purposes of prophecy is to confirm to believers what God has already said to them. Under the old covenant it was mainly only the kings and the prophets that were filled with the Holy Spirit. Now under the new covenant all believers can be filled with and be led by the Holy Spirit. In 1 Corinthians 13 it says we know in part and prophesy in part. Isn't it interesting you heard God tell Martin you were a governor and a prophetess? I only received fifty percent of the revelation and Martin who was asleep heard none of it."*

Beena stood up and stretched. The wooden chair and her pregnancy were taking their toll. She would have to rest for a while to relieve her back pain. As she left the room she mentioned it was Biju her older brother who had just phoned. "He's coming over to join us," she said. "He said he has something very important to share with you."

3

The Rubber Hand

Thampy and Mariamma have four children. Their names are Biju, Bini, Beena and Binu. I know what you are thinking but please don't go there, don't even think about it. This is India with its own values and customs. No ethnocentric attitudes please. And hey, I have fourteen children. I know all their names backwards, forwards, upwards and downwards. Though now and then their mother experiences some difficulty. When under pressure, she'll say to one of the offending boys, "John? . . . Patrick? . . . David? . . . whatever your name is - stop that right now!" while one of the girls may find themselves on the receiving end of, "Mary? . . . Hannah? . . . Ruth? . . . whatever your name is - get off that telephone immediately!"

It could also be a lot worse. Beena's husband Martin's siblings are called Marshall, Merlin, Merin, Mercy, Marlow and Marvel. I'm only asking you to get to know Biju, Bini, Beena and Binu at this juncture. No trouble to you if you have read this far. Did you know only 13% of readers ever get beyond the first chapter? You're a winner if you've got this far! So let's go.

Biju, male, the tallest and eldest, has studied at Bible School in England. He is principal of the Bible School in Goa. He is married to Secu. They have a son called Timothy. Biju is full of giftings and confidence being a singer, teacher, preacher, evangelist etc. My call is he's an apostle. Like his father he plants churches, lots of churches. Bini, the eldest girl and second child is married to Shibu. They have one daughter called Ashlyn and at present they live in the state of Oklahoma in America. I have never met Bini but look forward to it. Once Mariamma said, "Oh Brendan, Bini is the best one for stories. You haven't heard anything until you've talked to her. Even when she has finished she'll say, 'Oh and just one more thing.' She is like a preacher that has difficulty finishing a sermon."

Because I haven't personally spoken to Bini she appears in the pages of this book only in the stories of others. Another day another race, for Bini and I. Beena is the third child and second daughter. She is the *dreamer of dreams* we've been listening to in the last chapter. She is married to Pastor Martin. They have one child called Daniel who sports a great smile. She is pregnant at the moment with her second child and with a growing vision for a great work of mercy among the poor and needy in India. Binu, the youngest son and youngest child is on his way home after spending three years at Bible School in Australia. He is a visionary, a man of change, a man of ideas, and a man for the future. When God is doing a new thing Binu will be one of the first into it. He may suffer much for this pioneering spirit that he has inherited from his parents.

Beena arose and we had lunch. Biju had joined us by then. Like myself he enjoys humor. I brought up the issue of Thampy's alleged kidney trafficking. Biju laughed, "Johnny was one of our drivers at our headquarters. One day a local fellow came and said, 'Johnny I need some money. Do you think Pastor Thampy would buy one of my kidneys?' Johnny told him he didn't look too healthy so his kidneys might not be worth too much. He said unfortunately our freezers were crammed full of kidneys at that moment. But he promised if we ran out of stock and if demand picked up he'd get back to him.

"Another believer, also named Johnny, worked for us. He maintained the property and looked after the milky cows. He was always happily going about his duties singing and saying, 'Sthothram, Sthothram.' (In the Malayalam language Sthothram, means 'Praise the Lord.' If you ever go amongst Christians in Kerala, you'll hear it often.) Johnny didn't have a bicycle. He walked everywhere. One day a few fellows were standing at the corner of our road in Kottayam. As Johnny sauntered past one of them remarked, 'Look at that poor man. He has no energy at all. Thampy has taken most of his kidneys. Now he has only four or five left.' People used to joke on the buses. When they'd stop outside our property, they'd call to one another, 'Be careful at Bethesda. Keep a close watch on your kidneys.'

"Another story is told of an imagined trip to London. The customs people at the airport supposedly opened Dad's suitcases. They discovered a big brown paper parcel they made him open. With shivering hands he slowly unwrapped it and, lo and behold, inside was a fresh and quivering kidney. Other rumors claimed there was a huge wanted poster of Thampy at Bombay

Airport. My sisters and many of the church children were being badly teased and picked on at school about this 'kidney stealing.' For me the whole thing was very funny, but for Beena and Binu, who were younger, it was a very difficult time."

Beena said, "Many of the older people didn't know what kidneys were. Nevertheless they were very frightened by the whole thing. Whatever few kidneys they had they wanted to keep. People were saying things like, 'There are no kidneys left in the whole of that church.' There was lots of misinformation and confusion everywhere. We even got phone calls from America and the Gulf countries inquiring about what was happening. It's amazing how fast bad news travels. People would ring up and say, 'We have heard Thampy is in jail for stealing kidneys. What is going to happen?' It was a terrible time for me personally. I was so embarrassed.

"Dad wasn't at all bothered by any of this. That year thirty new churches were birthed in the midst of all this persecution. He was too busy getting on with the work of the Lord to pay attention to these accusations. That year, after one Sunday service, about five hundred of our church people decided to conduct an open-air meeting in our town. This was the day before the start of our national convention. One of the men who'd started the kidney rumors was a believer. He'd been talked to about his behavior in regards to an affair with a woman. He was very angry for being corrected and set out to spoil the name of the ministry. It is thought a denominational leader, who was very much against Dad's ministry, egged him on in this. He printed leaflets against Dad and distributed them far and wide. While our open air celebration was taking place our enemy and his supporters climbed onto a high building and rained thousands of these leaflets all over our worshipping people.

"On the third night of the convention they attacked us with fiery rockets launched at the pandhal. (A large covering for a crowd of people made of dried coconut leaves.) This happened twice during the convention. Dad brought one of the rockets to the pulpit and holding it high where everyone could see it, proclaimed that all the fiery darts of hell could not stop the work of the Lord. Our opponents also set off loud firecrackers during the preaching to distract the people. In the end it turned out badly for the main rumormonger. He lost all peace and committed suicide by drinking poison. Another rumormonger, a young man in his late twenties, got drunk and caused uproar by jumping up and down in front of a senior pastor's house. He was shouting, 'Thampy, kidney, Thampy, kidney. Your leader is a kidney thief.' Afterwards he went home and fought with his father who beat him to death. Another man ended up with huge debts and committed suicide by jumping off a train. Eventually all our persecutors were gone and believers came and bought their properties. Now the whole place around us is filled with believers. In the end, despite all the harassment, what the enemy meant for evil the Lord turned for good."

Our talk turned to how Satan and his hoards will always try to prevent the work of the Lord going forward just like the enemies of Nehemiah who did all they could do to discourage him from rebuilding the walls of Jerusalem.

Beena said, "When I was sixteen, I was sleeping with Mum because Dad was away on a missions trip. The whole time I was praying, *Lord use me for Your Kingdom.* I was speaking in tongues for maybe three or four hours. Mama, a great prayer warrior is my example. Even in the night when she is sleeping she continues to pray. If the least noise happens she wakes up and begins speaking in tongues and praying. As I lay there trying to sleep, because the next day I had to go to college, a strange thing happened. I heard a female voice but I also sensed the presence of evil. At that time I was trying to grow my hair longer for my wedding. The voices of angels that I hear are all feminine. This voice gave a mocking laugh and said, 'Beena you are looking good with your long hair.' As it spoke my hands lost all sensation. I couldn't talk as it began to scoff at me. It asked, 'Who is this Jesus to you?' My hands and legs went totally numb. Although I was conscious I couldn't open my eyes. My tongue went down. I felt paralyzed. Only inside was I active. I've had a few other experiences like this. When the evil spirits come to attack me it's as if my whole body is paralyzed. In my spirit I began to speak in tongues. Then the taunting voice said, 'You are not going to do anything for Jesus.' In my heart I was saying, 'Jesus is everything to me. I will live my life totally for Jesus.' 'Ha, ha, ha,' it laughed. I continued speaking in tongues and my strength returned. I was able to awaken my mum. When I thought about it I was encouraged by this experience because I realized the enemy was trying to stop my prayers. It showed me the devil knows certain things about us. The voice knew my name and spoke of the long hair I was trying to grow.

"Another time Mum went to Jaipur in North India for a final exam for her masters in Divinity. My exams were also going on at this time. I had to get up early in the morning, 5 AM, to study. The previous night, alone in my room, I'd prayed for a long time. Suddenly my whole body became paralyzed. I couldn't move a finger. I was lying sideways on my bed. I got this strange feeling that something or somebody was holding me very tightly. I thought, *What is this? I'm sleeping alone in this room?* I had the courage to reach down and touch this hand. It felt like rubber. It had fingers, but no bones. It felt like a rubber hand. Immediately I started speaking in tongues. After I got released I sat up and prayed for a long time. Then I went and told what happened to my family and our intercessors. The next day I also told my college friends about this strange thing. Mum came back from Jaipur and before she even put her bags down, she said, 'Beena you will not believe what happened to me.' She had experienced the exact same thing, the same day, the same time. She'd had the same phenomenon: a hand around her middle, no bones, like rubber, so soft but nothing inside. Even now I'm not sure why this happened to us? Later someone told Mama that for devils there are no bones but I don't know. Mama has a gift for the discerning of spirits. When she goes to a place she knows if there are evil spirits there. Mama has discerned spirits in thousands of people."

"Have you ever physically seen angels or demons?"

"Never physically. I've often seen the manifestation of demons in people's lives. I've seen blood coming out of people's mouths and teeth coming down."

"Teeth coming down?"

"Yes, one girl's teeth came down. During her deliverance two big teeth came down and blood came out of her mouth. I also saw one woman's tongue come out of her mouth - over a foot long. There is a certain bloodthirsty demon that exhibits this trait. When the people are manifesting demons they can't look at Mama's face. They say things like, 'No. No. I can't look at you. I see Jesus in your face.'"

Biju, who was quietly listening, said, "The hand of the Lord is mighty but the hand of the devil is weak. It is only a rubber hand. It doesn't have a bone. Nevertheless it's not pleasant when it comes to frighten you. The Lord's hand comes upon us to preach and prophesy and move in the Spirit. The rubber hand comes only to paralyze and cause fear. Fear is the main weapon of the enemy. So often in scripture when angels appear the very first thing they say is, 'Fear not!' The purpose of the rubber hand and these experiences from the enemy is to immobilize believers. I personally have never encountered the rubber hand but I've had similar experiences where my body became paralyzed. Sometimes, when the presence of the enemy is strong, I've experienced a choking sensation where my tongue seems stuck in the back of my throat. Many times, when we go to a new place for ministry or when God is using us powerfully or when things are really happening, the enemy will go all out to stop us. He seeks to scare us. The Bible talks about the two main jobs of the devil. First, he is the deceiver and second, he is the accuser. In reality he cannot do very much against the believer, so he seeks to deceive us and frighten us.

"There was a little temple on the property in Ponda that we bought for our Bible School. After we acquired this land we had to face a lot of attack in the spiritual realm. One night when I was sleeping there I felt as if a snake was crawling all over me. I woke up put the light on and shook the bedclothes. Though there was nothing to be seen I could sense a very evil presence in the room. I was really tired so I went back to sleep. Then I was awakened by the sound of many feet running. It sounded like a big army. I jumped up, looked outside, but there was no one there. Again I went back to sleep. Suddenly something came and choked me by the throat. I awoke and was fully conscious but I couldn't speak. My tongue just went down. My hands were frozen. My legs were paralyzed. All this time my inner man was completely conscious and in my spirit I began to plead the blood and the name of Jesus. I kept saying, 'Jesus, Jesus, Jesus.' Eventually my tongue was released. I was able to pray aloud. We are accustomed to this sort of happening especially as we take the gospel into unreached areas where it has never been preached before.

"When I was at Bible School in England I'd sometimes tell my fellow students and teachers about experiences like this. They wouldn't believe me. They had theological reasons why these things can't happen. In Bible School there was a guy called Oliver (not his real name). He was about thirty years old and from Edinburgh, Scotland. He had links with the Chinese community. From them he learned Kung Fu and became a ninja black belt. Oliver had been a Satan worshipper before he was saved. He was an unusual guy, very quiet. He was going out with a girl named Linda (not her real name) who was about eighteen years old. She was pretty but childish and immature while he was just kind of weird. In the West whether people go out together or not is their personal decision but that sort of thing would never happen in India. One day I was reading a newspaper when Linda came running into the room. She said, 'Biju I need to talk to you. Oliver and I went for a walk in the woods tonight. All day he has been depressed. All of a sudden he began to make strange noises. Then he fell flat on the ground. He's lying near the bridge. I'll show you.' This all happened just five minutes walk from the college. I told her to stay in the college while I went and looked for him. My friends Sam Mooney, from Northern Ireland and, Nicky Charles, a West Indian from London, were there. We ran to the bridge shouting, 'Oliver, where are you?' I felt a strong sense of evil. When I discern evil my entire body feels it strongly. Don't make a theology of it but this is my experience. I kept shouting Oliver's name. Moonlight was streaming through the trees.

"Suddenly I heard a growling noise like a tiger. I rushed over to where it was coming from. I said, 'In the name of Jesus, stand up!' The next moment Oliver was standing in front of me. He lunged and tried to punch me with all of his strength while screaming at the top of his voice. He was trying to smash me in the face but his hands couldn't make contact. It was as if a shield was covering me. Sam and Nicky were frozen to the spot. They didn't know what to do. I realized a guy from the Bible School screaming at the top of his lungs was not a good witness to the local people. So I said, 'In the name of Jesus, shut up!' He fell silent. The three of us carried him back to the college. When we arrived Linda had fainted and was lying in the middle of the corridor. We couldn't get past her. I still remember Nicky grabbing her by her hands and dragging her into the dining room.

"Later a German student called Reinhardt told us Oliver had been reading occult books over the Christmas holidays. Since then he'd been depressed. It was probably through this that the devil had found an opening in Oliver and had begun to oppress him. Next day a college official called me to his office. He asked what the problem had been. I said, 'Sir, Oliver was demonized.' He replied, 'No, no I don't believe that Biju. It's just some psychological problems.' His worldview hadn't much room for the reality of demons. Anyway, we'd prayed for Oliver and he had been released. What else do you do for a Christian who is demonized?

"At college, issues like this were difficult for me. I come from a world where spiritualism is part and parcel of daily life. In India, supernatural activity is happening all the time. If you talk about spiritual warfare in the

West some people are shocked. Here in India, people experience the reality of spiritual warfare day in day out. On the other hand, one of the great things about being at Bible School in the West was that my own worldview was challenged. A chicken in an egg thinks the whole world is in that shell. When it hatches, it thinks, *Man, that was nothing. This is the real world now.* I was fairly ethnocentric myself when I first came to England. I thought my views on what was appropriate about worship and life-style were the right ones. I believed our Indian patterns and systems of Christianity were the only way to go. I think I've become less legalistic on matters of dress and jewelry. I've had to come to grips with the cultural significance of things. One of the great things about Bible School is you meet people from many different nations and walks of life. You realize God is a God of great variety and cultural expression."

Beena said, "There are so many similar experiences of the works of the enemy we could tell but you must talk to Mama. She is the real prayer warrior in our family. Dad always says she is the backbone of the ministry. She has won so many victories in prayer. She has also suffered many attacks. I remember one that happened when I was eleven years old. Dad was away ministering in Malabar. Binu, my younger brother had accompanied Daddy. My exams were taking place so Mama woke me up to study at 4AM, after seeing them off. She was lying on the bed praying. I was in the corner of the room studying. Suddenly, Mama heard a voice that sounded just like Dad's. 'Mariamma, Mariamma,' it called. Dad came in wearing the same clothes he'd worn going out. He walked into the room, sat down beside Mama on the bed and started talking. Immediately Mama began to feel the way she does when the evil spirits come. She noticed his feet weren't touching the ground. She started rebuking this evil spirit until it disappeared."

Biju said, "It's so much easier if you don't believe in the supernatural. Then you don't have to do anything about it. Then there is no need for spiritual warfare. You can just sit at home and read your Bible. Then you don't need to set up churches and you don't need to pray for healing or deliverance. The devil's job is to deceive us into believing we are doing something when in reality we are doing nothing. As Dad often says, 'We get full of beef and unbelief.' The Christian writer C.S. Lewis said one of the subtle deceptions Christians fall into is in believing they have accomplished something when in fact they have only read about it. They confuse knowledge with action.

Knowing something is not the same as actually doing it. In fact, the Scriptures say if we know what to do and do not do it then for us that is sin. Knowing you should love your neighbor is not the same as actually loving your neighbor. Whenever there is a powerful ministry operating there will always be a counter attack. The day before you came Brendan, five or six things went wrong in our house. Secu slipped very heavily and hurt herself getting out of the shower. Now God is using you here, but what is happening to your family at home? Are they being attacked? The devil will always try to get at your weakest point. If you are teaching on prayer, then the enemy will attack your prayer life. If you are teaching from the word of God he will attack your Bible reading. Satan wants to stop supernatural activity in our lives. We must always be careful to cover ourselves and be covered in prayer when we are doing something for the Lord. We have to be aware of the works of the devil. I'm not surprised when I hear of men of God falling. We have to learn to live fearfully before the Lord as we handle the word of truth. That is why Paul tells us to be careful we don't fall and to be careful about our doctrine. Scripture also says when we help somebody caught in a sin we need to be careful, lest we ourselves fall."

Beena said, "It's the same thing when you are praying for someone. As you pray and intercede for them the enemy might well attack your family or your husband. Nowadays I pray the blood of Jesus on my family before I even begin to pray for others. The enemy will always want you to drop your guard so he can get to you."

One of the sounds coming from the church in India is that of suffering and struggle. It's the constant background noise of daily life. In the West we rarely talk about suffering. Our culture is one of comfort and convenience. Our background noise is the piped music in our supermarkets where we, "shop til we drop" experiencing "retail therapy" for our pain. In the West we lay down our lives to get comfortable. Even our deaths are eased by drugs like morphine. In India, death is an ever-present reality. Biju and I were traveling in and out to the college at Ponda. We saw a dead dog lying at the side of the road. Each day the dog became more and more decomposed. Back home it would've been removed immediately. In the West we don't want to be reminded of our mortality. Nor do we want to talk about hell anymore. Biju said it was the same at college. If anyone mentioned hell they were considered a radical. In India there are constant references to the Second

Coming of Jesus in the everyday talk of the believers.

Beena said, "In Kerala, if you preach on the Second Coming of Jesus, people get very excited. Here in India there is so much suffering in our daily lives that many people will be so glad of the Second Coming in order to go to a better place. In the West people are looking forward to their retirements and their pensions. Here in India we look forward to the Second Coming of Jesus and going to heaven."

Biju said, "Have you heard the story of the doctor, the lawyer and the engineer? There was a very old, rich, greedy man who was going to die. So he called his three sons, one a doctor, one a lawyer and one an engineer. He gave them 100,000 rupees apiece. He told them when he was dead they were to put the money into his coffin. He didn't know what was going to happen to him after death but he thought, *I have lived with money and I don't want to die without money.* After this greedy man died his three sons got together and asked one another if they had kept their promise to their dad. The doctor said, 'I really only put in 5,000 rupees and spent the rest building an extension at my hospital in memory of Dad. We put up a nice plaque.' The engineer told of how he put in only 10,000 rupees and gave the rest to an orphanage in memory of his greedy father. The lawyer said he put all of the 100,000 rupees into the coffin. He said he'd written the full amount in a check, 'The money is in my account and when Dad needs it, he can have it.'

Biju laughed and added, "The main problem is people don't want to lose control of their lives but when we die we have no more control. The only thing we will have then is whatever we have invested for eternity now. We need to hold material things loosely in this world. Our security needs to be in the Lord and in heaven. This can only be done when we live with eternity stamped in our eyes. We need to live in the light of eternity. We need to have an eternity perspective."

Beena said, "Recently Mama's sister, Aunt Valsala was sick. She was dying but we didn't want to let her go. I was praying, 'Lord why does this have to happen? We love her. We need her in the world.' One day God really spoke to my heart. He said, 'Beena I am more concerned about your eternal life.' God sees everything from an eternity perspective. God was telling me this world is only a shadow of the things yet to come. We must look to eternity and do whatever we are doing for the Lord with all our hearts.

I was sharing these thoughts with Tanya recently. We don't know when she'll go to heaven. We don't know how long she'll be with us."

"Who is Tanya?"

"She is a believer who has AIDS," Beena replied. "She was staying with us until yesterday. I'll tell you about her later."

Biju said, "Although Tanya has AIDS we need to realize that God still heals the sick and raises people from the dead. Signs and wonders are still following the preaching of the gospel."

Beena became excited, "Oh yes! This happened recently to one of our church members; a poor lady from Andhra-Pradesh. Her name is Maria. She comes from a village called Noorkappally. She is around forty years old. She and her mother were recent converts from Hinduism. She'd been visiting people in hospital and contracted typhoid fever. Then she herself was put into the hospital. The doctors said there was no hope for her. Soon afterwards she died. Her only relative was her mother who was too poor to afford a funeral. The body just lay at home for two days. It started to stink with ants crawling all over. One of our pastors, Abraham, went to their home and saw the sad state of the mother. Compassion and strong faith was stirred up in him. He began to talk in tongues. Speaking directly into the dead woman's ear he commanded her to come back to life in Jesus' name. After some time her toes began to move, heat came back into her body, and she opened her eyes. She said her soul rose up when she died. She was able to look down and see her body lying on the hospital bed before her spirit rose up through the clouds. She told of how evil spirits called out to her, but Jesus came and took her to heaven. Jesus showed her things in the garden and in the golden city. When Pastor Abraham's prayer was heard Jesus told her she had to go back to earth because her time had not yet come. She begged not to be sent back again because everything was so beautiful in heaven, but she had to return. Now she is a powerful witness for the Lord in her area. A few months back she traveled with Mama to different villages testifying about Jesus. This is all I remember of this story. Mama may remember more."

Biju said, "About seven months back, Mama, Dad and I were at a convention in Andhra Pradesh. At the end of one meeting a lady, called Bhavani, came up to my parents and invited them home for dinner. We were in a big hurry so we told her perhaps we'd visit next time. The pastor was one of our Bible School students from Goa. He explained to us this lady had been healed from AIDS. In the rural areas of Andhra they don't have hospitals. In most of these villages they only use witchcraft for healing. In the last stages of illness they normally put the sick person outside the hut. Bhavani, who was only thirty-five years old, was put outside to die. She'd been unable to eat food for over a month. She was unconscious. While she lay in this state she had a dream in which two angels came and told her Jesus was going to heal her. At this time Bhavani and her family were Hindus. They knew nothing about Jesus. The angels also told her there was a meeting in such a place (this was the convention we were attending). Although she'd been unconscious for many days she rose up and started to ask for something to drink. Her mother gave her water and listened to her dream. They dressed her and brought her to the convention where she gave her life to Jesus and was totally healed, just as the angels had said. Afterwards she went to the doctor for a check up and was found to be completely clear of AIDS."

Beena added, "The Lord is moving in so many ways. It's hard to remember all He's doing. This morning when I talked to you I was very encouraged. Remembering the dreams and visions the Lord has given me strengthened me. Remembering what the Lord has done is good. Cancer patients, AIDS patients and all sorts of patients have been healed. Mama can explain all that to you. Last week the same thing happened to one of our church members here. That fellow had some crabs for lunch. After eating them he developed an allergy. He was having the itching on the whole body. I phoned Martin. By the time he came the man was swollen and shivering like a malaria patient. He was breathless. He is the first son. His mother was squealing in fear. When Martin prayed for him the man felt a current going through his body. Then his soul went up and he could see his body lying in the bed and Martin praying for him. He could hear Martin saying, 'In the name of Jesus, be healed.' You know what happened? He went up to the clouds. He saw lots of figures in black dresses. They were like devils. They were pulling him and saying, 'Come with me, come with me.' Then all of a sudden he saw someone with a golden stick coming towards him. It was Jesus. Jesus said, 'Go back your time has not yet come.'"

Biju nodded, "We all have an allotted time on this earth. We all have a work to do." Oh by the way Brother Brendan, this is the last night you and Dad are staying together in the hotel. Tomorrow you will stay in our house and Dad will go with my brother Binu to a friend's home. Binu is arriving at Goa airport later today. Do you want to come with me to collect him?"

I thought for a moment. I said, *"No I'll see him later. I want to hear about the girl Tanya who has AIDS. I'll have one last talk with Beena and Martin if that's OK."*

"No problem," he said.

"Biju," I said, *"Beena mentioned you had something important to tell me."*

"Oh yes," he beamed, a large smile creasing his face. "I nearly forgot." My son Timothy said, 'Papa,' today for the first time. Secu and I are so proud of him. Isn't God good?"

4

Holy Beena

Biju rushed off to collect his homecoming brother. Beena said, "I easily feel embarrassed when I talk about my dreams and visions. When I was younger my brothers used to tease me terribly. They'd call me 'Holy Beena' and 'Saint Beena'. Mum shared the 'rubber hand' experience with them. They said things like, 'Beena, watch out for the rubber hand. The rubber hand will get you if you don't say your prayers. Beena, have you seen the rubber hand lately?' One of them might be reading the newspaper and joke; 'It says the rubber hand was sighted in Sri Lanka last Tuesday. It was playing a six stringed banjo!' They got great fun out of this but their jokes made me shy to share my dreams with them. Mum would never laugh. She was always excited about my dreams. She'd encourage me to seek out their meanings and to pray about them. She believes God speaks to us in dreams and visions."

"She's absolutely right," I said. *" In Acts 2 the scripture reads,*

'In the last days, God says,
I will pour out my Spirit on all people.
Your sons and daughters will prophecy,
Your young men will see visions,
Your old men will dream dreams.
Even on my servants, both men and women,
I will pour out my Spirit in those days,
And they will prophecy.'

If the Bible said, 'In the last days, God says I will pour out my Spirit on all people. Your sons and daughters will speak in Irish, your young men will see visions in Irish and your old men will dream dreams in Irish,' then

36

those who wanted to know what God was saying would make a big effort to learn Irish. These are the last days. Nobody disputes that. These are the days when God is speaking to us in prophecy, dreams and visions. It would be prudent of us to take these things seriously. Your mother is a wise woman. Maybe she is a prophetess as well."

Beena said, "She used to prophesy in church. Last week I had a dream in which I was back in our home church in Kerala. There were lots of people gathered. We were all praying. I have always longed to fall down in the Spirit but this has never happened to me. In the dream, as we were all praying I fell backwards in the Spirit. When this happened I saw Jesus appear as a big light in the shape of a human being. I started shouting, 'I can see Jesus! I can see Jesus!' Then I woke up. It was so refreshing for me to see this light and Jesus in front of me."

"When you see Jesus in your dreams did you particularly remember anything about Him? What He looks like? His features?"

"I don't remember any details like that. Often in my dreams figures and faces are not clear. I just know this or that person has come. Some dreams are so obvious you know minute things but others are not so clear. I do remember the eyes of Jesus though. I always remember His eyes. It's more the way He looks at you. His eyes are always full of love and acceptance. I can never forget the eyes of Jesus. They are so very wonderful. But His face I can't remember so well."

"Maybe your feelings of inferiority come from the time you suffered persecution at school?"

"Maybe? When I was eight years old I went to a Catholic primary school run by nuns. In Kerala the Pentecostals don't wear jewelry whereas the Hindus and others wear lots of jewelry. So a Pentecostal female is easily recognizable. Mama had a prayer group going in a Catholic hostel. Some of the nuns, who were my teachers, lived there. They knew all about Mama's ministry. One particular nun took a dislike to me and started picking on me. She'd make me stand for hours in the classroom for small mistakes. I began to dread going to school. I think it was from this time my inferiority complex came. In front of the whole class she'd make me go and stand in the corner. She'd embarrass me by saying that Mum and Dad were doing bad things. One of my Catholic friends called Fuja - she was so small - used to tell me not to worry. She said, 'Beena, every time somebody speaks evil about you, then you will get one more reward in heaven.' Other classmates would ask why I wasn't wearing earrings. They'd say, 'Are you in a cult?' This harassment went on for two years before Mama found out about it. Then she came to the school and made a big complaint. After that this nun was transferred to another school. As I got older others would tease me about being Pentecostal. 'Pentecostals don't do this or that,' they'd say. In India many people believe that only the low castes become Christians. They claimed poor people only got saved in order to get money. They often said to me, 'You are with low caste people so you are low caste.'

"I was not familiar with the caste system because in our home Dad treated every one the same. In many houses in India if low caste people come they have to go around to the back door. As a rule, they don't get into the house. Dad didn't treat people like this. Anybody could sit in our kitchen or in the bedroom and talk to Dad. It didn't matter. I was never taught I should treat certain types of people differently. When I was married this caused a bit of a problem because Martin's family were more aware of caste protocol than I was. In India you call some people by their first names and other people you give respectful terms to. I didn't know this. I treated everybody respectfully. Eventually Martin got used to this. Dad always taught us to treat others as we would treat ourselves. He also taught us not to be fussy about food. Sometimes there'd be hundreds of people in the house. We all ate the same thing. In Changanacherry we used to have everything in the house; the meals, the prayer meetings, the office and the church. If people wanted to go see Mum and Dad they had to walk through our bedroom. Mama might be changing her dress and someone would be coming through to the office.

"There was no caste system in our home. I believe the caste system is very wrong. I believe all people are equal. When I was picked on at school I didn't like it one bit. How would you like to be treated as an untouchable person by others? It was bad enough for me having dark skin. At school some kids would tease me about my skin. I felt so inferior in that sense. My sister Bini is much fairer than me. For boys it doesn't matter so much but for girls it is a big thing. I was always fearful nobody would propose to me. I was insecure. I used to say to Martin after we married, 'Do you really love me or did you just marry me because I was the pastor's daughter?' He'd just laugh because he loves me so much. When I was younger I couldn't even speak to people. I'd rather escape into my room. Before I was married I used to go into my room and close the door. When people came to the house I shivered. But God is changing me. Praise God for that. It's for His glory. I feel Martin has a strong personality. He tells me. 'Beena you also are strong.' People have prophesied that I make wise decisions and that I help my husband to make wise decisions. I feel Martin and I blend together although we have very different personalities. It has taken us four years to begin to understand one another. Martin is a great encouragement to me. Because of my feelings of inferiority I get easily embarrassed when I stand at the front of a church. I feel too shy to share with the people. My face blazes with embarrassment.

"One Saturday evening Martin said, 'Tomorrow, in church, you are going to share something about your experience with God.' I argued, 'I cannot do it. I cannot speak. Why are you doing this to me?' Martin said, 'I don't care if you shiver or fall down. Tomorrow you are going to share.' I thought, *There is no point in arguing with this man.* I began to ask God for strength. Throughout that whole night it felt like I was literally fighting with a person. In the morning I was exhausted, but I felt I'd won the battle. When Martin called me to speak I was able to talk before a congregation without fear for the first time in my life. Afterwards many people said they were really touched by the things I'd shared. From that day forward fear was conquered and God gave me a new confidence. This happened in *Christian Revival Church* at Wagga Wagga in Australia. It was only after this that I began to tell my dreams and visions during services.

"When we came back from Australia, God guided us to Goa to look after the church there. It's called *New India Church of God, Panjim.* When we left for Australia there were twenty-five people in that church. When we came back there was only four left. One day when I was traveling with Martin, somebody spoke to me and said, 'Beena, what is all this Christianity really about?' That started me thinking. I began to ask, 'Is it salvation? Is it the faith we have in Jesus?' Then God began speaking to me. He said, 'Christianity is about love. Its foundation is love.' The scripture came to me, 'For God so loved the world that He gave His only begotten Son.'

"When we receive Jesus, we are receiving love and compassion for people. God started revealing lots of things about love to me. He told me to read the words from I Corinthians 13 three times every day. Whenever I had a chance to speak I'd share about the love God has placed into His church. Wherever Jesus went He had compassion on the people. He also said the world would know us by our love. In my dreams of heaven I've felt so much love. Whenever Jesus came to me in my dreams I'd always feel pure love and acceptance. The most important thing is the love. For three years God continually spoke to me about this. Whenever I'd speak, I'd speak about love. I began to think people would be fed up with me speaking about love. The greatest commandment is that we should love God and love one other. If we have the faith to move the mountain but have no love we are nothing. Many times, in the church, people say and do things that hurt us. But the more I looked into love the more the Lord gave me the ability to love even those who had said and done hurtful things. God said love doesn't envy. God showed me we love our children very much. If somebody speaks good things about our children we are blessed. It should be the same if somebody says good things about our brothers and sisters. We should feel so blessed. The more I thought about love the more I realized there needs to be a practical outworking of it. I felt the Lord leading us to work with women and children, especially HIV positive women and their children. Last year Martin was fasting for twenty-one days. I joined him for the final seven. It was then I shared with him my desire to do something for these people. He suggested we bring it before the Lord with all the other things we were praying about. 'Let us see if it really is from God, don't worry, He'll show us, he said.'"

Martin said, "Early morning, Saturday of the twentieth fasting day, a phone call came. It was from a pastor who was trying to place some orphans. He had nowhere to put them. Someone had given him a brochure about orphanages with my name written on the front cover. Beside my name, they had written, 'If you need any questions answered talk to this man.' When he phoned I asked him to come and visit for I didn't want to just pass the buck. I thought, *I should be fair to this man and see if the Lord is talking to us or not.* A children's home was not one of my priorities but if the Lord was confirming something to my wife I felt I should be obedient and listen."

Beena said, "As we put this before the Lord He began to speak to us through other people. An older couple from England, Jack and Eva, called and told us the God had given them a vision of a large building for mothers and children with HIV, in India. We became very excited about this. As we talked our vision began to grow. Martin said we'd need a big building and cottages for the people. He said we'd also need accommodation to offer hospitality to God's people who'd pass through. Next day a man of God came. He was a prophet from Kerala called Suresh Babu. He knew nothing about our situation. He'd just come to pray for my back pain. While praying he began to prophesy, 'Beena, God will speak to you through dreams and visions.' I cried bitterly that day. I felt God was doing something in my heart. I always thought I had nothing to offer God. Suresh Babu prophesied, 'You have always believed you are the least in the family but God has chosen you to do great things for His Kingdom. God has given you a broken heart. God has led you through brokenness because He wants to heal many people through you. God will heal many broken hearts through your brokenness.' I was poor in studies. I thought I didn't have anything to give. Often I felt rejected. I now believe God allowed these things to happen so I could identify with the broken hearted. Suresh Babu also said God had given me a deliverance ministry. He prophesied, 'God will also give you a children's home. I can see cottages with lots of acreage. I also see a large house where you can give hospitality to men and women of God.'

"After that, as a step of faith, we began to rent a small flat as a start for our children's home. Roosa from Kerala and Jisha from our church are looking after the children. The children now go to a good Christian school during the day. Now another nine children, age three to nine years old, have come to be looked after in our home. These are very poor children who have no parents. One of our church members, Anita Pereira, is working as a counselor for HIV positive people. Sometimes she takes us to share the gospel and pray for these AIDS victims. Many sick people, particularly prostitutes soon to die, come and speak with her. They are all very concerned about the future of their children. They want someone responsible to look after them when they die. Yesterday a prostitute came with her two children aged three and six and asked if we could care for them. I told her I'd pray about it. I'm believing in two or three weeks we'll be able to take those children. We are looking at a bigger place for our children's home. I have a heart to believe we can start a home for women also. Many deserted wives have approached us to see if we can get them accommodation or work. We are hoping to start a tailoring school for women because a lady in our congregation is a tailoress who could teach them. We believe God wants us to step out in faith before all the prophesied buildings and cottages materialize. It all started when an elderly lady in our church, called Doris, had a massive heart attack. We took her to a government hospital at 11PM and had to wait with her until she was seen at 4AM the next morning. Martin had to go into the X-ray room with her. I couldn't go because I was pregnant. He also had to lend a hand to help remove her clothes."

"They don't teach you that at Bible School," said Martin.

Beena smiled. She said, "I believe God was showing us we had to do things first before we could expect others to do them. Doris was in the hospital for over a month. We visited every day. The hospital is free, but the medicines have to be bought by the patients. We'd to buy everything for her. Doris also had diabetes that affected her kidneys and bladder. At the same time, a twenty-one year old, girl called Tanya came to us after her boyfriend had abandoned her. She was 7 months pregnant and HIV positive. She became a believer before she knew she was either pregnant or HIV positive. She only found out she was HIV positive after a blood test to determine her pregnancy. The only place we had to put her was in our children's home. I wasn't too pleased about this but there was nowhere else available. Tanya went into the same hospital as Doris to have her baby. The hospital staff were happy to deliver the baby but were cautious because she had HIV. They'd only do a C-section. We had to buy five AIDS kits for them; masks, gloves etc. Because of the HIV, the nurses wouldn't go near Tanya. Martin got the job of picking her up and putting her from the stretcher to the bed etc. I couldn't help much. I was regularly vomiting because of my pregnancy. The nursing staff kept looking at Martin strangely. When the baby, Esther, was born we had to buy baby milk to feed her. She wasn't allowed to be breast-fed. Tanya was in the hospital for eight days. The staff didn't want to take food or anything to her. We had to buy and do everything for her. They began to think Martin was her brother. They said it was good to see a brother looking after his sister. They were surprised to learn he was not her brother but the pastor of our church. God gave us an opportunity to show His love to Tanya.

"Esther is a beautiful little girl. I was able to give some of Daniel's baby clothes to her. I also gave Tanya some of my own clothes because she had nothing whatsoever. The hospital gown they'd given her was badly torn. It was something they weren't ever going to use again. She even had to eat from her own bowl. She was treated like an untouchable. I'd hoped the Lord would have given us a house by the time she got out of the hospital but God has His own ways. Instead we had to take her home and keep her in one of our rooms. At that time I'd to have one month's total bed rest due to internal bleeding. When Doris was discharged we also had to bring her to our home. She had nowhere else to go. Around then Martin visited Kerala where fasting and prayer was going on.

"A prophet called Joeboy prophesied to him that God wanted us to look after sick women with AIDS. He said first of all God would make us look after them in our own home. Only after that would God open the doors wider. Joeboy had no idea we were already doing this. This was a confirmation and an encouragement to us. I'd been feeling disappointed that God had not provided a proper home for us to put Tanya and her daughter in. Our son Daniel loved little baby Esther. He used to run up and down to her room, kissing her and holding her. I was a bit nervous. I didn't know too much about AIDS. I tried to make sure Daniel had no cuts so there'd be no blood contact. Tanya would come to my room and I'd read the scriptures and talk to her about Jesus and eternity. I shared the various dreams and visions God had given me.

"Now Doris and another lady are sharing a house together. I've found a small room near here for Tanya. We managed to get in contact with Tanya's mother and have them reconciled. Her alcoholic father is now dead and her two younger brothers are in hostels. Tanya's mother didn't want to see her but she changed her mind after we told her of the transformation that had occurred in Tanya's life. I explained we were not in a position to financially help Tanya. I would love to, but we didn't have the money. All this happened the day before yesterday. I was able to give Tanya a mattress from our house and a few little pots and pans and two buckets. We bought some provisions and paid the rent for her. We are still looking after her. Yesterday, Tanya phoned to say she was out of the baby's formula. Martin went and bought some more for little Esther."

Outside the crows cawed loudly as the monsoon clouds darkened. Martin turned on a light. Beena stood up and gave a long slow stretch and a deep sigh. She sat down again on the hard wooden chair. Martin said, "All these things began to happen before I felt ready for them. I always pray that God will give me a big heart and a strong spirit. I don't mind helping out but where it will lead to and what it requires I don't honestly know."

Beena said, "We can't sort out all the problems of the world. We can only respond to what God wants us to do in our own lives and be faithful and obedient to His challenge to us. When God tells us to do something, it is always beyond our natural ability, but in faith, we do the little bit we can and He will do the rest. We are focusing on women right now. Men can go anywhere and sleep but HIV positive women are the most vulnerable. They are the innocents because most of them get it from their husbands. When the husband dies, many times the in-laws put these women out of their homes. But, wonderfully, God is providing. Even yesterday a miracle happened. We became penniless; nothing in the hand. I prayed, *Lord what am I going to do?* Tanya's mother had asked how we'd get the money for the milk. I told her we'd get it somehow. Just then the phone rang. It was Jack and Eva from England. Eva asked me how I was. She said, 'I feel in my heart you need some money.' I didn't know what to say. She said, 'I feel strongly I need to get some money to you today or tomorrow. How can I do that?' I told her to ring back in ten minutes after I had spoken with Martin. Through credit transfer she was able to send us £60. This was a great miracle for me. When we have a need God does things like this because He doesn't want my heart to be troubled. This is how God is leading us."

This trip after I first met Beena we were all sitting together in a restaurant when the Lord gave me a vision of her standing in front of congregations in America, Canada and Australia. I'd assumed she'd be speaking about the church in India. Now I realized it'd be about AIDS victims, orphans and other needy people. I looked across the table at Beena. I said, *"You are pregnant with a baby. You are also pregnant with a mercy ministry that will bless thousands in this nation."*

Martin nodded in agreement. He said, "I feel God will use Beena in a different way than He uses me. I believe the love and compassion in her must find an expression. I've been telling her about going to all these countries the angel talked about. She must go. The person with the vision must speak it out."

Beena said, "The whole issue of money is a difficult one. When Martin and I went to Australia we were often embarrassed. We didn't know what and how to share. Martin was new to the family. He wasn't sure about the workings of the ministry. We didn't communicate much about the work in India. At times I felt so discouraged. There are great needs in India.

44

Money from the West is really multiplied in strength here. The £60 that Jack and Eva sent will go a long way here. Their sacrificial giving is immediately increased in value. There is a vast need for finance but I find it difficult to ask for money. God has not called us to be beggars. There must be a way in which God gives wisdom. I'm not a person that can just go and ask. When Mama was in Australia she heard of one preacher from India who said he'd started an orphanage. He was not telling the truth yet people were trusting him. Unfortunately when the deceit is exposed then people who give with a good heart feel cheated. They think everybody from India is like him. There is, I'm sure, a proper way to ask. We need God's wisdom for that.

"During my present pregnancy I started bleeding. The doctor said I needed injections that would cost 1,000 rupees every week. He also said I'd need other injections that would cost 150 rupees. I didn't want to waste money on these injections - money we didn't have. One day, I heard a voice saying, 'Beena you don't have any problem. The child in your womb is perfectly okay.' These words strengthened me. Next day an intercessor called Daisy, came to visit. She confirmed God was saying the baby would be OK. Afterwards I went to the hospital for a scan. They still wanted me to take the injections but I choose to trust God. Mama and Dad have been great examples to us of people who pray and trust God for everything. Mama prays for hours and hours. Near our house in Changanacherry there was a little bridge over a river. When I came home from school, as I neared the bridge, Mama's voice could be heard speaking and singing in tongues or shouting in warfare. If my friends were with me I'd always be embarrassed because Mama would be so loud. My friends thought she was a little mad and I suppose she was. She was mad at the devil.

"I believe the *New India Church of God* ministry has flourished because of Mama's faithfulness in intercession. She is a woman who knows how to stand in the gap. We had a big breakthrough revival in Changanacherry in 1979. Cliff Beard from Australia was at that crusade. There was over a lakh of people who came to the Lord (Lakh: one hundred thousand, usually rupees or people, written 1,00,000). Before that convention, for six months, day and night, Mama was interceding. She was praying when we went to school and when we came home from school, when we went to bed and when we got out of bed. I used to ask her, 'Mama when do you get any sleep?' If I'd waken during the night I'd still hear her praying. She even prayed in her sleep. Sometimes I asked Dad, 'Don't you get bored with Mama and all this praying?' Many times, when I came home from school, I longed to sit and talk with her but at that time her priority was prayer; prayer, prayer, prayer. Nowadays she is used very powerfully among the women. She is a great breakthrough person. She breaks up the fallow ground with her prayers. God is also using Mama in a deliverance ministry. Whoever she comes across will get saved. She has a real call for personal evangelism, even stronger than my dad. He is more for talking to hundreds and thousands of people. I used to cry when I heard my dad preach and wept when I listened to the stories he told to the people to get them saved. But for personal evangelism Mama is the best. Every day people would bring five or six persons to talk to her. She'd get them saved. The conviction of the Holy Spirit would always come upon them. Nowadays when Mama visits me I always take her to those who are interested in the gospel. She will always lead them to Christ.

"I'm so happy I've been born into a Christian family and I've had the good example of watching Mum and Dad live their lives sold-out for Jesus. I have watched my Mum at prayer and intercession. This has encouraged me. When Mum shares her testimonies of how God has worked with her and Daddy they have a powerful effect upon the people. Dad loves everybody - rich and poor - he treats everybody the same. He has a great heart. He gives to many people. As a youngster I remember we needed money for school fees and personal things. Dad's priority was to make sure the pastors and their families were financed first. His main concern was not, 'First my children and then the rest.' His priority was always the work of the Lord. In those times I might have been angry with my dad and complained that he didn't care about us, but his desire to seek first the Kingdom of God has always been a great example to me. The way he handled money made us closer to God as we relied on Him. Whenever we were sick the first thing Mum and Dad did was pray over us. We've seen miracles in our family. Sicknesses were healed. Often when we needed money someone would come and give Dad the money right before our eyes. To us this was a miracle. Time after time, as we saw God supplying our needs, we children were encouraged to believe God would also answer *our prayers.* He is no respecter of persons. God has no caste system.

"When I was twenty years old, and doing my third year degree, Dad went to Australia. I had a real burden to protect him in prayer for some sort of deliverance. God told me to fast every day until 3PM until Daddy came back. When Daddy would call I'd ask how things were going. He'd say God had to do a miracle so the needs of the ministry would be met. I kept praying, *Lord let Your will be done. Don't let the devil have any victory over my dad.* Dad was in Australia for three months. He had asked the Lord for a specific amount of money for the ministry in India. He didn't know I was fasting. Just before the last meeting he was very far from his financial goal. The final get-together was a prayer meeting in a small fellowship in Adelaide. There was no collection taken. Afterwards one man came and gave Dad an envelope. Inside was a check for $35,000. This money was from Mr. Sheppard. He has twelve children. His wife was pregnant again when I last saw her. She said she wants to have more. They are not rich people. This was sacrificial giving on their part. When Daddy came home I went to pick him up from the airport. Over breakfast he explained these things to me. I was so encouraged he'd been able to meet his financial targets. Fasting is a powerful thing. Mum fasts often. Usually she'll do two twenty-one day fasts each year. When Dad goes on ministry trips she'll always fast for him. When we were small she used to fast every Wednesday until 4PM for us. In Australia, I never heard a sermon on prayer and fasting. Mostly they were prosperity messages. Those are wonderful messages but for people to grow spiritually there has to be fasting and prayer. Sit at Jesus feet and fast and pray and then you'll get things directly from God and not just from other people. It's so good to get food directly from God. Every dream and every vision I get from God is a great strength to me in times of trouble. I remember, too, when my heart is troubled then Jesus' heart is troubled. I don't want to trouble Jesus' heart. When you receive something from God it is yours and it lasts forever."

I asked, *"Beena, what will things be like in ten years when we sit here talking?"*

"I don't know. God's ways are always higher than our thoughts. I don't know, but I know it will be good. From childhood my dream has always been to have a home for people. Over the years I've seen so many people come to our house with broken lives and broken hearts. So many have been mistreated by life's circumstances. I've always prayed, 'Lord use me to bring people to know You so they can enjoy this life and the life to come.' I believe God has given us this life so we can know and enjoy Him. We all have an emotional, spiritual and physical tank within us. These three tanks have to be filled. It is not enough to be spiritually filled and emotionally and physically weak. A lot of women in India do not enjoy their lives. They just sit at home with very little purpose. Their husbands may be bad to them. Always I've dreamed of having a big home for such women. As a child I'd dream of all the rooms and what they'd be like. There'd be rooms for all the ill people we could look after. When I'd see people along the roads, sick and crippled, I longed to take them home and care for them. I wished I had a hospital to bring the sick people to.

"As a child I was going to a friend's house when I met an old lady who had fallen down and couldn't get up. She was crying very sorely. She said her children didn't look after her. She said, 'I am old. My feet and legs are all swollen up. My son's house is there, but his wife doesn't want me. But I have to live somewhere until I die.' I felt so sorry for her. I helped her home and put her on her bed. Nobody was there. She said, 'I'm so thirsty.' I went to the kitchen. All I could find was coffee so I made her a cup. I left the house quickly. Maybe they'd wonder what a stranger was doing in their home. I asked the Lord to allow me to help those types of people. Nowadays this vision is beginning to happen. It was wonderful to look after Doris and Tanya and little Esther in my home. I was so happy to have them. Sometimes people are not grateful. I've always known that. Sometimes people take things for granted when you help them. That's the way it is. Many times I have taken Jesus for granted as well.

"I used to think that when I was forty-five or fifty these dreams would come to pass. For the first four years of our marriage I didn't tell Martin about my dreams. I have waited for God's perfect timing. Just recently another pregnant lady with AIDS came for help. Her husband has just died from AIDS, leaving her helpless and homeless. I am searching for a house for these ladies and their children. In God's time He will do it. A lot of the ladies are professional prostitutes. People don't even want to look at them. But the Lord loves them. In the Bible He always went and spoke to them. Many of these ladies are prostitutes because they have no other way of making money. It must be so terrible for them. Tomorrow two prostitute's children and two children from Poona are coming. I pray the Lord will bring the right children to us. In India there are so many people who need help. We are praying the Lord will bring genuine needy children to us. These children who come to us have never been loved or cared for. When they receive love they run with open arms shouting, 'Mama,' 'Papa.' They are so happy. We hug them. They talk to us and tell us all the things that are happening in their lives. When I had to take bed rest I missed them so much. I had them brought to me so I could play with them. It is really great fun. They have so much to talk about. It's a lovely experience. There are many Portuguese houses, here in Goa that are boarded up. The owners have gone abroad and left them empty. We are praying the Lord will give us some of these houses for the poor and needy. If we could get a couple of houses it would be wonderful - one for boys and one for girls."

"It all takes faith," I said.

"Brother Brendan," said Martin, "Do you want to hear how God took us from a poor country to a rich country in order to teach us about faith?"

"I always love a good story. If you're talking I'm listening."

"In that case," said Martin, "I'll make more coffee. Beena will start the story."

I gave myself a good stretch and shifted into as comfortable a position as the wooden chair would allow. *"So what happened?"* I asked.

5

Learning Faith

Beena said, "After we were married we began praying for an opportunity to go abroad for Martin to study. A friend of Dad's, from Australia, called Gary Clarke rang up. He said there was a chance for a couple to come for a one-year course at the Hillsong Bible School. There was a scholarship that would cover food and fees. We had only to get in faith for the air tickets. Daddy thought this would suit both of us. When we were praying about finance, a man called Bob Uden came and said he'd buy the tickets for us. I was under four months pregnant and still able to get a visa. We arrived in Australia wearing summer clothes in winter. We had no other outfits. We didn't have any money with us. The church blessed us with $90 each week. This was enough to cover rent, bus fares and food. There was no money for warm clothes. For the first two weeks I didn't go near the college. I couldn't bear the cold. Afterwards the Lord used one person to provide some cozy garments. The college people were really worried about me being pregnant. I didn't have money or a medical card or anything like that. They were concerned about the cost of giving birth."

"In fact, they were quite silent about the whole matter. They weren't sure what we were going to do," said Martin.

Beena said, "There was a doctor for the Hills church. They suggested I go and see him for a check up. The problem was this. Each time we went we had to pay $40. This really knocked a hole in our $90 allowance. We went four times but stopped when told in order to proceed we'd have to have a scan costing $150. He was a good doctor. He tried to find out if there were any organizations that could help us. We also learned we'd have to pay $5,000 to have our baby born in an Australian hospital."

Martin said, "That means they'd have charged you $70,000 for the births of your children Brother Brendan. How would you have liked that?"

"God take care of us," I intoned.

Beena said, "We were advised to book in early for the birth. But having no money our hands were tied. Eventually, under pressure, we booked an appointment to have the $150 scan. It was scheduled for a Monday morning. We were not worried. We believed the Lord would provide. On Sunday we were asked to share at a service. Afterwards a family took us home for lunch. As we were leaving they put money into my hand. It was $150; the exact amount needed for the ultrasound. On the following day we were so excited by God's provision we forgot to ask about the sex of the baby. When I was three months pregnant God gave me the name Daniel for our baby. Although I didn't like the name at first, I knew God was speaking strongly to me. Throughout the entire pregnancy I never once thought of a girl's name. When I would speak to the baby in my womb, I'd always say 'Hello Daniel. Jesus loves you Daniel. We love you Daniel.' I had God's word rather than the doctor's scan to go on.

"Six months into my pregnancy I didn't know how or where I was going to deliver my baby. There is a Christian Camp called *Obadiah* about six hours from Sydney. It's on the way to Brisbane, near a place called John's River. There was an elderly couple named Daryl & Joyce who were father and mother to the camp. They were friends of our family. I'd previously met them in India. One day they called and asked where we were going to have our baby. I told them I didn't know. This was my first baby and the first grandchild for our parents yet we didn't know where it would be born. It was a new thing in our lives. There had been no money for iron or calcium tablets, injections, medicines, or check-ups. Joyce told us there was a male midwife at *Obadiah*. She suggested we come over and talk to him. We were delighted at this news. This midwife's name was Barry. He also delivered the calves on the campsite. He knew Dad and he was very friendly to us. He said he'd be privileged to assist in my delivery. The cost for a midwife in Australia was $1,800. Barry said, 'You won't have to pay me anything. If you need stitches you will have to pay for those because normally a doctor has to do that.' We sang all the way back to Sydney. We were so happy God had provided a way for our baby to be born. In India $5,000 or $1,800 is a king's ransom. We never had so much money in our lives. In India even the extremely poor people can go to a government hospital and have their baby born. Our worlds are so different. September 4th 1997 was my delivery date.

51

We planned to go to the camp one week before our baby was due. During this time I had plenty of strength and faith to have my baby well. Those were good days. We felt the presence of God with us.

"Each morning, we'd lay hands on Daniel and pray for his safety. We were so happy when Mama managed to come to Australia to minister and to be with us during the delivery. On August 26th, Mum and I went to Camp Obadiah to prepare for the baby. Martin was to follow on the next day. We thought we had plenty of time. Daniel wasn't due until a week later. We were all so relaxed and at peace. That evening Mama went off somewhere to minister for a couple of days. Barry and his wife borrowed a mobile home and went off on holiday to a place about four hours away. If anything unexpected happened we were to ring a certain telephone number."

"A mobile phone in a mobile home?" quipped Martin.

Beena said, "At 5AM the next morning, I was alone in the house when the contractions started. At 10AM I phoned Joyce and told her I was having some pain. She advised me to wait and if it increased to phone her back. Three hours later the pain was much stronger. I rang again. At that point she contacted Barry. Mama, who was three hours away, was also informed. By the time she came the contractions were very severe. Soon afterwards Barry arrived with Martin close on his heels. They needn't have rushed. In the end, it took me thirty-eight hours to deliver the baby. Daniel was in a military position, which means the baby's head is up and its feet are downward. Daniel's head was *really* up. I was praying, *My goodness Lord, help me!*"

I joked, "*Maybe he was in the military position because his great-grandfather was a Brigadier General in the Salvation Army.*"

Beena smiled, "Maybe there was some pride in him. I don't know. A doctor, I spoke to in India, said the military position is very dangerous because of the long duration of the labor. Also, the umbilical cord was around Daniel's neck. For me, the pain was so severe it has taken me four years to get up the courage to have another baby. Barry said when one is having a baby it is very dangerous to wait two sunsets from the first contractions. In my case, it was 5:30PM, nearing the second sunset of my labor. Barry said we'd wait for another fifteen minutes and then we must go to the hospital. The pressure was now on. I didn't want to have suffered all this pain only to go to the hospital and get into $5,000 worth of debt. Everyone was praying really hard. It was like a spiritual warfare meeting. Mum was crying and praying very loudly. Barry kept taking her out of the room to try and quiet her down, but it was no use. You can't stop Mum when she starts praying. They were walking me about the compound to try and change the baby's position. Barry pushed and pulled at the baby. Then at 5:40PM, in the midst of all this commotion, Daniel was born to great shouts of, 'Sthothram! Sthothram! Sthothram!'"

"There was quite a battle over this little soldier."

"So much struggle," said Beena. "Recently I heard one of my friends in India had a baby in the same position. She had to have a caesarean section. Usually with the military position you have to have a c-section."

"Did you have any stitches?"

"Barry gave me five stitches. There was some complication. The wound gave me a lot of pain and I couldn't sit down. We went to the hospital with this problem. They said they'd have to cut open the wound and do the stitches again, which would cost us $500. We didn't have the money. We just prayed for healing and within two weeks the pain totally left. So, that's how we had our baby, Daniel.

"A month before we returned to India we were invited to speak in some churches. In one morning service I had an opportunity to testify of how the Lord had provided for our baby. At the evening service, an elderly gentleman asked the pastor if he could speak. Turning to me, he said, 'Since you shared this morning I've had a picture of your baby in my mind. I can't get rid of it.' He said God had given our child a great name like Daniel because He was going to use him mightily for His purposes in Australia. The sense was I had gone through a lot of pain to bring forth this child. There had been a lot of resistance to him being born. The old man also said, 'Everything was under God's perfect plan and timing.' Two ladies came forward and confirmed these things. One said we were to faithfully protect Daniel with prayer until his eighteenth birthday because God has a big purpose for him. The other lady had a vision in which she saw a snake try to wrap itself around Daniel. But due to our prayers it lost its strength and had to release its grip. 'Let us all pray for Daniel and give him into the hands of God', the pastor said. At times I'd wondered if it was God's plan for us to go to Australia at all. He had always provided for us, yet there were also difficult days of no money, no food, and no clothes. But that evening as those people shared I finally felt assured it was God's plan and purpose for us to be there."

Martin said, "I believe God took us to Australia to teach us faith. Had we been here in India our parents would have somehow managed to get us into a good hospital. They'd never have allowed us to go the way we did. We would not have had this experience of having to trust God. I thought of it like this; *God had taken us from a poor country to a rich country to teach us faith. God's ways are not our ways.*"

Beena said, "Afterwards we met the original doctor. He asked us if we'd paid by cash or check. We told him we hadn't paid anything. He was surprised. This was also a big shock to the college people. They couldn't believe it. 'You're joking,' they said."

Martin said, "I remember going to Hills church. I had $20 with me. It was the only money we had left."

Beena said, "I was eight months pregnant and very hungry."

Martin said, "In India our currency is rupees. While we were in Australia we kept comparing the cost of things there with those in India. We would convert dollars into rupees all the time. When an Australian comes to India he finds the cost of a good meal to be very cheap. For us it is the reverse. We find it outrageous that people pay $10 for a lunch. To our minds that is incredibly expensive. So I put the $20 in the collection plate for the work of the Lord. I told Beena we'd go home and cook some rice. I forgot we had no money left for the bus fare."

Beena said, "I thought, *How are we going to manage? He's not even thinking of me or my baby.* At the end of the service a boy named Brendan offered us a lift home. On the way he took us to McDonalds for a take-away meal. This happened on Saturday. When we arrived home a lady rang. She invited us to speak about India in her church next day for Missionary Sunday. She said she'd take us to and from the service. This was great news because we didn't have the bus fare. After the service they took us to a good Chinese restaurant. This was the first time we'd been in a restaurant since we arrived in Australia. When they drove us home they gave us a check for $200! Since then we've been to many good restaurants. It seems like we got a breakthrough. It was a bit like the widow who gave the two coins into the temple coffers and Jesus saw it. God saw Martin give the $20 and next day he gave us $200 back! Experiences like that strengthened us. I have always heard Mum and Dad's testimonies about how God provided for them but it's very different when you are involved in the story yourself. It's like giving birth. You experience the pain and the joy in your own self. Sometimes one of us gets upset over the others faith. I thought Martin didn't care about me when he put the $20 into the offering. Things like this can cause big struggles but in the end I was glad Martin had been obedient. We must learn to make space for each others faith."

Martin said, "There were many lessons for us in Australia. We were in a new country, and I wanted to try everything. But there I was with my new wife who was large and slow and pregnant. *Can you not hurry up?* I thought. Sometimes Beena would complain about me not taking her anywhere but we didn't have the money. We saw so little of the many wonderful sights in Australia. In the end the only tourist place we visited was the Sydney Opera House."

Beena said, "Sometimes I'd get so upset with him. It was a learning period for both of us. We were only newly married. The Bible says Jesus learned obedience by the things he suffered. Isn't it?"

Martin asked, "Some more coffee, brother Brendan? I'm sure you're thirsty after all that listening."

"So I'm staying with Pastor Thampy one last night in our hotel room and then I'm moving somewhere else?"

"That's what Biju said," nodded Beena. "As this is your last night with Daddy why don't you ask him to tell you about Chester Bieson and Cliff Beard? They are two men from the West who really helped him in the early days of his ministry. Daddy is at his best when he is preaching to crowds of people but if you ask him about those men that will get him talking. He's always ready to share about those who have helped him in the ministry."

"Thanks for the advice, Beena. What do you think Brother Martin?"

"I think you're a happy man Brother Brendan, you didn't have to pay $70,000 to get all your fourteen children born. "

6

Help From Afar

Over breakfast in our room, I asked Thampy. *"What's on your heart these days?"*

"What do you mean?"

"What do you want to do with the rest of your life?"

"Easy," he said, "Christ for India, India for Christ."

Thampy is a quiet man, maybe even a shy man. Mariamma is full of stories. Breakfast with her is a two-hour conversation. Like myself she thinks aloud. Thampy on the other hand processes his thoughts internally before he speaks. A couple of years previously I was sitting with him on his veranda late one afternoon. He has a locally made chair that has extra long arms upon which you can rest your legs and feet. He was chilled out on this thing. We weren't talking. A chorus of Kottayam crows was rehearsing in the background. I broke the silence, *"Thampy, what's the most important thing for success in ministry?"*

"Dedication. 100% dedication," he said. We went back to silence with me listening to the singing in the trees. I always remember my conversations with Thampy.

The previous night after leaving Martin and Beena's home I'd read through an in-house publication celebrating twenty-five years of ministry of *New India Church Of God*. It was jam-packed with photographs and names of people and places that held no meaning for me. Hundreds of people each with their tale to tell; hundreds of people laying down their lives for the gospel in India. People whose story I'll never know until I get to heaven or until Mariamma comes back. Some of the language was a little antiquated and vague as in:

'With exceeding happiness and great burden,
I began to study the word of God...All of us

in the school, united would stand together,
pray, and help each other when in need or
sickness. Above all we used to spend a lot
of time with the Lord   interceding for the
perishing souls. That enhanced our relationship with the Lord. That year was one filled
with joy that can never be forgotten in my
life.'

I wanted to know details. Who was sick? Who was saved? What
caused the joy? What was it like? What were the names of the perishing
souls? Oh, Mariamma, where are you with your facial and tonal changes and
all your little feminine intricate details and asides that bring the characters to
life. Stop *Waltzing Matilda* and come home from Australia immediately.
Brother Brendan hath need of thee. Remembering Beena's advice I said,
"Thampy, tell me something about Chester Bieson and Cliff Beard." He
reflected for a moment. I closed the windows to dampen the sound of the
monsoon that had just kicked in.

He said, "At the very beginning of my ministry although I had no
means or tools for evangelism I was full of enthusiasm. So strongly I felt the
call of God to preach the gospel. I had a dozen young disciples with me. We
would go from village to village preaching, teaching, and evangelizing.
Sometimes the villagers would give us something to eat; sometimes they
would drive us away. At such a time a small team of Americans came to help
us under the leadership of Cliff Beard, an Australian missionary. There was
an American Presbyterian Christian among them by the name of Chester
Bieson. He was 75 years old. When the crusade was over and the others had
returned to America he said, 'Pastor Thampy, I have three more weeks to
spend in India. May I travel with you and see what's happening in your
ministry?' I told him that would not be a problem.

"Day after day Chester traveled with me. He became very interested
in our work. During the day we would conduct meetings in the streets and in
the market places. In the evening we would have a village campaign. Normally
we would get sixty or seventy people at the cottage meetings. I took him to
a rural area called Ranni in the hill country and arranged for three nights of
meetings. Each night the crowd grew larger. The final meeting gathered

about one hundred and fifty people. This was in a small cramped hut. People were standing and sitting in the kitchen, outside, inside, everywhere.

"Chester said, 'Thampy you need some sort of place to have your services. You don't have a building. You don't have a bicycle. You have nothing.' He asked me how much it would cost to buy a small piece of land and build a prayer hall. I told him according to the situation at that time it would be about $5,000 American. He said, 'Is that all? Ten years ago my mother died and she left me $5,000. She told me to use it for the good of God's Kingdom. All these years I have been watching and waiting but I haven't yet found what to do with the money. In America $5,000 is hardly enough to build a toilet for a church.' Chester was very happy the money would buy land and a church in India. He rang his wife Vivianna and asked her to send the money over. We bought the land and started to build before he went back to America. Chester had been a senator as a young man and a professor in political science at the Pacific University of Washington. He was a Colonel in World War II for the British Army. He was a highly educated man who had retired from a municipal corporation.

"When Chester returned to America he wrote, 'Thampy, since I have returned from India I cannot sleep well. Whenever I go to bed I see masses of Indian people in front of me. They are asking for light and bread. I don't know what I should do. I am retired and I am old. All my money and time has gone. Even in the daytime when I am going to the store I am in tears. I cannot sleep. My eyes are always wet. I feel God is speaking to me to be a part of the work you are doing in India. Please pray for me.' Three weeks later he wrote again, 'Thampy, since I have been praying I have found an employment opportunity as a noise control officer. I went for the interview and I was hired for the position. You can count on every penny from that job for the ministry in India.'

"That man invested his life for India. He began to save every single cent out of his job. After two years he returned with the money. Before he came he wrote he would be in India on a certain date. His letter said, 'Please conduct a mass crusade where the gospel has never been preached. Arrange a good band for singing. There will be no other preachers other than you and me. Arrange for workers to look after the children and teach them good Bible stories. Make them happy.' Always in our crusades there are a lot of children. Chester was very concerned about children. On the first night there were over 5,000 people at the crusade. I announced that Chester Bieson, the great American evangelist, was going to preach and proclaim the word of God. I introduced him. He stood up in the pulpit. He said, 'Thampy is the man of God with the vision and the passion for the people of India.' Chester told them I had a great message. He asked the people to listen carefully. Then he sat down. I preached for an hour and I challenged the people. I explained the wonderful message of salvation. The people of India are very religious. Though they are worshipping millions of idols and gods they are still ignorant and very hungry for God. I explained how simple the love of God is for us. I told them of the great sacrifice of Jesus. At the end of my message I asked them to respond. About eighty-five percent came forward. Night after night the crowd grew. The Spirit was moving, demons were screaming, and the sick were being healed. At the end of those meetings there was a big revival in that area. Chester was really blessed. He said this was his confirmation that God had sent him to India. For two months he stayed with us. He asked me what my priorities in the mission field were. I had two-dozen young men going from village to village on foot. Chester bought them bicycles, PA systems and gospel literature. He built two more village churches. In three months, he spent all his money. Then he returned to the USA. For the next ten years that man invested all his life and time for the ministry in India. He did a big job.

"In India," Thampy continued, "we have a lot of Hindu and Muslim people that are kicked out of their homes for believing in Jesus. The women particularly become homeless and destitute refugees. We were looking after such people, feeding and housing them in our own home. One day Chester said, 'Thampy, look at these poor women put out of their homes for Jesus. They need a refuge. How much would that cost?' Then an acre of land and a building to accommodate one hundred people cost around $50,000. He said we should pray, 'God somehow must give us that money otherwise you cannot manage all these things. You have a lot of needs. You are not affiliated with any denomination or mission society. You live by faith, so let God help us.' A few months later he wrote, 'Thampy, God has given us an open door for our refugee home. I've received a letter from my attorney informing me my cousin has died and left me $50,000. That is the exact amount we prayed for. What a prayer answering God we serve.' Chester sent the money and we bought the land and built some buildings we called *Vivianna Life Centre*. It is next door to our headquarters. We have widows and refugees there as well as a Ladies Bible School. There is also a tailoring school for the women. Now these poor women who have been thrown out of their homes for believing in Jesus have a place to live and pray. In 1987 Chester Bieson passed away. He was a man after Christ to me. From time to time God touches the hearts of people in different countries to support us and to be a partner of the ministry. In all my life, God has never allowed me to affiliate with any denomination or mission. I think He wants me to depend on Him alone. I am still trusting God and our ministry is growing bigger and bigger every time. We don't have any visible resources other than God. I think that is the best one for me."

> *"Tell me about Cliff Beard."*

"Cliff Beard was an Australian missionary who had immigrated to Canada. I first met him in 1972. He asked me who I was and what was I doing. I said I was a Christian minister called to evangelize India. He explained his friends had gone back to Canada but he had one week left before his own flight. He asked me to arrange some village campaigns for him at short notice. Next day I called my disciples. We went to the border of Tamil Nadu and started a campaign. On the first night we had 500 people. Cliff Beard had a mighty anointing on him for casting out demons and healing the sick. The second night we had a few thousand. Third night we had 5,000. On the fifth night we had 10,000 people.

"All this happened without any publicity apart from word of mouth. Cliff was really stirred up. One night he woke me up at 2AM He said, 'Thampy, God is speaking to my heart to support you and to be a partner to you. I don't have any church or any connections. I am just an itinerant traveling minister. All I can do is take you to Canada and America and introduce you to some Christian people we know. Perhaps they can help you.' I asked him, 'Why should I leave India when it is the most needy country in the world for the gospel? India is closing to missionaries. Hinduism, Islam and Communism are pretty strong. Only the national people can do the job. God has called me to preach the gospel in India. Why should I go to Canada and America?' He said, 'Thampy, God is speaking to me. You don't have a bicycle or any resource.' I said, 'God is my resource. God is my support.' Cliff said, 'Of course He is, but God always uses people.' We argued for a couple of days. I told him I knew no English nor did I have any desire to go to Canada or America. Finally he convinced me to be open to God doing new things in my life. It was arranged we would meet in Vancouver.

"When I landed in Montreal, immigration officials began to ask me questions, 'Who are you? Why are you here?' I told them I was a Christian minister from India on a visit for three months. They told me a lot of people from India and Pakistan come to Canada and then vanish and never go home. They said they had decided not to take any more visitors. They said they were going to deport me. I told them God had sent me and they could not send me back. They said they were Canadian immigration with the power and the authority to decide who stays and who goes. I told them I was the servant of the Most High God. As He had sent me they could not stop me. They were mad at me. They asked who my sponsor was. I showed them my letter from Cliff Beard. When they contacted him they found out he was an Australian without money or a church to look after me. They said he was not eligible to sponsor me so they put me in jail for five days.

"When Cliff found out they had imprisoned me he argued with them. He even called an attorney to try and get me released. The Canadian Immigration authorities were angry and decided to deport me. They booked my flight for the next day. I told them, 'God Almighty sent me. You cannot send me back.' The Canadian Immigration chief said he was the supreme authority in Montreal immigration. I told him God was my supreme authority and I was His servant. He said, 'Wait and see.'

"Up until then I had been fasting and praying. I said, 'God, why did You send me here? They are going to deport me back to India. I didn't want to come to Canada or America. I didn't have any desire to come but Lord You put pressure upon me. You sent a man over to India to meet me and open the door for me. That is why I am here. Now they will deport me. I don't want to go back to India as a failed soldier for Jesus. During the last ten years I had no material possessions but I never failed. I enjoyed Your victory all the time. Lord, please don't let me fail now.' The Lord strengthened me. He reminded me that many Indian Bible students had come to Canada and America. When they saw the luxuries there they compromised with the world and never returned. God asked me, 'What will you do? Will you stay too?' I told the Lord I would not stay. I said, 'My mission is in India. India is my country. I will go back to India.' He asked me if I was sure. I told him, 'Yes Lord, don't worry.' The Lord told me no immigration authorities would be able to stop me. Later, I was invited to a tribunal. Ten officers began to question me. They asked me the purpose of my visit. I told them I was there to preach the gospel.

"The officers asked me why I had come to preach. I said, 'Because Jesus said to go and preach the gospel to all nations.' They said, 'India is a heathen country. Go and preach it there.' I told them, 'The Bible says all have sinned and fallen short of the glory of God.' They asked who would look after my wife. I told them my family lived by faith. Then they asked, 'If you preach the gospel in Canada what is your reward?' I told them I lived by faith and that Jesus was my reward. They were confused. They said, 'Thampy, Canadian immigration is not spiritual. It is political. We cannot write on our forms about Jesus and heaven and spiritual things. So forget Jesus, the Bible and heaven and answer our questions properly.' That was too much for me. I said, 'Sir, I cannot forget Jesus and His words and heaven. That's the only hope I have. Don't worry about me. Send me back to India. I am ready to go. I will not deny Jesus in order to gain entry to Canada.'

"I walked out of that office ready to return to India. I had no more to say. A while later the chief officer came and put his arm around my shoulder. He said, 'Pastor Thampy we have found you are a man of God sent by God. We have decided to give you a visa. Then he booked my seat to Vancouver. He called my friend Cliff Beard and told him I was allowed through. I met Cliff and his wife Helen at Vancouver Airport. Everyone was shouting and praising the Lord. Now as soon as I go to a foreign country I always feel the presence of the Lord. I say I am a man *from* India *for* India and as soon as my mission is finished, I must go home. God touched the hearts of a few faithful people and they organized *Christ for India* in 1974. They registered it as a charity in Canada and America. It is not a big thing. There is no publicity. God speaks to the hearts of people from time to time when I am in great need. Some who know me will send a check for *Christ for India*. We get a little money from here and there. All the time we have to trust God. We have to look to Him for our daily needs. He is always faithful.

"It was Cliff Beard who introduced me to Neil Milne from Australia in 1978. Neil was an olive farmer who helped Cliff in the ministry. I stayed with Neil and his wife Joy for a week. I poured out my heart about my burden for India. At the end of my stay Neil said God was speaking to them about coming to India. A few months later they arrived in Kerala with their three little children. Neil became a full time missionary, traveling, preaching and helping with campaigns, crusades and minister's seminars. Neil and Joy were a great strength to us. Sadly a great tragedy happened. Their second boy, Judson, was killed in an accident. He was only eleven years old. While on a school outing the boy slipped from a rock and fell ninety feet to his death. I remember doing the funeral. Neil and Joy were bold enough, singing and teaching during the funeral, though no doubt their hearts were heavy. They continued ministering here until the Indian government made a law that evicted all foreign missionaries. They went back to Australia leaving the tomb of their son as a memorial to their sacrificial work here. Neil became a pastor in Australia and later became the director of the whole *Australian Christian Revival Crusade* of three hundred churches. They are still serving the Lord. They are a wonderful couple who taught and helped in our ministry. They are keeping busy for the Lord. Once every few years we still manage to get a chance to meet each other and remember things. From time to time God has sent good people from the West to help us. There have not been so many in recent years since the new government has come to power. New laws forced us to discontinue all our non-Indian missionary activities. Now it is the Lord's season for the nationals to do the job. In the past we've had wonderful evangelistic crusades with hundreds of thousands coming to the Lord. But that's only the beginning. After a crusade is over the new believers need to be cared for and brought to maturity. That is why church planting has gone along with our evangelism. Now we have over one thousand churches in *New India Church of God*.

"Nowadays there is a great need for Christian brothers and sisters from the West to come and see the work and to catch the vision. Then, God may touch their hearts to become partners with us and support us by prayer and finances. Our workers are trained and ready to do the job. In India there are thousands of different ethnic groups all speaking different languages and dialects. They all have distinctive cultures. Only the national people can do the job. So we train the nationals. We equip them and we keep them alive and encouraged. We enable them to continue the work. But we need the tools and the support. If we can get enough tools we can do the job."

"*What are the tools?*"

"Things like Bibles, jeeps, PA systems, generators and motorbikes.

I used to buy bicycles all the time, but I now realize they are too slow. With a motorbike people can do the job very speedily. Now we have lots of teams organized in different areas. Already we have bought a few jeeps and minibuses. We have teams with generators and movie projectors showing the *Jesus* film. They go from village to village conducting evening campaigns. These teams get a few thousand people at each meeting. They show the movie and make an altar call. Hundreds of people come to the Lord every night. These villagers are ignorant but they are innocent. When they know Jesus Christ is the only savior and the only One to die and pay the price for humanity, with tears they come to the Lord. We have a good response in our village campaigns. Time is short. The militants and the communists are very strong. They try to stop Christianity. Their eyes are everywhere watching against white missionaries.

"A few years back religious fanatics burned alive an Australian missionary called Graham Staines. He was a worker here for over thirty years with lepers and orphans. They became jealous of his influence. One night when he was sleeping in his jeep with his two little sons, fanatics came and burned them alive. They challenge, 'No more Western missionaries in India.' I know the West is a sleeping giant. If God opened their eyes and touched their hearts they can be anything for us. Just like Chester Bieson. This old man was not a preacher or a missionary but for ten years he was a resource behind me to support and build the ministry. He was a man with the heart of Jesus for India. During those ten years a good foundation was laid on the mission field. I have been able to build on that foundation. Now the ministry has grown into twenty-one different states with over one thousand churches and nine Bible training schools. But all this is just a drop in the ocean in India. We still have a long way to go.

"India is the second largest populated country in the world with well over one billion people. Two thirds of the people in the villages have never heard the name of Jesus. In over 500,000 villages generations have lived and died and gone into eternity without ever hearing the gospel once. My ministry is reaching the unreached for Jesus. It has cost me everything: finances, tools, even my health. All these years my life was threatened, but I am still alive. God is with me, and if God is for me who can be against me? Wonderful God. Most of my enemies have converted to the ministry. The rest of them are dead. That is the way God has blessed me and used me in India."

Help From Afar

"I hear you have been kidnapped."

"Yes, it happened after I had conducted a few days of prayer and fasting meetings in a village. People got saved and there was a revival. This made some people very angry. Afterwards while I was walking home some fanatics grabbed me and took me on their shoulders. They carried me over one kilometer and locked me in a small room. They said I was an evil man coming to convert their people. They told me they had been watching and waiting for an opportunity to catch me. They said, 'You have to make a vow to never come back to this place and preach this gospel.' I told them I couldn't do that. I said, Jesus had commanded me to go and preach the gospel to the whole world, to all peoples. I explained these villages were included in that commission. They said if I returned they would kill me, 'We will shed your blood.' I told them Jesus had shed His blood and paid the price for me. I am not afraid to die. When I die I will go home to heaven. They beat me up and tried to force me to take an oath never to come back. I kept saying, 'No way.' In the early hours of the morning a local woman heard the noise of the beating and she came and knocked on the door. She stood up for me. She said, 'I have seen this man walking through the streets with a Bible. He is a Christian man. What are you doing with him? He is a good man. Leave him alone.' Her complaining awakened the neighbors. They came and rescued me. I have been persecuted and beaten several times. But always there was disunity between my persecutors and always God has allowed someone to come to my rescue. Wherever I go there is opposition and persecution but God will always touch some hearts to help me. He still keeps me alive."

"How did you first hear the call of God in your life?"

"Ever since I found Jesus I was full of enthusiasm because my sins were forgiven. I could not hold in the joy. I went to the streets and I talked to the people, 'Look at me, I'm forgiven.' People asked me how much it cost. What had I done? I told them, 'Nothing.' They said in India there are gurus and yogis that have been chanting and suffering for decades and still their sins are not forgiven. How could I say my sins were forgiven and it cost me nothing? I began to tell the simple story of John 3:16. It's all I know. For God so loved the world that He sent His Son to die for our sins on Calvary's cross. I have seen people touched by God's power and crying. All I know is John 3:16 and my little testimony. I was thrilled with the people responding and receiving Jesus in the street. Each night as I prayed I felt God was saying to me, 'Son, lift up your head and look to your own people. They live in darkness. They are under the bondage of sin and Satan. Go and share this good news. Tell them what God has done for you.' I said, 'God I don't have a church; I don't have a Christian friend. My parents are not Christians. Where will I get my money? Who will support me? How can I serve You in a country like India where the people hate Christianity and persecute Christians? It's not a good job for me Lord. Call somebody else. I am not educated. I was a bad boy in my school and in my home. My mum did not like me. My teacher did not like me, I was thrown out of my school. I am good for nothing. It's enough for me to be a good Christian. Please call somebody else for Your service.' Night after night God said, 'Follow Me! Follow Me! Give up your job and come be a full time minister in My vineyard. I will support you. My just shall live by faith.' Finally I had to submit. I realized the love of God. Jesus had died for me. I submitted to His will for my life.

"I still remember those days. I was walking from village to village and sleeping in bus depots. Often I did not have a proper meal for weeks. One day I was sitting alone. For almost a week I had not eaten. My mum was on a farm only two kilometers away. She had plenty of food. Perhaps she would give me something to eat. I knocked at my mum's door. I said, 'Unless you give me some rice I might die tonight.' She said, 'Evil boy, get out! What shame you have brought on our family. I have nothing for you. Get out!'

"I fell to the ground and prayed, 'Lord, even my mum doesn't want me. How am I going to serve You?' I lifted my head. Our family dog was eating rice from a bowl. I chased the dog and ate the rice. I began to cry like a child but the Lord comforted me. He said, 'Son, follow Me. If you follow Me in this life I will give you a hundred times more mums, dads, sisters and brothers. You will enjoy My presence and My power. Do not worry. Follow Me.' God has kept His word to me. He has given me mums, dads, brothers and sisters a hundred fold even in this world. What a wonderful God! Jesus said, 'If you follow Me and serve Me, I will bless you. I will look after you.' He is a good God. He is good all the time to me."

"How did you come to know the Lord?"

"When I was twenty-one I had a job in a rubber plantation. A Christian Anglican minister named Joseph came and talked to me about Jesus.

He was an Indian. I argued with him but that night I couldn't sleep. I saw my sins like on a movie screen. By midnight I went and asked that Christian man what I should do. He was awake praying for me. He taught me about Jesus; the One who paid the price for my sins. The One who died in my place. He told me to call on that wonderful name. I simply cried, 'Jesus, Son of God, have mercy on me.' Instantly my burden was lifted. My sins were washed away. I was set free. Since then the joy and fire in my heart is still there."

"How did the Holy Spirit come into your ministry?"

"Joseph, who led me to the Lord, was a Spirit filled man. He taught me how to pray, to serve, to read the Bible and how to be a good Christian. He was sharing with me about God's ministry and God's love. One day he said, 'Thampy you too can be a witness of Jesus Christ. You could be a good evangelist.' I said, 'I don't think so. How can I be?' He replied, 'Through God's power. Through the Holy Spirit who is God's strength.' He took me to a prayer meeting where a dozen people were fasting and praying. They were speaking in languages I had never heard before. I asked Joseph what was happening. He said, 'These people are worshipping God. They are speaking in tongues.' I said, 'What? Speaking in tongues? In India we have eighteen major languages, hundreds of sub languages and thousands of dialects. Why should these people be speaking something else?' Joseph answered, 'They are speaking the language of God. They are communicating with God in His language. If you do that your spirit communicates with God. Then you receive the supernatural power of God so you can serve Him more effectively.'

" 'Oh,' I said, 'In that case, I also need it. I want to communicate with God. I need God's power.' I knelt down and began to weep. I cried, 'Help me Lord.' I was praying for about three minutes and holding onto the leg of a table. I cried out, 'God, I love You. I want to serve You. I need Your power. I need Your strength. Anoint me Lord.' The power of God came upon me. I jumped over the table. My body was shaking. I was speaking a new language I'd never learned. For almost three days I couldn't stop. I was shaking and speaking these new languages. People thought I had gone mad. Only after three days could I control myself. Since then that fire of God has kept me in the midst of many trials and troubles. Oh praise the Lord! He breaks the chains of the enemy. He keeps me alive."

"Do the people under your ministry get baptized in the Holy Spirit?"

"Oh sure! Sure! Wherever we go we lead them to the Lord. Then we lead them into the Holy Spirit baptism. That is the only way forward for the Church in India."

Thampy was on a roll. I thought I'd keep him talking. I asked, *"How did you meet your wife?"*

He said, "In 1969, I was invited to speak at a convention at Mariamma's native place in Nagercoil, Tamil Nadu. Her whole family had just been saved and filled with the Holy Spirit that year. They were all at the convention. At the end of one meeting they invited me home for dinner. Mariamma has one brother and five sisters. She was the eldest. She had just graduated from University. Her parents ran the local post office. Her father told me, 'Mariamma thinks she's been called to the ministry. I don't know. As a girl how can she serve the Lord? It could be a consideration if she finds a boy like you who is a full time minister.' I told him I was not the person for his daughter. I was an uneducated nobody without resources. I didn't even know where I was going to sleep the next day. I said I would pray for a husband for his daughter. Then I walked out. A few weeks later we met again. He said, 'Pastor Thampy, we have been praying and praying and God still puts you in our hearts. We think you are the person for Mariamma.' Again I refused. I had no desire to get married. I was just a wandering street preacher. I said, 'I only have heaven over my head and the earth beneath my feet. If I marry your daughter she will have to suffer starvation and many trials.'

"Later, I returned for another convention. Again I was invited to their home. I had a serious talk with Mariamma and her father. I explained I was a man kicked out of his family home. I had nothing in the world. I told her, 'If you marry me, you will have to starve and endure persecution. All your life you will be suffering.' She said, 'I am called for that.' I told them I would pray about it. For the next three months I did and finally I felt it was God's will.

"My family was totally against me marrying a Christian girl. They wanted me to marry into their community. They didn't come to our wedding on October 6th 1970. Only Christian people helped. Even the next week after marriage we had to sit in the bus depot all night. We had no money, no home and no place to go. Yet we were happy. We were praying, preaching, and distributing gospel literature. Later we managed to rent a room. It's a long story. God is good. He blessed us with four beautiful children. All of them have surrendered their lives to serve the Lord. Three of them are in full time ministry. Bini in America is waiting for full time ministry."

"So Mariamma is a good wife: a woman of faith and prayer?"

"Busier than me sometimes. She is much in demand from women's groups all over India. She is a woman with a passion for souls. She loves the Lord very much. She is a great intercessor. She is the backbone behind the ministry. Prayer and fasting have been very important in our ministry. We started with prayer. That was the only resource we had. We believe in prayer. Prayer touches the hearts of the people. Prayer is power. God answers each and every prayer. The first thing we built at our present headquarters was the prayer tower. It is our powerhouse. All the time our intercessors are praying and seeking the Lord. Prayer is the tool of the Christian to touch the heart of God. Only by prayer can we put God in action. Prayer is continually going on. It is the only weapon against the powers of darkness. Here in India there can be no progress without prayer. The weapons of our warfare are not carnal. Their power is prayer. Whenever we pray the strongholds of the devil are pulled down. Then we see tremendous things happening.

"Women play a great part in our ministry. We have about forty women's missionary groups. Here in India, many Hindu and Muslim women have to stay locked up in the home like dishwashers and washing machines. They are forbidden to speak to men. Only women can deal with them. We train our women for one year in our Bible School. Then we send them out two by two into unreached areas. From morning to evening they knock on village doors handing out gospel literature and witnessing to the village women. Many of these women are depressed and disappointed with their lives. Our lady missionaries minister to these women and win them for Jesus. They follow up and organize women's meetings and so on. These Bible women need about $10 per month to live on. If they get more they think they are well off. They don't have any more clothes than two saris each. They are happy from morning to evening going door to door talking about Jesus. A lot of village churches have been started through their ministry. We can do the job if we have enough means and tools. The harvest is plenty and the laborers are there but we need the resources."

"Is sending money the best way for the West to help?"

"No. The first and best way to help is to pray for us. Money and people can be stopped but the effects of prayer can never be stopped. Always I need the portion of the Holy Spirit. I need the guidance and the power of the Lord. Secondly, we need financial support. In India there are a lot of workers, but the problem is the workers need to be trained, equipped and supported. For example, monthly support of around $50 can keep a pastor or an evangelist and their family in the ministry full-time. Many of our workers are struggling financially. Many of them don't even own a bicycle. I have fifty overseers who pastor their own churches as well as oversee other churches. Most have only a bicycle. With a motorcycle they could be much more efficient. There is a great need for motorbikes, jeeps and PA systems for our outreach. We also need generators. In the villages there is no electricity. When we show the *Jesus* movie we get hundreds maybe a few thousand people each night. They cry when they see Jesus persecuted. They say they have never seen such a good man as Jesus. He loves and heals the people. They say, 'All *our* gods demand blood, money, silver and gold. Jesus is the only God we have ever seen that heals, loves, and feeds the people.' When they see the crucifixion they weep and shout, 'It should not happen!' When they see Him raised from the dead they jump to their feet, clap their hands and rejoice. Then we make the altar call. They come and receive Jesus.

"My vision is to equip all our teams and leaders with jeeps, generators, PA systems, Bibles and literature and a little support to keep them going. We have a long way to go. We have to reach a nation of over one billion people. Jesus is the only answer. The gospel of Jesus Christ is the only hope for our nation. We have another problem. We usually start off in someone's home. Later as we grow we have to build a church with a cemetery. When the religious fanatics realize people are turning to Jesus they always kick us out from our rented places. So, unless we buy our own land we cannot get established. We also need somewhere to bury our dead. These responsibilities are on my shoulders. The poor village people cannot afford these things. Please God they will be able to someday but at present the new believers look to me and I look to God."

"How much does a church cost these days?"

"In a village we can build a basic church for $2,000. In a town it can cost as much as $20,000. In a village we can build with bamboo and mud. In urban areas we have to use stronger material and land is more expensive. All of this is a heavy burden. Beyond that, we have our part in reaching the unreached millions in this nation. I also have to help look after the people we already have. I must stir them up and keep them encouraged."

"Were you ever reconciled to your parents?"

"Yes. They were led to the Lord through our ministry. Dad was saved fifteen days before he died in 1979. My mum was saved in 1984. I baptized Mum in water. She lived with us until her death five years later. Three of my brothers were saved and went into full time ministry."

There was a gentle knock on the door. A waiter came in and quietly took the breakfast dishes away. I stood up intending to go for a stroll on the beach. I wanted to let Thampy rest for a while.

He said, "Did I ever tell you of how a communist man helped me in my early ministry?"

"A communist man?"

"Yes, a communist man helped me multiply the effectiveness of my ministry and he never ever knew it. He also got me into big trouble with my mother."

I sat down again on my small wooden bed, *"So what happened?"*

7

Tree Preacher

Thampy chuckled at my curiosity. He said, "In 1957, Kerala became the first state in the world to elect a communist government. One morning I was praying under some coconut trees when I saw a man walking purposefully by. There was something hanging from his shoulder. I became interested to know what he was doing. I climbed a tree and watched him. Nearby there were hundreds of poor women working in the rice paddies. He took the instrument off his shoulder and put it to his mouth. It made a big noise. He shouted, 'Children of the soil, rise up! The landlords are suppressing you. They are taking advantage of you. Stand up! We must fight for our rights. Follow me. Leave planting the rice and follow me. The revolution will have the victory!' The women all followed him to some big labor rally shouting, 'Victory! Revolution! Victory for Communism!'

"When I saw this, I was stirred up. I thought, *If hundreds of people can be so quickly challenged to follow this philosophy that sheds innocent blood, why then can't I preach Jesus to these same people? I need one of those tin instruments. How can I get one?* Then I remembered a big kerosene drum my mum had. I went home and poured the kerosene into various pots. I then took the drum without permission. I rolled it to a smithy about a mile away. I told the blacksmith, 'Make me an instrument like the one the communist man has.' He didn't know what I was talking about. He called his son. The son explained the communist leader had a loud speaker made out of tin. 'Oh, you want a megaphone,' said the blacksmith. 'Okay. I know what it is, but I am too busy today and tomorrow. I have too many things to do. Come back some other time.' I replied, 'Unless you make the megaphone, I will not go away for the Kingdom of God badly needs one.' I put pressure on him, so he began to make it. It took about three hours. When it was finished I used it to preach to him and his workmen. Then I went into his kitchen to preach to his wife and children. I was so happy with my new tool. I preached to all the houses I passed on my way home. I felt like a hero. By now my mum was very mad that someone had stolen her drum. I arrived home like a champion who was speaking about Jesus. She met me with a big stick. 'Bloody evil boy,' she said, 'I don't want you. Get out.' She whacked me hard. 'I'll break your feet if you ever come back!' she shouted.

"After that I began to go to the paddy fields where thousands of people were working. I preached, 'Children of the earth rise up! God has sent His only begotten Son to forgive your sins and to bring a revolution.' Jesus has said, 'Come unto Me and I will give you rest. I will give you peace.' I'd walk miles and miles to the paddy fields where I'd see crowds of people. I'd challenge them to come to the Lord who could give them rest. I declared, 'Marx didn't say he'd give you rest. Engels didn't say he'd give you rest. Mao Tse-tung didn't say he'd give you rest. Only Jesus of Nazareth the Son of God said that. He died on the cross on Calvary so your sins could be forgiven. He paid the price for your sins. Marx did not pay the price for your sins. Millions of people on five continents have found Jesus as their savior. They have had their sins forgiven.'

"During the monsoon season these isolated paddy fields are flooded. They look like an ocean. It was necessary to get a ride on a boat out of these flooded areas. One day I went to a landlord as he was leaving and asked for a lift in his boat. He said, 'I'm not helping you. I heard you preaching. You are interrupting my laborers. Don't come here with your new religion.' I was broken and sad. I started to cry, 'God, I haven't eaten for three days. I've been serving You. I can't get out of this place. I can't swim through these deep waters.' Some of the poor laborers came over and asked me how far I had to go. I told them I had to travel over one kilometer out of this big canal before I could begin to walk. They decided to help and buy me a meal in a country restaurant. Then, ten of them got a big boat and paddled me to the land. I felt like Jesus and His disciples going through the waters of Lake Gennesaret.

"After that I began to pray for a boat, *Lord, there are millions of people in these backwaters. They are living on small islands isolated from the mainland. I need a motorboat, Lord.* I prayed this same prayer for seventeen years. Once in a while, during these years, I would hire a boat for a day. With some of my disciples I would go and preach in the islands. It was expensive to hire a boat. I could only do this every three or four months when I got enough money. After seventeen years of prayer God performed a miracle. He got me a motorboat. A small team from America under the leadership of Tim Marsh, a pastor of *Idaho Christian Center,* began to send support of $50 per month. Then they came to Kerala for some mini-crusades. We had one on a backwater island. We took a government boat. This boat returned before midnight. The first night we had five hundred people at our meeting. Many people were healed and many gave their lives to Jesus. The second night we had well over one thousand people. They had heard about the healings and of the demons being cast out.

"This went on for five nights. Every night the crowd was getting bigger. But always we had to stop the meetings so we could catch the government boat back home. On the last night we waited and waited for the government boat but it never came. It had broken down. Eventually we awakened a countryman who owned a small boat. He rowed us to the mainland. This took five hours of steady paddling. The American team were uncomfortable. They had no food and they couldn't sleep with the mosquitoes biting them. They said, 'Thampy you need a boat. You definitely need a motorboat. We don't have a big church or lots of money but we'll pray about it.' They went back to America and began to tell their story. They presented the need to their small congregation of forty or fifty people. The people said, 'Surely we could raise some funds to buy a boat to help spread the gospel in India.' Some men worked overtime and gave the money for India. Some of the women found part time jobs and gave the money to India. Even the children responded. They gave up coca cola, candy and ice cream and sent the saved money to India. In only two months they had raised $7,000. They called me, and said, 'Thampy, we thought it would take us a year to raise the money. But after we rose to the challenge we found we were able to do it in two months. The money is here for the boat.'

"The West is a sleeping giant. Though many hearts are closed in the West there are still a lot of open doors. In India, the doors for missionaries are closed but the hearts of the people are still open. They are hungry for God. There is plenty of manpower to preach the gospel but we don't have enough tools or support to do the job adequately. I believe the Western people; people in Europe and America, have a lot of potential. They have a lot of opportunities. In India and Africa people are hungry for the gospel but the harvesters need support to strengthen their hands. Australians, Europeans and Americans; really they are sleeping giants. *Idaho Christian Center* was a church that couldn't find an extra dollar per month for missions. Then they saw the need and rose to the challenge. Within two months they were able to be the answer to a prayer I had been praying for seventeen years!

"For months I searched for a craft within the price range. One day I found a boat in a dry dock that was exactly the size we needed. The owner told me it was not for sale. He did business with Europeans. Afterwards he'd take them for a drive in the boat to make them happy. So he wasn't planning to sell. I was disappointed. It was exactly the size we needed. A couple of weeks later this man called me. He asked if I still wanted to buy his boat. When I went to see him he said, 'It's yours for $15,000.' I told him I only had $7,000. He chased me. I continued to pray. He called me again. He said, '$14,000.' I told him honestly, 'I only have $7,000.' He worked down to $10,000. I kept telling him I only had $7,000. Later he phoned me. He said he had a big tax bill from the government. If he didn't pay it they would take the boat and everything anyway. So he gave it to us for $7,000.

"That boat was only made to hold about thirty people. Usually over one hundred would be crammed onto it as we went from island to island preaching the gospel. For thirteen years, this boat moved through the backwaters. During that time we raised up a dozen churches in those areas. Nowadays most of those islands have been connected by road. A few years ago we sold the old boat. From two months of sacrifice by that little church in Idaho a dozen churches were raised up here in India. Because the little children sacrificed coke and candy for two months many people here have come to know Jesus. I bought the boat in 1983. I called it *Eliada*, a Swedish name meaning 'God's Love'. During the heavy monsoon rains we took clothes and food to the people on the islands. They were completely cut off and starving. I'd challenge them, 'I know you're flooded and famished. I have something to help you with. Come here.' They would line up in front of the boat. I'd preach the gospel for an hour. I'd tell them, 'I know you are hungry. I know you have nothing. I can help you by giving you some rice and clothes. But this is only a temporary help. It will only last for a few hours or days. But I have something else to give you that will last you forever. I can give you the bread of life, the Gospel of Jesus Christ.' Hundreds of people would be standing patiently with their containers as I preached to them. Along with the rice and the clothes we'd give them gospel literature. We'd also pray for them. Afterwards we would do follow up work. That is how we raised up churches in the backwaters of Kerala."

"How did you get started in ministry?"

"In the early time of my ministry my school friends and neighbors thought I was a fool. They believed preaching was not a good job for me. No one wanted to listen. There was no income. They didn't understand the call of God upon my life. Even I didn't fully realize what was happening. All I knew is that God had called me and I really didn't have a choice. In those days I would regularly pray all night. My mum didn't like me doing this. I'd be speaking in tongues. She would say, 'What are you speaking? What is wrong with you? You're acting like a mad man. My son is crazy.' But I was full of enthusiasm. I would pray and pray. Night after night God would waken me and have me intercede for the lost people of India. Then He'd give me a burden for a certain village many miles away. I would travel through the darkness and the silence. By 4AM I would reach the village. Sometimes I would climb up a mango or a small coconut tree and set my megaphone toward the crowded places. I would sing a small chorus, then begin to talk about Jesus, 'For God so loved the world, God loves you, God loves the people. Humanity is fallen. We are separated from God by sin. There is a big gap between God and man.' I explained the love of God and how He had sent Jesus to the earth. I would preach for an hour and make an altar call, 'If you open your heart right now and ask Jesus to come into your heart you will be saved.' I was just like a television evangelist talking to the people. I couldn't see them but I knew there were people out there listening. I would say, 'If you are sick I'm going to pray for you right now.' I couldn't see them and they couldn't see me, but by faith I preached the word of God. Sometimes a few people would come out of their homes to see where the voice was coming from. They'd sit about in their blankets listening. When the dawn came they'd see me. Some said, 'We thought you were an angel come to talk to us early in the morning.' Sometimes they'd give me a little coffee and talk friendly. Some joked, 'Come every morning and we will be on time for our bus. You are better than an alarm clock.' Young children would ask me to come everyday so they could awaken early for school. One night, God told me to go to a certain village about five miles away. I arrived about 3AM. I waited for an hour, then climbed a mango tree and set my

megaphone toward the crowded huts. It was still dark. I couldn't see anybody.
I spoke a strong message about salvation and the love of God. I remember
nobody was about that night. Nobody came to the tree later on. I made an
altar call and left. I had done my work.

"Years later I was sharing my testimony at a big church when I told
of how I used to preach from the trees before daybreak. I named many of the
villages I used to visit. After the meeting a woman came to the front of the
church with her husband and children. She was shaking and crying. She told
me, 'Fourteen years back I lived in one of those villages you mentioned. At
that time my husband was an alcoholic. Every day he'd get drunk and abuse
me. One night he beat me so badly I was unconscious until 2AM. For years
he had been persecuting me. That night when I awoke I decided I couldn't
take the beatings any longer. I kissed each of my children. I'd made up my
mind to kill myself. At the back of our house I tied my sari around a tree to
hang myself. I had no hope. I knew my family couldn't afford to receive my
children and me back. I had nowhere to go and I couldn't face the beatings
any longer.

"Suddenly, out of the darkness, I heard a voice speaking which said,
'Jesus loves you no matter who you are or what your problem is. No one in
the world may care for you but He cares. You may be a person who is fed up
with life and cannot cope any more. You may be a person who has no hope
for the future. You may be a person who is thinking of suicide. Killing
yourself is not the answer. Jesus is the answer. God loves you. Jesus loves
you so much. That's why He came to earth. Give your life to Jesus.' I was
so shocked. I just stood there in the darkness with the sari around my neck.
All the time the voice kept talking about Jesus. I thought God had sent an
angel to speak to me. I loosened the noose. I lay down under the tree sobbing.
Then I gave my life to Jesus as the voice told me. Immediately I was filled
with new hope and joy. I didn't want to die any more.'

Thampy continued, "She told me as the years went by God gave her
the strength to endure. She prayed for her husband and children. Eventually
her whole family committed their lives to Jesus. She never understood the
experience. She always thought an angel had spoken to her. Then after hearing
my testimony the mystery was made clear. She said, 'Thampy, I would have
been no more in this world unless you had come that morning to my village.
Now we all believe in Jesus. Will you please come and baptize us?' I was so

happy when she told me her story. It helped me realize we should be obedient to the Lord whether we see the results or not. That night I had no idea if anyone had listened to me. Always I was preaching in the darkness. Faith doesn't need to see in the natural. But God is good. Sometimes He pulls the veil aside to encourage us. He helps us to keep on believing that our faith will be rewarded."

I stood and walked over to a window. The rain was teeming again. I watched and listened to the downpour for a while. Thampy had been lying on his bed throughout his story. I turned to him, *'Well Brother Thampy, this is the second time we have shared a room together. Tonight I'll be staying with Biju and Secu. Maybe they'll tell me what it's like to have an Indian marriage."* He didn't answer. He was sound asleep. I lay down and continued listening to the monsoon. I wondered what my family was dreaming about in the middle of their Irish night. Were they missing their Dad? I sure hoped so.

8

The Young Bride's Story

Biju and Secu are temporarily staying in a converted gangster's home. The pictures on the walls are not exactly Christian but I like them. Biju has left early for an emergency meeting at the Bible School. Secu's dad, who is visiting, is out on the veranda enjoying the early morning coolness. He is humming to himself. In the kitchen I can hear the sound of Gracie, recently arrived from Mariamma's Ladies Refuge, singing to Timothy, their son. Secu and I are seated at the kitchen table.

"Tell me a bit about yourself."

"My Mum was from a Marthomite background. She didn't believe in praying to the saints or the dead. Neither did she believe in baptism by immersion. My father prayed to saints and believed in baby baptism. His family were very orthodox. Neither one had the anointing of the Holy Spirit."

"They didn't speak in tongues?"

"Nothing doing. They weren't baptized in the Holy Spirit. They had a love marriage. They both studied together at university in Andhra Pradesh and they liked each other. So they came back home and made it look like an arranged marriage though they had fallen in love beforehand. They kept this a secret from their parents because love marriages are not normal in our society."

"They probably got it the right way around, for Saint Paul said, 'If I speak in the tongues of men and of angels, but have not love, I am only a resounding gong or a clanging cymbal.' They had the love before they had the tongues."

Secu laughed, "I'm afraid there was also plenty of clanging cymbals in our home. Dad was a work-a-holic. Once he was hoping to be promoted in a situation when instead he was demoted. Some co-worker gave a bad report about him. It was such a shame. He was so disappointed. He had many problems at this time. Mum never encouraged us to go to church because she didn't want us praying to saints and such. We grew up without much Christian influence. My sister Prima and I had always been used to Mum and Dad's continual rows. After Dad's demotion there was also big problems with family, in-laws and finances. At one point things got so bad my parents thought of poisoning us all and finishing with life. Their trials and troubles seemed all too much. At this stage a man came. 'Why don't you go and see such and such a pastor who lives in such and such a place?' he said to Dad.

"Usually, if Mum talked about anything religious, Dad wouldn't listen. But this time she told Dad, 'Why don't you go there. They are believers.' To people outside, believers, are low caste. In India mainly only the poor people have become Christians. It's only very recently that high family people are turning to Jesus. In the main, Pentecostals have been farmers and fishermen, very low caste people. That's the major reason my mother's two brothers backslid. They became Christians when my mother was studying but returned to their traditional church so they could find suitable wives. They had both been filled with the Holy Spirit and both had begun prophesying. They were gifted and on fire for God but all of a sudden when it came to marriage, they realized they wouldn't get suitable partners from the Pentecostals. So they went back to the old Marthomite churches in order to get a wife. Now one of them has come back to the Pentecostals. The other is strong in church in social activities and so on. Anyway, to Mum's surprise Dad said they'd both go and see the man of God. Dad had been so upset and troubled. He became so thin you could hardly recognize him. As soon as they stepped into the house Dad felt the peace of God. The pastor talked to him, from I John, about the love of God. Dad was really moved. That day they both committed their lives to the Lord. When they came home we were expecting the normal fight but, to our surprise, they were both very good. I was about eight years old and Prima was about thirteen at this time. I thought, *Wow! What has happened to them?*

"My parents said we were all going to church on Sunday. For the rest of that week they didn't fight once. Prima and I were excited to see what sort of a church it was that caused such a change in our parents. We went and we just loved the place. This was the *Church of God* in Cochin. The smiles on the peoples' faces were so welcoming. They were all so loving. Dad became like a small child. All the anger and tension just left him. He became so soft and nice, just like you see him today. One day a visiting pastor came to conduct a service. He gave an altar call for salvation. There were just the four of us, Mum, Dad, Prima and I that went forward for salvation that day. After seeing the changes in Mum and Dad's lives I knew Jesus was the answer to all our problems. Dad's newfound faith caused healing between him and his brother. Old problems no longer had the power to defeat him. Our home became a happy place. Dad began getting promotions. In May they went to the church and in August they were baptized. Next year Prima was baptized. When I was twelve, I also was baptized. I got baptized in the Spirit before I was baptized in water. Our pastor would come to visit and pray with us. One day we were praying together in our home and I was filled with the Holy Spirit and spoke in tongues. Our pastor had the gift of healing. Prima would see visions and pictures in the Spirit but she couldn't interpret them. Our pastor would come and pray with us when he needed some guidance. Prima would see and explain a picture from the Lord, then pastor would be able to interpret it."

"Is it easier now for high families to get a wife than it was in your uncle's time?"

"Much easier. Now lots of good families are coming to know the Lord. Before, you couldn't even imagine a city Pentecostal church. They used to be only in the villages among the poorest people. Pentecostalism now includes higher social levels."

"Who was it that told your Dad to go and see the Pastor?"

"We never met that person again. Sometimes we wonder if it was an angel. If Dad hadn't gone to see the man of God that day, our lives would be so different now. Thank God he and Mum went."

"What's it like to join a family like Biju's?"

"I feel it is God's plan. I feel God has brought me to the right place. But sometimes things seem much too fast. Being in the ministry is not a nine to five job. In India, it's a twenty-four hours a day job on fast forward."

"What age were you when you received your marriage proposal?"

"I was eighteen. I'd just written my first school year exams when the proposal came. I wasn't ready to get married. My sister married when she was twenty but I was thinking, *There is no way I am getting married that young.* I said to Mum, 'What's wrong with you trying to get me married off at this age? No way am I going to get married.' Mum told me to calm down. She said to pray about it to see if it was God's will. The proposal came on a Saturday. The next day I decided to put a fleece before the Lord. As I went to church, I asked God to allow the pastor to speak on the verse from 1 Corinthians that says, 'No eye has seen, no ear has heard, no mind has conceived what God has prepared for those who love him.' My fleece was that our pastor would speak those words. During the sermon he was speaking on some other topic altogether when all of a sudden he quoted this verse and spoke about it. I was so shocked. My heart began to pound so hard I thought everyone in the church could hear it. Then after the service two or three people came up to me and during our conversations used the same verse. They said things like, 'Don't worry, no eye has seen nor no ear heard the things God has prepared for those who love him.' In the normal course of conversation there is no way people would use that verse. I was knocked for six, but at the same time I also felt a real peace that God was confirming to me this marriage was from Him. Had it not been for this confirmation I'd probably not have married so young.

"At this point I hadn't even seen a photo of Biju. Next Sunday his mum just turned up at our church. I felt a little overwhelmed that things were moving so fast but since God had answered my fleece prayer, I also felt strangely at peace about it all. At that time, Pastor Thampy was in the hospital in our home city of Cochin. He had had an angioplasty for his heart problem. The day after Mariamma's surprise visit to our church he was discharged. Mariamma, Biju and Thampy dropped in to see us on their way back to Goa. Biju was allowed to talk to me for a few minutes. He asked me a few questions like, 'Where do you study? Do you play any instruments? Are you called for the ministry?' Mama asked me to sing a song, which made me awfully nervous. I didn't expect that in a marriage interview. Thank God, Biju got me off the hook by telling Mama not to embarrass people like that. Then, because their car was causing an obstruction, Biju had to leave to move it. That was how my marriage interview ended. Some photographs were taken and by the time Biju came back they were all ready to pray and leave. On our first contact Biju and I had only a few minutes together."

"How did you feel when he was talking to you?"

"Scared. Very nervous. My heart was thumping. At the beginning I was quite cool until Mama asked me to sing. After that I nearly forgot my own name. When they'd left, Mum asked me, 'Do you mind dark guys?' I said, 'No,' because my father's dark. My brother-in-law is also dark. Biju was darker than them. I said skin color didn't bother me. Beforehand I hadn't really liked dark skin but when I saw Biju it didn't seem to matter. In India people tend to prefer light skin. Dark skinned girls are not really appreciated. It's probably a cultural thing. That afternoon, I went back to college. The next weekend when I returned home Mama and Beena had come to see me. Dad was working in Orissa at that time. Again I was asked to sing. This time I was a little more prepared. I sang, *I'm Forever Grateful.*

"Beena tried to scare me. She said Biju was ten years older than me but none of that bothered me. That same weekend Bini and Binu also arrived. The next Saturday they all came to visit. That's when Biju talked to me for a little longer. He talked about the ministry. He said life in the ministry was not easy. He said we'd have to go to North India to poor villages. 'It's not going to be a life like you have now,' he said, 'It's going to be hard. You might cook a special dinner for me but I may possibly not turn up. Someone else may have invited me to their home. If that would lead them to the Lord I'd have to go.' He also talked about hygiene. He said it wouldn't be very clean in the villages where one might have to sit on a floor made of cow dung. He told of an incident in Karnataka when after a meeting they were having rice in a believer's home. They asked for water. A boy with a runny nose wiped his nose with the back of his hand. He grabbed three glasses and dipped his hand and glasses into the bucket of water. They had to drink it without comment. All those things he told me. I didn't feel too yucky about it so I said, 'OK.' In the past I had committed myself to the ministry and I was ready to do whatever was necessary."

"When was that?"

"When I was sixteen. The state overseer was visiting at a public meeting. It rained that day, so we had to go inside. He intended to do an altar call for salvation but things changed. He made an altar call for ministry instead. He challenged us, 'Who will go to Africa and North India for the Lord? Many want to go to America, but who will leave all to follow Jesus?' I felt as if someone pushed me forward. I arrived at the altar steps in tears. My heart was broken. I said, 'Here I am Lord, send me, use me.' After that, nothing seemed to change much. I just continued with my studies. If I'd kept on in the way I was going I'd have turned into an academic. Mum is a lecturer in a university. She teaches Zoology. Dad is a marine biologist with the Government. Although I'd committed myself to the ministry thoughts of studies and jobs began to fill my thinking. My vow to God was pushed well to the back of my mind though apparently not to the back of God's mind. At the right time He pulled me out of the system. I was studying Computer Science. I thought my career would be along those lines. I imagined I'd be either a programmer or a teacher in a Computer Institute."

"Didn't Mariamma see you in a vision?" I said, half remembering something someone had said.

"Yes. During our talk she asked me what my legal name was. She knew my pet name was Secu. I told her, 'My name is Secunda Mariam Verghese.' When I said this she and Beena gave each other a knowing look. I had no idea what they were thinking about. Later, I learned when Mariamma had prayed for a bride for Biju, she had heard the Lord's voice saying, 'Let one more Mariam come.' Mariam means Mary. In earlier times, in India, ladies got Amma, meaning mother, added on to their names. Even when they were just babies Amma was added to their names. So Mariam and Mariamma are basically the same name. Then the next week I got married. My parents used to say, 'If it's the right proposal then all of us will feel a peace about it.' They were right. We all had a great peace about Biju. This was also a confirmation."

This concept of arranged marriage is pretty foreign to us in the West. Once I mentioned this to Biju. He asked me how I'd met my wife Angela. I explained I chanced on her at a dance I'd never been to before in my life. It had been a spur of the moment decision to go, even though I wasn't dressed for the occasion. In those days, in Ireland, one had to wear a shirt and tie in order to be admitted to the community dances. I was never much of a shirt and tie man. I was more of a Hippy, an Irish Hippy with shamrocks in my hair.

Biju had laughed and said, "I could never imagine my dad saying, 'Biju, go down to the dance and get yourself a wife.'" The whole idea was totally ludicrous to him. I didn't bother trying to explain that I hadn't gone to the dance to look for a wife, nor had my mother sent me there for that purpose. In fact, she hadn't wanted me to go at all, but as they say in Ireland, "Every cripple has his own way of walking and every tinker his own way of dancing." It says in Proverbs 19, that houses and wealth are inherited from parents but

84

a good wife is from the Lord. It doesn't mention the way God chooses to get the good wife to the husband. I was happy enough to leave it at that.

Secu said, "I was eighteen when I was married. Within a month I got pregnant. I wasn't prepared for that. The first three months were very bad. I could hardly get off my bed. I was sick all the time. Every hour I'd throw up, but after three months I began to feel better. Then Biju and I went to England. While there the sickness returned. Before meetings was especially difficult. Sometimes as we were going out the door I'd feel nauseous. I'd cry to God, 'You told me to get married. Now I'm pregnant and sick. Why are You doing this to me?' Biju didn't know I was feeling like this. One day we had an appointment to see an English prophetess called Deborah. We'd never met her before. A friend of Biju's family, Marion Copp, had made the connection. As we entered Deborah's home I felt the presence of God. Soon after being introduced, she started prophesying to me. She didn't know I was pregnant for I didn't have a tummy then. She prophesied, 'Secu, your marriage is not a mistake and the baby in your womb is not a mistake.' Nobody but God knew I was grumbling about my condition. God was saying, through Deborah, 'It's okay Secu, this is all part of My plans for you.' Before this word when people used to pity me I also used to feel sorry for myself. I'd say, 'Oh God, I'm only eighteen. How could You do this to me?' When I heard this prophecy I was really encouraged. Afterwards, when someone came to sympathize with me I'd say, 'It's the will of God I'm having this baby. My marriage and my baby are gifts from God.' I was able to see things differently and because I saw things differently I behaved and felt differently. The prophetic word of God restored peace to my heart."

"Have you any plans to finish your education?"

"I intend to. Before I got pregnant, Biju and I talked about going to Canada for further studies. He thought of doing an M.A. in Theology and I thought I might study Psychology. Nowadays in India a degree is the basic qualification. People expect you to have at least that. I read that five million Indians graduate each year. My parents expect me to study some more."

I said, *"Earlier this year I finished an M. A. in Irish Literature after leaving it on the back burner for twenty years. Life has a habit of interrupting our plans. I have faith as it says in Joel 2 that the Lord can restore the years the locusts have eaten. I also believe, as in the book of Esther, that people are raised up for certain times and certain purposes. God's plans must come before our own goals and agendas. It was a hard thing for Esther to submit to God's plans, yet in the end, her obedience saved the whole Jewish nation and kept a people alive that the Messiah would be born through. Esther had no notion her surrender to God's will, would affect the future of all creation for the better."*

Gracie came in and offered more coffee. Timothy had fallen asleep. I said to Secu, *"It's one thing talking about hardship. It's quite another thing experiencing it. Have you sat on any cow dung floors yet?"*

She laughed, "We went to Madhya Pradesh last February and traveled amongst the tribal peoples. The food was strange and the roads were terrible. The place we visited was called Bastar. This is the biggest tribal region in India. Inside the jungle there are people who don't wear clothes. We even saw adults and small children armed with bows and arrows. If they feel threatened they will shoot their arrows at you. I felt like a time traveler. I couldn't imagine people still living like this, eating leaves and bamboo shoots. I saw one woman kneading bread and breast-feeding at the same time. We had to travel for hours, by jeep. We drove along dried up streams and riverbeds. We were all travelsick. We also got diarrhea from the food. Because we were special guests they gave us chicken. They boiled the water and just dipped the chicken in and out of it quickly. It wasn't cooked properly. They used a lot of chili pepper. All the food was extremely hot and the rice was sticking together. With their hands they grabbed a gooey lump and put in on your coconut leaf plate. I could hardly bite into the chicken. It was so hot and raw. We had to finish everything in order not to offend them. I enjoyed the strangeness of it all.

"We have some churches there. A pastor and some people traveled out from that region and moved into the city. Now they are a bridge between the people and us. There's a lot of witchcraft in that area. There's a particular demon that is known for drinking blood. These people have devised magical powers so they too can drink people's blood. They might walk alongside and throw a thread onto you. You won't notice this thread but in the night they are able to use this point of contact to drink your blood. In the morning all your blood will be gone. Many people have died from this ritual. We met two ladies who became Christians after losing their blood. They got their lives back and were saved."

"Do they drink all your blood?"

86

"To the very last drop."

"Sounds a lot worse than the rubber hand." We burst into fits of laughter. It's easy to be brave during daylight hours.

Secu said, "The Bible says the life is in the blood. When these two ladies were dying from their blood loss their families called upon two of our pastors for help. They went and prayed. The two ladies were saved and healed. They were in good health when we met them. Going there was a great experience. It's good to see all the many different ways God is bringing people to know Jesus. It's very exciting."

"More exciting than a degree in Psychology?"

"I don't think psychology would have helped those two ladies get their lives back," she smiled.

9

Seeking First The Kingdom.

In the early morning as we walked to the car we passed little shrines with fresh flowers. Women were coming to the communal well with their water jars. Secu holding baby Timothy on her left hip carried a case in her right hand. Biju was hauling a fold-up pram. He said, "I never realized until I was in England how difficult it must be for Westerners to visualize a lot of the scriptures, like the woman at the well, animals being unequally yoked, etc. They must have to use their imagination an awful lot. Here in India things are still very much as in Bible times; sheep and goats are being herded, cripples are lying in the street, fellows are begging, demons are coming out of people, oil lamps are still functional and so on. Here, Bible stories are very much in context. In the 500,000 unreached villages of India a life-style very similar to that of Jesus' time goes on daily. Even in the West you don't have arranged marriages like in the Bible any more."

"Do you think Mother Teresa is in hell?" I asked. He laughed at my typical Northern Irish sectarian question timed to throw him off balance. Back home, a fellow Christian had asked me the same question. He'd been deadly serious. I was interested to hear how Biju would answer.

As we drove along the narrow road Biju said, "Mother Teresa was one of the most powerful leaders the world has ever known. She did not assert herself outwardly. Her influence came from real internal authority. She showed the whole world you don't need expensive clothes to create an image. Her only outfit was the uniform worn by the scavengers of Calcutta. She went to the White House and talked to the President of the United States of America in that uniform. She went to Buckingham Palace and had dinner with the Queen in that uniform. She went to St. Peter's in Rome and talked to the Pope in that same uniform; the cheap sari worn by the dispossessed of

Calcutta. In India, the scavengers are a despised people yet Mother Teresa was proud to identify with them. She gave them dignity by taking them to her heart and wearing their clothes. She won India by love.

"I heard a story about the early days of her ministry when she had no money. Once, in order to help the aged and dying, she asked an Indian pharmaceutical shop owner for some medicines. He angrily abused her, 'Get out. You are a foreign missionary who has come here to convert my people. I won't help you. You are a Christian. India is a Hindu country. Get out of my shop.' She never flinched. With outstretched hands she quietly repeated, 'Please give me something for the dying.' The shopkeeper collected a big glob of spittle in his mouth and spat it full on her face. He thought she'd just walk away humiliated. She didn't move. Her expression didn't change. She just kept her hands open. 'Thank you,' she said. 'That was for me. Please give me something for the dying.'

"That was Mother Teresa. She is one of my all time favorite ladies. If she didn't have the love of Jesus in her heart she could never have achieved what she did in India. In the end she won the hearts of the people. When she died the whole of India mourned. Even the Hindu government honored her ministry by giving her a State funeral. She established her missionary society in over one hundred different countries, not because she was a loud person, nor because she had five telephones on her table but because of the love of Jesus and the eternal confidence she had in her relationship with her Lord. That was what kept her going. I heard her clothes were full of stitch marks. When she died her only possessions were three white saris and a bucket. This was her bucket for water to cleanse the sores of the lepers."

"Was she a little like Gandhi?"

"They were similar in some respects but very different in others. Their visions were different. Gandhi was a political revolutionary. His vision was a free India. Her vision was to show the love of God to the people of India. One common thing about them was that they were both completely sold out to their visions. Nothing could distract them, neither material things nor positions of power. When Mother Teresa went to America someone gave her a brand new Lincoln Continental car to use in her work. She immediately auctioned it and gave the money for a new home for lepers in India. That was Mother Teresa. When I talk about her I get excited. Her commitment to her vision was exemplary."

India - One Act of Kindness

"Has AIDS affected India much?"

"AIDS is a growing problem especially in Bombay, Delhi, and other large cities. In the Sangli district of Maharashtra, where we have a work, I personally know many people that are HIV positive. AIDS is a growing disaster in India. The government, like many other governments in the third world, tends to play down the extent of the epidemic in order to prevent panic. I believe it'll become one of the great challenges of the twenty-first century. At present we have three children in Goa, in our Bethesda Life Centre, whose parents have AIDS. The father is missing. We don't know whether he is alive or dead. Thankfully none of the children have AIDS but now the poor mother is unable to provide for them. She's too sick to work so we're taking care of her and her children. This puts an extra financial burden on us but what else can we do?

"In the Gospel we read Jesus taught the people for three days and then he fed them. I believe our number one priority in India is to preach the gospel but I also believe there is a social aspect to this gospel as well. James warns us not merely to say to someone in need, 'Go I wish you well; keep warm and well fed.' Rather he encourages us to give to the needs of the poor, warning us that, 'Faith without works is dead.' In Jeremiah 22:16 it actually says caring for the poor and the needy is the act of knowing God. Mother Teresa lived by this reality.

"Yet there is also a subtle danger in this for one can get sidetracked into only doing social work instead of preaching the gospel. That is a big trap of the devil's. If you are just feeding people without giving them the gospel they are merely going to hell on a full stomach. To only give education without sharing the gospel is not a very clever thing to do. The main food people are starving for is the bread of life. Jesus Christ has to be preached. The gospel has to be proclaimed so people can receive eternal life. We may receive healing but it's only temporary. We will die sometime. Our stomach can be full but we'll get hungry again. Clothes will eventually wear out. Preaching the gospel is the most important thing of all. But it's not an either/ or choice. It's a both/and situation. We must help people in need because we love them. The love of Jesus compels us to do so. We don't give food to people so they will listen to the gospel. We give food to the people because we *love* them. We preach the gospel to people because we *love* them. Over the years many organizations have come to India with social ministries but at best they have only been of limited value. The gospel is the only answer to India's problems. In Romans 1:16, it says, 'I am not ashamed of the gospel, because it is the power of God for the salvation of everyone who believes: first for the Jew and then for the Gentile.'"

We talk about how easy it is to lose the simplicity of the gospel. Biju and Secu are eating apples as we drive along. Timothy is sucking on a biscuit. Biju begins to talk about liberal Christians. He said, "There was one fellow from Kerala who was on fire for the Lord. Then he went to Bible Seminary in Bangalore where they taught him about world religions. Now he believes one can worship Jesus and Krishna, Jesus and Buddha and Jesus and Mohammad. Such nonsense. Now he's just lukewarm and totally confused. What I'm trying to do in our Bible Schools is to focus on simple faith. A couple of months back our Bible School students presented a drama. When our students first come to us they are all on fire for God. After finishing Bible School some are acting as if they were theological graduates. In the drama one guy says, 'Let us pray.' Another guy starts praying loudly, 'Jesus, Jesus.' Another guy interrupts him and says, 'You can't pray to Jesus. You must pray to the Father in Jesus' name.' So confusion and discord breaks out.

"Knowledge puffs up. That's not what Bible Schools are supposed to do. They are there to equip the saints to do the work of the ministry. The Liberals in the West say, 'Religion is very personal. You can't push one faith over another. One religion is as good as another.' That is Liberal theology and I don't agree. It takes more faith to believe in liberal theology than to believe in the miraculous. They say, 'Five thousand people came with their lunch packs, waited three days and then ate their sandwiches. Mary went to the house of Elizabeth and Zechariah and got pregnant by Zechariah, the father of John the Baptist.' I read that in a book. It's a lot of rubbish. These fellows neither know the scriptures nor the power of God. They even have theories against the virgin birth of Jesus. That stuff makes me angry.

"During my time in England I attended a Church of England service. The minister was speaking about the ascension of Jesus. He read a portion of scripture, 'Jesus ascended to heaven.' Then he said, 'Of course it didn't happen that way. Elijah going up in a chariot of fire? Of course it didn't happen that way. Tongues of fire coming down from heaven? Of course it didn't happen that way. They are all pictorial allegories to help us understand

91

ideas. Jesus didn't really rise from the dead. He just became the center of our thinking.'

"Listen Brendan, if Jesus didn't rise from the dead then you and I had better shut up and go and sell hamburgers or vegetables in the market place. We should do some other work to get some money. This is why so many people come from the West to follow Indian gurus and babas. At least here they see the supernatural at work. If Jesus isn't risen from the dead then Christianity is no better than any other Indian religion. They have more philosophies than us. Miracles are happening here in India. Baba is doing miracles and teaching philosophies. Lots of spiritual leaders come from India. They have thousands and thousands of followers. They talk about love, they help the poor and they build hospitals. They do all these things. But they all die and remain in the grave and that's the end of their story. People build shrines to them. Mother Teresa did a lot of good work here but now she is dead. What makes Jesus different is that He died and He rose again. That is the message we preach. Otherwise the death of Jesus is a failure. They crucified Jesus on a cross. If Jesus didn't rise again to life then Jesus is a failure story to Hindus. Many of the heroes in their epics were attacked but won great victories in the end. What chance has the Christian story against such heroic tales if Jesus didn't conquer death, defeat the devil and rise again from the dead?

"Rising again from the dead is what makes sense of the whole crucifixion story. He died for the sins of the whole world. He shed His blood. Nobody could kill Him. He laid down His own life. He rose again. He has the power. That Church of England preacher with his, 'Of course it didn't happen like that,' ideas would be of no use whatsoever in a spiritual country like India. The people would laugh at him. He has nothing to offer. By denying the miraculous and the resurrection he has made void the word of God. Liberal theology is a load of rubbish with its notions like, 'The Red Sea opened up because the tide was going out.' It takes more faith to believe stuff like that than to believe scripture. I believe in the Bible 100% because I see it at work in India every day. Jesus said we would do greater works. He said we would see the dead raised and the blind seeing. We see these things happening here in India. The gospel is still the power of God to salvation to everyone who believes.

"There are some things in the scriptures that we find hard to understand. It says in Deuteronomy 29:29, 'The secret things belong to God, but that which is revealed is for us and our children, that we might walk in His ways.' Only the things that we need to know so we can walk in His ways are revealed to us. In Jeremiah 33:3 it says, 'Ask of Me and I will teach you unspeakable things you do not know.' The Holy Spirit will teach us, not the commentaries. Commentaries are good to get the background and the context but you can't build your whole ministry on commentaries. The Holy Spirit must lead us. These kinds of things have to be taken seriously. Unbelief is a thief that creeps into the Church. If you go according to this liberal theology or extreme Calvinism then there is no motivation to go and evangelize. Why should you go and evangelize if God knows who is going to get saved anyway? Better to sit in your home and spend time with your wife and baby."

Biju said, "There are two influences in India; the influence of the gospel and the influence of the cults. The Church in the West needs to make an impact in the Western world. Otherwise the cults and the gurus will make an impact for them. In the West people say religion is a very private thing, meaning we can't discuss these matters. If it's only a personal thing then how come the gurus are making such inroads in the West? Jesus said, 'Go and proclaim, preach the gospel to all creation.' He didn't say, 'When you receive the Holy Spirit you will receive the power to sit in the church and say Hallelujah!' The whole purpose of the Baptism in the Holy Spirit is that we may receive power to be witnesses and not just to have a happy-clappy time. Its not a case of, 'Come to the church every Sunday and run to the altar for some blessing.'

"We need to see people coming to the altar to get saved; not to get soaked. We must remember, 'A land that takes in much water and doesn't bear fruit is in danger.' India is hard work. It's not Christian entertainment. Liberal theology talk is useless in India. Here without prayer nothing works. When we go into new unreached territories we pray and intercede. Our intercessors especially pray all the time. There is a spiritual blindness like a veil that stops people from understanding the salvation message. Salvation is not an intellectual convincing, it's a revelation in which the inner eyes of a person have to be opened. As the Bible says, 'The god of this age has blinded the minds of unbelievers, so that they cannot see the light of the gospel of the glory of Christ, who is the image of God.' Intellectual convincing and reason alone cannot break spiritual blindness.

"Of course there is a place for reasoning. Paul reasoned night and day with the Bereans but for a person to come to a saving knowledge of Jesus as Lord, logic is not enough. We can argue and win the argument, but lose the person. We can lose the argument but win the person for Christ. There've been times when I've had to tell people that I don't have all the answers, but I know that Jesus is the answer. I believe spiritual blindness can only be broken through spiritual warfare. By prayer and fasting. Intercession is vital. We see this in Reinhard Bonnke's ministry. While he is preaching salvation on top of the platform as many as one hundred people are interceding underneath it. People are holding him up in prayer. Prayer is vital. Again it comes back to the fact that we can't do it in our own power. 'Not by might nor by power, but by My Spirit, says the Lord Almighty.' It's got to be Jesus.

"We must come back to the apostolic kind of witnessing and preaching. Peter preached the gospel and 3,000 people got pricked by the Spirit in their hearts. He preached the message without compromise. A while back I was really concerned about some problems our churches in Kerala were experiencing. I asked God, 'Why are there so many problems in so many churches?' The answer came, 'The quality of the believer is going down because the quality of the message is going down.' God really convicted me. We must come back to the apostolic kind of preaching, 'You crucified Him. The same Jesus whom you crucified.' We must share the gospel with boldness. The early apostles were talking out of assurance. That kind of preaching has to come back. This concept that it's all very personal and all very private is a big lie of the devil. Here in India gurus and babas are pushing their beliefs. They are telling people about their philosophies and winning people to follow their gods. In the West there is a huge vacuum created by an absence of the true gospel message. I believe the church in the West has to stand up and make an impact otherwise these religious teachers from India will fill that vacuum with their new age philosophies. If you go along to these cult places in India you'd think you were in the West because of the number of Americans attending. There were thousands upon thousands of people from Europe and America at these meetings. It's big business. These centers have high quality conditions. All very clean and very posh, built with money from America."

"*A bit better than your Bible Schools,*" I joked, referring to the rather Spartan conditions of the latter. Biju was in no mood for repartee. He looked hard at me. He said, "I don't think so. I don't think they are any better than our Bible Schools. Better in the land of famine with the promise than the land of promise with the famine. The way to darkness is broad. The way to destruction is wide. The way to heaven is narrow. Where are these cults and gurus getting their money from? They are being financed from the West. Finances are pouring in to assist the spread of these myths. The truth is the Western nations, which are supposed to be Christian, are the very ones supporting the various cults in India. These cults are the very people who stand against the Christians in India. These cults and their new age darkness are being fueled and financed by the West. That is where I believe there is a role for the Christian church and the people in the West. I am convinced we can make a vast difference if the Western churches will stand with us. God is raising up apostles, pastors, teachers, prophets and evangelists in India. These are native people who know the languages and cultures of India. Surely they are the people who deserve support from the West and not the gurus who are enemies of the gospel. Things are the wrong way round at present.

"It seems most people don't know how to help us. When I go to places, in England for example, I can become very frustrated. After I share about the needs in India they regularly respond, 'We will come with a team of people to help.' Now I understand and appreciate their heart in this matter but that's not the best use of resources. On one hand it's good that the team of mostly young people should come and have an exposure to what is happening in India. On the other hand it really isn't the best use of money and manpower. The cost involved in covering fifteen to twenty people's airfares, travel, and so on would keep thirty to forty full time workers in the ministry for a year. This would be a much more effective use of resources. Managing a group like that can also be very difficult for the church here. They need an interpreter. They need to go shopping. They want to phone or e-mail home. They get Delhi-belly. They have to go to the doctors and pharmacies and so on."

"Sounds a bit like me."

"You're okay." said Biju. "You're low-maintenance, high impact. I know peoples' hearts are good and that some folk need to see what is really happening in the mission fields of India. But in many ways it's a case of, 'Blessed are those who have not seen and yet have believed.' A lot of people have sacrificially sent us financial support without ever having seen the harvest here. I've no doubt they will receive a great reward in heaven for their giving. We must give our efforts to that which is most effective. As Paul says, 'All things are permitted, but not all things are useful.' So I say, 'Let key people from the West come. Let those with influence come.' People like you, who will pour out their hearts and preach and pray and prophesy. Yesterday at the Bible School, you saw the need. You really lifted up the spirits of the students. You greatly encouraged them. What we need are two-way influencers. People, who can motivate and build up the body of Christ here and then go back home and educate the people there as to how they can best help the work in India. They are the people we've got to give time and space to. So instead of twenty people coming, tying up our resources and costing lots of money rather let us learn to use time, energy, finance and manpower to maximum use. I pray for these dual impact people, who will impact here and then impact at home. They are the people who will make a real difference. They are the people we need to work with."

"Is there a place nowadays for teams like those Cliff Beard brought here in the 1970's & 1980's?"

"Those big teams were great for their time but not for today, for a number of reasons. Most importantly, nowadays we have plenty of trained indigenous leaders ready to go into the mission field. Also, many people in positions of power and various anti-Christian organizations are stirring up a lot of opposition against outsiders preaching the gospel. There have been no foreign missionary visas issued in India since 1984. From that time it's been unlawful for foreign missionaries to work in India. We don't want to be under the searchlights of these anti-Christian fanatics. We just want to be allowed to get on with the job of getting people saved, baptized, filled with the Holy Spirit and discipled. When foreign teams come they don't want to go and minister inside our churches. They want to go as missionaries into the villages where all the action is. I understand their desire for this but the very fact they are Westerners can cause a lot of violent opposition. After such a team returns home the government spotlight can shine on us and prevent us from getting on with our work. These teams regularly want to go to the very places where they are least equipped to be effective. They can't speak the local languages, and many have great trouble with the living conditions out in the field. They can so easily become very high maintenance and very low impact groups. Our biggest problem is when the police begin to take notice of us because we are hosting a large team of Westerners. When foreigners arrive the Central Bureau of Investigation sends spies to every meeting. We cause enough trouble ourselves without provoking them further by breaking the law and using foreigners to evangelize."

Biju said, "We have also discovered that smaller meetings are much more effective than large crusades. It's like in business; small investment, large profit. In a mega crusade one could spend maybe 5,000,000 rupees. You can get thousands of people lifting up their hands in response to an altar call. In the end you might only have twenty or thirty new believers who are really committed to following Jesus. With all this money you could have had five hundred smaller meetings. They would have been much more effective. In local outreaches, local believers know all the people who have lifted up their hands in response to an altar call. They can do follow-up work much more efficiently. That's what we focus on nowadays. Large crusades look good on video, in photographs and on television screens. In reality they're not a very effective use of resources and manpower. We are talking about good stewardship here. We are not out to get publicity. We just want to do the job.

"We want to be effective for the Kingdom of God. We must be responsible with the widow's mite. We must continually look at how well we are using our resources and our giftings. Time is short. There is a big job to be done in India. The harvest is plentiful and the laborers are ready. The resources are few. Pray that our Lord will open people's hearts and minds so that they may become partners with us in this great work. When we take white people to villages the accusation is that we are using native people in moneymaking ventures. Our opponents say we are selling photographs and videos of our people. One reason for this is as soon as some Western groups come they get their video cameras out and start recording without being sensitive to the dignity of our people. This can create a big unnecessary fuss. I get cross with certain people. I remember we were praying for the sick when one Western girl shouted, 'Come over here with the video camera. This woman had a back pain. Now she's been healed by me praying for her.' That is so inappropriate. Give God the glory and leave self-promotion alone. It's all about Jesus. I don't want a video camera being a stumbling block to someone coming to Christ."

"What type of people should come to help in the work in India?"

"Let key people come and see the work. Let John and Cliff Beard come. They do a great job of honestly presenting our needs to the West. Can a team come? Of course they can come and see how things are being done but they can't expect to come and function as major evangelists. They could spend time encouraging our workers. A team must come for the right reasons. I brought a team from Mattersey Bible School when I was studying there. Four months before we came we began to fast and pray once a week for the meetings. We planned to work alongside a local congregation in India. We wanted to plant three new churches. I told the team while they were in India they'd be expected to do things the Indian way. We discussed the need to abide by proper dress codes, proper spiritual protocol and basic good manners. Every Tuesday, after first praying, we'd discuss various matters particular to India. This was a good and effective time of learning. When we came to India we worked alongside the local pastors and succeeded in our goal of planting three new churches. Another major problem with some people from the West is that often they want things done their way. Instead of coming with a know-it-all attitude they should simply come and seek to help the local church. An ethnocentric attitude and approach will not work in India. We can all be effective in our own way in our proper place. Somebody who genuinely wants to help the work in India must first ask God's permission and secondly ask the local leaders how he or she can help?"

"Can you give me an example?"

"Yes, one of my Bible School teachers Vernon Ralphs, came to me and said, 'Biju, I can come to India for a month or I can give you £1,000. Which do you prefer?' I told him to come and teach because he has a great gift of teaching and moving in the prophetic. He can influence the lives of so many people for good. Now if someone else had sincerely asked that same question, then the answer may well have been, 'Please send the £1,000.' It's not all about money or gifts. It's about the most valuable use of the talents and resources the Lord has given us. We must be frank and grown up about these things so we can be successful soldiers for Christ. We want the Body of Christ to be working together in a proper way. In all of this we must be open to the leading of the Holy Spirit because the Lord still uses the weak things of the world to confound the wise. He chooses unlikely people, like Chester Bieson to help us enormously in our ministry. Today is a time of great opposition to the gospel in India. It is also a time of great harvest for the gospel in India. We need the right people in the right place, doing the right thing. People who are willing to give financially into this mission field with a no-strings-attached attitude are crucial at this time. A few dollars used in India may well be more effective than $100,000 back in America. We are not making merchandise out of God's people. We need money but we cannot be controlled by that need or by those who want to give with strings attached. It is wise that people want credibility and accountability but many other conditions such as, 'We must do the preaching, the videos, etc.' are inappropriate. Sometimes we have to say, no. There was a time and a season for the big crusades. Many of our churches were planted through this method, but nowadays God is raising up indigenous workers. I have learned to keep my mouth shut when I go to other states in India where I don't know the local language. Let the native people do the job. Let us support and stand behind them. There is a type of colonial Christianity in which one does not trust the local people to do the job. This has to change. It's a new day. We can't continue making the same old mistakes in brand new ways. Of course there is a need to make room for teams that are standing with us, to come and visit. We are starting children's homes. They can come and help there maybe. People like Gaenor Hall who has come and helped with our administration have been a tremendous blessing. We need servants and soldiers, not tourists. Many people who have come have been extremely effective, like Gary Clarke from Australia. He brought teams to help plant churches but the political situation was very different then. It's a new day. God has used those days to prepare for these days."

"What do you mean by, 'It's a new day?'"

"In the past God used many missionaries such as Francis of Assisi and William Carry to lay a strong foundation for the Gospel in this nation. By the time the government of India expelled all the missionaries in 1984, God had already put His next move of indigenous leadership into place. He was one step ahead of the devil. Now God has begun to release these local leaders. This is the next wave of missions. It is a native missionary movement with nationals evangelizing the nationals. The role of the church in the West did not stop with this 1984 exclusion order however. It merely changed. Nowadays foreigners cannot come as missionaries any more but they can send support to the local people. There is still a huge role for the West to play in India. They can still help us finish the work in this great country. Rather than send people, they can send finances to support the locals to get the work done. In the past, so many people from the West, like the lady who led my great grandfather to the Lord, have come to India and laid down their lives. The blood of these martyrs has become the seed of the present day indigenous church. The West needs to understand and catch this new vision. As the door for foreign missionaries was closing God was already opening a new door for indigenous people to do the work."

"Is there not still a need for missionaries and their families to come to India?"

"I know one family from Belfast who came to Maharashtra. They sold their home and came here but they had to go back within one year. This was an expensive lesson. Another family are living here in a nice house. Their children are studying here. They brought everything from England because they couldn't cope with the local stuff. They have to use British things. Their children must study in a very expensive school. Again, the finances used in bringing them here and supporting them could easily maintain thirty to forty local missionaries on the field. This means we could put thirty to forty workers who don't need to learn the language or suffer culture shock into full time work for the same amount of money it takes to keep this family here. How effective is this is my honest question?"

At this point Timothy began screaming at the top of his lungs. Biju asked Secu what was wrong. "He wants another biscuit," she said, "but they're all gone." Biju pulled up beside a street vendor. He bought a packet through the car window. Timothy grasped the biscuit and put it to his mouth. Quietness and a contented sucking sound filled the car.

"That was definitively an effective use of resources."

10

Why Didn't You Come Here Sooner?

We sat around the ex-gangster's table. Gracie kept piling food on to my plate all the while looking inquiringly at me. I gazed quizzically at Biju. He told me, in India the server will keep spooning food on to a guest's plate until the guest indicates, 'that's enough.' "Another cross-cultural experience," he said as he eyed the fowl on my plate. "Have you heard the story about Leyamma's chickens?"

"No," I mumbled through my wishbone.

"Just before Mum gave birth to me, the Lord told Dad to go and preach in North India. We had two churches then, one in Ranni and one in Changanacherry. Someone had given Dad a Honda motorbike as a wedding present. Another church was needed at Thymaravumkara, so he sold the Honda and bought the land. He used the rest of the money to buy 100,000 gospel tracts in Hindi called *Who is Jesus?* He and his co-worker took the four-day train journey to Rajasthan on the borders of Pakistan. They stayed in a small church sleeping on the floor. Each day they preached in the market place. When their money ran out their only food was guava. This fruit was freely available. They just picked it off the trees. After several days of this they got dysentery. His friend fell seriously ill. Dad was the only one with any strength for the ministry. That day, as he was preaching, a postman approached and asked if he was the *Preacher Man Thampy* from Kerala. He handed Dad a money order for fifteen rupees. 'Sthothram! Sthothram!' shouted Dad. Rice was quickly bought. The gift had come from a lady in Thalayar, in Kerala, who was saved through Dad's ministry. Her name was Leyamma. She was a poor widow with five children. Her only livelihood was a cow and seven chickens.

"What happened was this. As she was praying for Dad, the Holy

Spirit told her he was in need of money. She never had cash. She just used her eggs and milk to barter for whatever she needed. That morning she sold two of her chickens in the market for fifteen rupees. This was the money she sent to Dad. Upon his return the first person, apart from Mum and I, that Dad visited was the widow Leyamma from Thalayar. He knelt before her weeping and praying thanks to God. Later Leyamma became the most prosperous woman in her village. Her children did well at school. They all thrived and took care of their Mum. Four of them are working in the Middle East. One of her sons is in America."

"I heard there are many millionaires in America."

Biju smiled, "Millionaires are not the people we've met. The Americans we've met are ordinary people who have given sacrificially. Many are people who buy their clothes from second hand shops and send the saved money to us. That's how our ministry has been supported. It hasn't come from the rich people. Like Leyamma, their giving has cost them. Sacrificial and cheerful giving means a lot to the Lord."

Biju has a good word on America and Americans. He said Americans have been a great blessing to his family and their ministry. Americans are a generous people and a people of action. They didn't just talk about a thing. When fully committed they translate their ideas and promises into performance rather than just beating about the bush. He spoke about the barrels of clothes sent from Christians in America to the poor families in the church when he was young. He remembered the front row at church; filled with little boys in broad American collared shirts, sitting all smiles, thinking they were the bee's knees. He mentioned some people who'd disconnected their telephones so as to have extra money to give to the work in India.

At Bible School, when his fellow students went out to play pool, Biju would stay in his room to pray and study. Occasionally he'd have a game or go for a coffee, but he always felt guilty on these occasions. When his classmates complained that he was becoming unsociable Biju thought instead of Leo Little who had donated "hard earned money" for his school fees. In honor of Leo's sacrifice Biju felt he had to make the most of his time. He felt the short-term sacrifice of missing pool or coffee would be small compared to his long-term effectiveness in the harvest fields of India in the future. So he used his time to pray and learn. This is very much an image of the ministry in India. Here people are aware the time is short and the job is great. There is a strong sense among the believers that Jesus could be coming back at any time. These are not days to waste time or money on trivial pursuits.

We talked about how much it costs to put a student through the Bible School in Goa. Biju said, "For just over £1,000 someone could support a student through three years of Bible School and into the ministry. This year in Goa we have thirty-five students. We need about £1,000 per month but we have only about £500 per month in pledges. I'm standing in faith the shortfall will be met. We don't just have to feed the students. We also have to bring in different teachers and they in turn need food, travel and an honorarium. My faith is really being stretched this year. Everyone in *New India Church of God* is living by faith. We are walking on the water every minute of the day. We all function like a family. We say, 'In the family if there is food, everybody eats. If there is no food everybody fasts.' The most important thing is that we all stand together. If there is no food the child doesn't leave the family. They remain with their father and mother and brothers and sisters. We stand together and pray together. That's how we function."

"Tell me a little about your church planting activities."

"Last year, in Andhra Pradesh we evangelized over five hundred villages and planted forty-four new churches. If we had been a little more focused, we might have planted fifty-two churches. One church per week. Now we are concentrating on each team planting one church per week. It has being going well so far this year but now the monsoon season has slowed us down for a while. In Kolhapur, in Maharashtra, we have started another team. People are ready in Madhya Pradesh. I've been promised money for a jeep and when it arrives that team will be up and running. We support the team in Andhra Pradesh with 23,000 rupees per month, which is around £400 for ten people. They show the *Jesus* movie and preach in the villages. They are very successful."

"Someone mentioned you had a vision about evangelism and church planting."

"In my final year at Bible School I was praying one day. I knew God had called me to reach India's unreached but I didn't know where or how to start. I had a map of India on the back of my door. While praying, I had a vision of a compass that one uses for drawing circles. The needlepoint was in Goa. The first semicircle drawn covered all of Goa. The next semicircle covered parts of Maharashtra and Karnataka. The next semicircle touched parts of Andhra Pradesh, Karnataka and Tamil Nadu. In my vision the ever-increasing semicircles covered all of India and beyond, but the needlepoint remained centered in Goa. When I first saw this vision I wasn't sure what it meant. Four months later, I came back to India and began to seriously pray about it. I hadn't shared this with anyone. I wanted to make sure it was from God and not from my own imagination. Gradually God began to confirm this vision from different prophecies from various people. Now it is coming to pass. We are operating in many of these states at present. With God everything starts from a small seed like the mustard seed Jesus talked about. I often think of my dad, as a young man, alone in the middle of the night, preaching into the darkness. This was the seed he was planting. Even though he saw little results the seed being sown was quietly growing. Wherever he went and preached in those days now churches have been planted. Then he didn't have the bus fare as he walked from village to village with his megaphone. Later God used him to buy many hundreds of megaphones, bicycles, motorbikes, jeeps and minibuses for the Lord's servants all over India."

I remembered the first time I came to India with Lionel Batke from Canada and John Scott from Northern Ireland. We'd been preaching and prophesying in a convention at the conclusion of which fifty bicycles were going to be distributed among the assembled pastors. I vividly remember three pastors arriving on a motor scooter. The thin one, in the middle, in a striped shirt had been fasting for forty days in the hope of being allocated a bicycle. As it turned out he was not on the list. There was no bicycle for him. I remember the disappointment on his face. I also have a vivid memory of coming upon Thampy who was sitting alone with his head in his hands. He was crying. He was exhausted at the end of those hectic days and frustrated that so many of the pastor's needs were unmet. My final memory is of the three pastors on the scooter; a striped shirt sandwiched between two white shirts, as they sped off on their long journey home.

Biju said, "As long as I can remember I have always seen my parents trusting God for their needs to be met. Every day was a new step of faith. Time after time, as I was growing up, I saw God providing in the most miraculous ways. Yet, often they were tested by disappointments and discouragement. Like the kernel of wheat in John 12 that had to fall into the

104

ground and die they had to face many difficult situations. People who see them now see only the blessings. They don't see the cost involved in it all. Over the years God has touched the hearts of people here and there to help support the ministry. Have you heard of Chester Bieson?"

"Your dad mentioned he was a great support in the early days. Did you know him personally?"

"I knew Chester Bieson. He was a real gentleman. He was a very mild, soft-spoken person. One day, at a large crusade, in Trivandrum there were many demon-possessed people receiving deliverance. It was very noisy with lots of squealing and shrieking. Chester was involved in praying for the sick and oppressed. Dad overheard him say, 'Dear devil, why do you trouble this poor girl? Why don't you let her go?' He was calling the devil, 'dear devil.' Bless his heart. 'Don't call the devil "dear devil." Cast it out,' said Dad. Then Dad commanded the demon, 'Get out in the name of Jesus!' Chester said, 'Ah don't talk to the poor girl like that.' Dad said, 'I'm not talking to the girl, I'm talking to the devil.' Chester was such a gentle person he didn't even want to hurt the devil." Biju laughed.

Next morning we heard news that Mariamma, Biju's mother, was on her way home from Australia. Quickly it was decided I should meet her in Kerala and make the most of my remaining time. Thampy and Binu would follow later. As Biju drove me to the airport we began talking about signs and wonders. Biju said, "I've seen many people getting healed spectacularly but I don't want to focus on that all the time. It is so easy to get sidetracked with signs and wonders. John 19:31 says, 'These signs He performed so that they might know that He is the Son of God.' The purpose behind signs and wonders is not that we should have a magic show. The person who gets healed will eventually die. All the people Jesus raised from the dead had to die again. Signs and wonders are not permanent. They merely point towards Jesus to confirm His word. The truth that Jesus is the Son of God is the thing that is being confirmed.

"In India, miracles and the supernatural are no big deal. But when you tell the people that Jesus Christ can save you just like He healed this person that's what makes it different. We tell them, 'When you call upon the name of Jesus - just like that blind man's eyes were opened - you can also receive forgiveness for your sins in Jesus' name. You don't have to go through endless reincarnations. You can be forgiven now.' In my experience, not everyone gets healed. I used to have a big problem with that. Now I don't. I have found that one spectacular miracle is usually enough for the whole village to turn to Jesus and get saved: one blind person seeing, one AIDS patient being healed, one cripple walking, one dead person coming back to life."

"It often says in scripture that Jesus healed all who came to Him."

"It also says He couldn't perform many miracles in Capernaum because of their unbelief. I believe there were many sick people at the pool of Bethesda but Jesus healed only that one guy. There are complexities but let's not lose sight of the truth. The biggest miracle of all is people coming to know Jesus. That's what it's all about. That's what Jesus came into this world for. That's the only thing, which is permanent. We can't only focus on physical healings – miracles, miracles, miracles. The greatest miracle of all is that of a life surrendered to Jesus. God wants people who believe Jesus Christ is Lord. He wants His Son lifted up and not just a magic show. Jesus is to be lifted up. He is to be exalted. He is all in all. We are nothing. Signs and wonders happen only to confirm the validity of the gospel of Jesus Christ."

"I totally agree but as my wife often quotes, 'What is easier to say, your sins are forgiven, or arise take up your bed and walk?' In the West we have endless talk about sins being forgiven but very little demonstration of the miraculous. Many of us are as your dad often says, 'Full of beef and unbelief.' Surely we need a demonstration of the miraculous in our ministry otherwise we're only one step up from those liberal theologians you're so fond of talking about."

Biju nodded, "Recently in Andhra Pradesh I prayed for a crippled man in front of the whole village. I told him, 'Throw those sticks away.' I took the crutches and said, 'Walk in the name of Jesus.' He hesitated. I commanded, 'Walk.' He began to walk perfectly. At the same meeting God healed a blind lady. Then we stood and preached the gospel. We told them, 'This is all about Jesus Christ, the only begotten Son of God. He is the One who has healed these people here today.' We proclaim Jesus as Lord and we teach what the Bible says about salvation. In most of these villages they've never heard tell of Jesus. Romans 10:14 says, 'How can they call upon the One they have not heard. How can they hear unless someone is sent?' The whole process is involved. People give us the resources and we go. We go anyway, but we can be much more effective when the body works together. Some man, woman or child in the USA for example, can be a partner with us here in India. Their giving can make a real difference to the eternal lives of others. Imagine meeting people in heaven who come up to you and thank you for making it possible for them to hear the gospel.

"One of our evangelists went to the only shop in a village. He asked the owner, 'Have you heard about Jesus?' The owner thought for a moment, then said, 'I don't know anybody in this village called Jesus. There's nobody here of that name. Maybe he lives in the next village but I don't think so.'

"I remember going to a village and saying to a man, 'We have come to tell you about Jesus.' He said, 'What is Jesus?' He thought Jesus was a product we had for sale. I said, 'Jesus is God.' He said, 'What kind of a god is he? What country is he from? What does he look like? Do you have a photograph of him? What kind of sacrifices does he require? What does he like – coconuts, flowers, blood?' These people's concept of God is of an angry God waiting to punish them. They believe they have to continually keep going to different temples to appease these gods. They think they have to go on a pilgrimage every year. Most of these pilgrim temples are on top of big hills. They have to climb these hills barefooted with a bunch of sacrifices on their heads. In many places the smell of the blood of animals and birds is a terrible stench."

Biju said, "In some areas they still kill children for human sacrifice. A while back I read in a national newspaper about a journalist who was traveling through the jungle to a certain village. He came upon the bodies of two little children lying in a pool of blood. He reported this to the police who came and made inquiries. The children had been killed by their own father. The police asked the dad, 'Why did you do this?' He said the Hindu priest had told him to offer his two children - a twelve-year-old boy and a three-year-old girl - as sacrifices. He hadn't wanted to kill them, but the priest claimed there was a curse on the man's family. He told the father, if he wanted a better life in the next incarnation, he'd have to sacrifice his children in this life. The father took his children to a temple dedicated to a Hindu goddess called Kali. He held them by their feet and smashed their heads on a stone. Bloodshed to appease the gods is very much a part of the Hindu psyche.

"In the villages we tell the people we have come with good news. The good news is that God is not an angry God. He is a loving God. Then we read, John 3:16, 'For God so loved the world He gave His only begotten

Son.' We tell them they don't have to go somewhere in search of God. Two thousand years ago God came to this world in search of them. They don't have to climb up big hills barefooted with heavy bundles of sacrifices on their heads. The Son of God, Jesus Christ, climbed a hill for them and carried the burden of their sins. We tell the story of Jesus: born of a virgin, lived a sinless life, public ministry, death and resurrection. He is not a blood thirsty God. He is a God who gives the blood. He shed His last drop of blood for your sins. Simple gospel. Jesus is not a dead idol sitting in the corner of the temple. He is risen. He is risen from the dead. He is alive for evermore. He has conquered the power of death and hell. Because He is alive, when you call upon Him then He can hear you. He is here. He is here right now. The Bible says, 'Whosoever calls upon the name of the Lord will be saved.' You don't have to keep on visiting the pilgrim temples. You don't have to wait until you have been born one thousand times in different cycles of life until you reach the nothingness of Nirvana. When you die, you can just close your eyes and go into eternity with Jesus. The blood of Jesus cleanses us from every sin.

"For Hindus this is a mind-blowing concept. They come forward saying, 'We never knew about a God who loved us. We never knew this.' Many times people have asked us, 'Why didn't you come here sooner? If only you had come a bit earlier many of our people wouldn't have died without hearing about this Jesus. They never knew. We never knew. We have wasted all these years worshipping dead idols. If only you had come sooner I wouldn't have had to sacrifice my little son.'

"This is the challenge constantly in front of us. Unless we go and preach, how will they hear? Unless someone sends us, how will we go? Unreached millions are waiting to ask, 'Why didn't you come sooner?' There are hundreds of millions of people like that. That is why we can't stop going. That question, 'Why didn't you come here sooner?' wipes out all the obstacles, all the tiredness, wipes out all the excuses for not giving or not responding. It keeps us going."

We got stuck in a traffic jam. Groups of policemen were taking lorry loads of illegally parked scooters to the police station. There was great excitement and activity. Hectic pleading and negotiating was taking place between surprised owners and custodians of the law. A time of reckoning had come like 'a thief in the day.' Money was changing hands and minds at a rapid rate. The circus-like quality of the occasion jarred Biju into a joke. He said, "An Australian visiting America decided to hire a motorcycle. Unaware they drove on the right-hand side of the road in America he happily took off at a great speed. A policeman spied him, raced after him and caught him. 'What do you think you are doing?' he shouted, 'Where are you from, outer space or somewhere?'

'No mate, I'm from Australia', he answered.

'From Australia? Have you come all this way *to die*?'

'No mate; I came yester*day*!' "

I wanly smiled not wanting to encourage him. I was afraid he might start on Irish jokes. Having studied in England he probably had a few of those up his sleeve. He began talking about his vision for building a new Bible School in a developing area close to the airport we neared. He said he could buy five acres of development land for around £60,000. His vision would be to have two hundred people, male and female, in separate dormitories. He hoped there'd only be around ten to a room compared to the twenty plus at present. Currently he has to turn females away from his Bible School because of a total lack of facilities for them. Seeing how powerful Mariamma is in ministry has convinced him of the importance of releasing women into their calling. His vision is for men and women to be in the same classroom. He believes they could both do the same three year course and both be given the same opportunities to minister. His sense is that one shouldn't keep people back from what God has chosen them to be. "You cannot fight against the anointing," he said. "One must recognize the anointing as a God given thing, sent for a purpose. The Body of Christ must learn to work together. Can a toe say to an eye, that one does not have need for the other?"

As we neared the airport, a herd of buffalo ran along the middle of the dual carriageway to greet us. Cars speeding along at eighty miles per hour casually swerved out of their way. A crowd of cows lay unconcerned in the middle verge of the motorway. We pulled onto a side road. Biju said, "This is very much a developing place." At that moment a sow ran across in front of us with two little piglets scurrying after her. They sped past a little girl hunkering down, relieving herself in the midst of it all. New penthouse flats were being built. Beside them, shanty worker's makeshift shacks appeared flimsy protection from the monsoon rains. Barefoot people with burdens on their heads stepped in front of brand new Mercedes. People in tents lived beside people in palatial homes. A herd of goats made us swerve. I loved the frantic activity of the quickened images that flashed past like a DVD player on fast-forward. Biju saw none of it. His mind was on future ministry needs.

He said, "We really need a publication wing to our organization. We need a printing press that can produce about 8,000 copies an hour. We are praying for this. We also require a good laser printer. We should send a regular newsletter to our supporters every couple of months. We could also do with an in-house publication going into our churches and keeping the whole movement in focus. We need it in three different languages, Malayalam, Hindi, and English. We could also print our own gospel tracts and literature and develop our Bible correspondence course. When gospel tracts go out with our address people write and request further information about Jesus. We have a real need for various levels of Christian literature. We have a youth group movement called YPCA. It is so important we focus on the youth today. We could also advertise our own conventions, crusades, outreaches, meetings etc.

"There is always a huge need for printing work. This could be done more efficiently in-house. Gospel literature has always been part of our ministry. We say every gospel tract is a mobile missionary that reaches places we never could. One of our pastors, Nooruddin Mulla, got saved through reading Gospel literature. He was a Muslim who had kept a tract very carefully in an upper shelf in his bedroom for many years. A time came when he was without peace and troubled. He brought it down, read it and gave his life to Jesus. We know of many people who've been saved through gospel literature."

When we arrived at the airport Biju went to buy my ticket. Standing in the airport doorway was a handsome, bearded man in bright white traditional dress. Accompanying him was an impressive looking lady; obviously a stunning beauty in her day. He was a distinguished looking man, crisp and clean in his native clothes. He wore glasses. He looked like a holy man or an academic. I kept an eye on my luggage. I saw Biju talking to him and shaking his hand. When Biju came back he was a little boy full of excitement. "Oh Brendan," he said, "that is such a big man. He is a famous singer. He has a wonderful voice. He is my favorite singer and musician. He is called K. J. Jesudas. Jesudas means *Jesus' servant*. He's famous all over India, especially in film music."

I was intrigued. I'd never seen this side of Biju. He went inside to put my baggage through. When he came out he was even more animated. He waved a piece of paper in my face with Jesudas' autograph on the back of it. On the front was a prescription for an infection that Secu had. I was delighted. Here was God's man of faith and power with his wife's prescription signed on the back by Jesudas. Biju was in a dilemma. Would he be willing to give away the autograph in order to get the prescription? I loved seeing the teenager in Biju emerge. Momentarily the man of vision, responsibility and action was replaced by a star-struck teenager. (Later I talked to Secu who said she didn't need the prescription. Biju had prayed for her healing instead.)

As I entered the departure lounge, Jesudas and his wife were sitting on their own at the edge of the crowd. I walked over to them. They both stood up.

I said, *"On behalf of the Irish people I would like to congratulate you on your great voice and your services to music and for making my friend Biju so happy."* Jesudas asked where I was from.

I replied, *"Ireland."* I showed him my Bodhran; the Irish drum I play. "Ah," he said, "Then we're from the same family; the family of musicians." He sounded like a man who had kissed the Blarney Stone. I couldn't help but like him. There were a few Westerners in the lounge blissfully unaware that a famous Indian singer - someone of the status of Bono or Paul McCartney - was in their midst. At Cochin airport Jesudas was standing talking to two men. As I passed by he recognized me. He shook my hand. "I hope everything goes well with your business in India," he said.

"And U2," I said, *"I'll tell Bono you were asking for him."*

He replied, "Thank you. Please do." So, if you are reading this Bono, why don't you and Jesudas get together and record a duet. It's sure to be a hit. It might even help your good case for the cancellation of third world debt. I sure hope so. Later I waited in the airport lounge for Saji, Thampy's driver, to come and collect me. An airport official approached and asked if everything was all right. She then asked me how I knew Jesudas. I replied I'd heard he was a great singer.

"He has the voice of an angel," she said. "He is God's gift to India." I could have prophesied that.

111

11

Only Jesus

I awaken. My things are where I left them; Bible open, pen with its top off, notebook, reading glasses, half empty bottle of coke and a novel. This is a rare experience for me. Two feelings; one of relief and one of loneliness always accompanies it. The relief is because I don't have to go searching for my stuff before I start my day. At home one of the kids could have taken my book to read. It might not resurface for months. Another would have finished *my* coke. Angela might be at breakfast reading *my* Bible with *my* glasses and writing her notes in *my* notebook. The pen top of course would still be there but *my* pen might well have gone. But today all my things are exactly where I left them. Something else is also here. Loneliness. Loneliness and order in a strange bedroom in India, while all the life my family brings is back in Ireland fast asleep. I enjoy both feelings. They each have their price. In Proverbs 14 it says, "Where no oxen are the crib is clean: but much increase is by the strength of the ox." Clutter comes with children but also life and strength. It's the same with some churches. They have a wonderful sense of order but absolutely no life or power. Yet if only I could get my wife and kids to listen to me and to leave *my* things alone I'd be a much happier man - *I think?*

Downstairs at Mariamma and Thampy's table I eat a breakfast of fried eggs and banana. Only Leelamma is here waiting on me. Smiles passing between us. Poor compensation for not being able to speak one another's language. In the background I can hear the sounds of hand clapping and praise from the prayer tower. I remember the first time I sat at this table, less than six years ago. Then all Thampy's children were unmarried and still at home. I had especially loved the breakfasts with us all jam-packed around the table listening to Mariamma's stories and laughter.

"Tell them about the demon possessed man that was so scared when he came here," Binu had said. "He saw fire all around the walls of the campus."

"Oh no!" laughed Mariamma, "We don't have time for that. You must go now or you'll be late for school."

"Please Mama."

"OK. Just one more."

And then she was off again. Casting out demons and healing the sick. *The Acts of the Apostles*, alive and well in India. Life bursting out at the seams. Now a few years later and all the birds have flown the nest. The crib is clean and I'm feeling homesick. I think of my own children who have left home. Their rite of passage into the big world has been by way of attending university. They leave. They come back at the end of the first term, but by then everything is changed. Some cord has been cut. Shann, Brendan, Nora, Aaron, Mary, Hannah and Ruth have all crossed this line. Before their final departure we have a last meal together. I acknowledge their time to move on has arrived. Then one by one we burst into tears at our sense of loss. Life changes. The river runs. The big sky moves. One of us is leaving and for a while we collectively share the pain. Jesus wept at the passing of His friend Lazarus. We weep at the loss of our sister or brother, son or daughter. We kiss and cuddle and sob deep tears. And although like Jesus with Lazarus we receive them back alive yet the reality that life will never be the same again is always sorrowful.

At these times images from their childhood replay in my memory like old home movies. Shann, all smiles and bouncing curls, rushing home with the Easter egg prize she won in the school raffle. Brendan, doing wheelies on his bicycle, oblivious to the raging bull rushing past him in its vain attempt to escape the butcher's knife. Nora picking up her dropped potato in the *egg and spoon* race on her way to winning the school sports shield. Aaron's relieved look as our van returns. We'd left him sitting in an isolated toilet in the highlands of Scotland and hadn't missed him until half an hour later. Mary, in her favorite red jumper, singing at the top of her voice on her beloved rocking horse, "Give Me Oil in My Lamp." Hannah pushing prams bristling with real live babies. They loved to see her tangled tresses coming their way. Ruth, like Frodo Baggins, leading her group of young friends into their next adventure. Then suddenly they are young women and men walking out my front door. Where have all the flowers gone? But soon enough it's back to,

113

"Where have all my pens gone? Who drank my diet coke? Did you see my glasses?" Life goes on and there are another seven kids to be reared. Yet sometimes sadness creeps into our hearts and days uninvited.

Suddenly a flurry of Bible School girls cascades into the kitchen dissolving my daydreams. They chatter excitedly in Malayalam to Leelamma. She gleefully claps her hands and runs to the front door like a young girl. Mariamma has arrived home. In the twinkling of an eye my loneliness evaporates. The circus has come to town. Women appear from nowhere like a flock of seagulls flapping around a merry Mariamma. Fussing, kissing, cuddling, the holding of hands, laughter and noisy hellos brighten up the forlorn kitchen. Within minutes, fish is being fried amid the pungent smell of spices. We're back in India. Mariamma sits at breakfast and eats like a starving woman.

I said, *"I read in a tourist guidebook people in Kerala have fish with all their meals except breakfast."*

Mariamma blushed. "Oh Brendan, you can't believe how much I have missed having fish. There's no fish like Kerala fish. Fish from *God's own Country.*"

"Back home we call Ireland God's own Country."

"Isn't it?" said Mariamma, "That's another thing we have in common."

We chat about my time in India; whom I have seen and talked with. She asks about Angela and my family. Then we talk about Thampy's health. She says, "In 1999 many people received dreams and visions Thampy was in trouble and that something bad was going to happen. We were all crying to the Lord and praying and fasting. God showed my daughter Beena a dream."

"She mentioned that dream."

Previously Beena had told me, "Two years ago Daddy had a heart attack. This surprised us. He was a strong man. He showed no signs of illness. I had a dream in which he was admitted to hospital. People were standing outside the hospital ward while Mama was going inside the room. Biju was in the corridor weeping as if the worst had happened. I told Mama this dream. She began to pray against it. After this the doctors discovered Daddy had a heart problem. He then had an angioplasty. They discovered some blockages. They did an operation to enlarge the valves. Next day, all of a sudden, he began to get breathless. Mama had gone to a meeting three hours away because

114

everything was fine. They had to give Daddy oxygen. When Mama came back, people were standing outside the room and Biju was crying in the corridor. Just like in my dream. Dad's feet went yellowish. His face went blue and his legs went stiff. The doctors kept saying his heartbeat was okay, but something was happening they couldn't understand. Returning from the meeting Mama was remembering my dream. She was very concerned. When she saw Biju in the corridor weeping she thought the worst had happened. She began to intercede. Outside crowds of Christians were fasting and praying. Suddenly, at midnight, everything returned to normal."

Mariamma resumed the story. "It was discovered Thampy had two blocks in his arteries. We knew this was a real attack from the enemy. Because of the prayer and intercession God helped us to come through it. Some people even saw visions of a funeral with a huge crowd but the Lord turned our mourning into dancing. The day Thampy was discharged from the hospital we went to see a girl called Secu. Within two weeks she was married to Biju. There were thousands here for the ceremony conducted by Thampy. Satan had planned it for mourning but God turned it into rejoicing. Through prayer and fasting, visions of a funeral were turned into the reality of a wedding. God warns us so that we may have victory over the works of the enemy.

"Recently there was another assault. A couple of months back, in a dream, I saw two men standing at the steps that go to Thampy's office. They were facing towards our house. I remember their faces so clearly. They wore turbans, white shirts and dhotis. I knew they were Muslims. They were doing some chanting. I thought, *Why are these people chanting against us?* I arose and interceded until I felt a sense of breakthrough. Beena had a similar dream. What I had rebuked here was seen by her in Goa. She rang and said, 'Mama, I had a dream about two Muslim men who were wearing turbans, white shirts and dhotis. They were chanting some witchcraft. They appeared in my room. I rebuked them and they disappeared.'

"Shortly afterwards I had a vision of a thin man with a cap standing in front of our Church door. I knew he was a Muslim. The Holy Spirit was showing me that Muslim witchcraft was being sent against us. Then I had to go to Australia. Three weeks ago I awakened with such a heavy burden. I got up and prayed for a long time. I knew I was opposing a sickness. I was speaking in tongues and interpreting myself: 'Sickness, sickness, the Lord rebuke you!' I was continually praying and breaking its power. After a couple of days I again felt really burdened about Thampy. I called home but nobody answered. I rang his mobile. He spoke. I asked him, 'Where are you?' He said, 'I'm in the hospital.' They had him on a drip. During this time I was so miserable and so much burdened. I prayed and interceded continually.

"When I arrived back this morning our intercessors told me they have been praying for Thampy this past month. One lady from our church rang saying she had a dream in which something bad had happened to Thampy. So they began praying, from six to seven o'clock each evening, for him. Idy is our main intercessor. Her sister rang and told of a dream she had about Thampy being attacked by the enemy. This was confirmed by others. So the intercessors have been alerted and are praying for Thampy's protection.

"Four days ago I had a dream in which Thampy had died. After praying and going back to sleep I had another dream that showed me Beena was in trouble. In this second dream Biju came and said, 'Mama, we will fast for three days.' So for three days I've been fasting. Always when I pray and fast for a specific thing the Lord will give me some confirmation that I've been successful. On the evening of the second day I rang my daughter Bini in America. Bini said, 'Mama, I had a dream last night about Daddy. In the dream I saw a poisonous cobra snake coming to bite him. It was trying to torment him from top to bottom.' The snake spoke. It said, 'I came to kill him. I tried to attack him from his head to his toes, but I couldn't succeed. Now I have received orders from above I have to stop my attack.'

"That was a dream from Bini. She didn't know anything about the situation here. When I heard this confirmation my burden was immediately lifted. My prayers had been victorious. I shared all this with Thampy. He'd been feeling pretty miserable, wondering what was going on. Bini's dream really blessed him. I rang Beena just a few minutes ago. She had a scan yesterday. The doctor said her new baby is just fine. God shows us things that are about to happen so we can be prepared. That's the secret. God warns us through dreams and visions. We must learn to take dreams very seriously. God reveals these things to us so we may pray against them."

Although she was tired after her long haul flight from Australia, Mariamma couldn't resist telling another story. It concerned a Hindu god called Ganesh. This chubby, elephant-headed god also known as Ganpati is beloved by many Hindus. He is revered as the 'remover of obstacles' and is usually worshipped first in religious ceremonies. He is believed to be a god of prophecy. His plump image is seen all over India. It adorns the thresholds of many homes and temples.

Mariamma said, "My sister Rajam and her husband have a church in Karnataka. She told me an interesting story about a couple called Rajiv and Chitra (Not their real names) who are members there. They were very religious and very rich Hindus who were totally devoted to their gods. In India there are said to be 333,000,000 gods and goddesses. This couple had only thirteen very special deities to which they were very devoted. They used to travel long distances, to different temples, to worship and offer sacrifices to these gods. This was their hobby. But as you know the roads in India are difficult.

"One day the thought came to Rajiv, *Why should we spend so much time and money traveling over hard roads to these temples. If we only can understand which is the most powerful god then we need only go to that place.* They decided to write down the names of their gods and put them into a box they'd then place before their statue of Ganesh. Then they'd ask, 'Ganesh, please show us which is the most powerful of all these gods.' Confident that Ganesh would reveal the name, they took a ceremonial bath and prayed earnestly as they wrote down their gods' names.

"While they were doing this their little girl, who was studying in a Catholic school, came home. Upon hearing what they were up to, she said, 'Amma, I know the name of another god. My teachers have told me about a god whose name is Jesus. They say he is a very powerful and a very loving god.' To please their little daughter the parents agreed they'd also include that name. So counting Jesus they put fourteen folded names into the box; Rama, Shiva, Krishna, Hanuman, Iyyappa and so on. Iyyappa was a special favorite. Over thirty times they'd traveled the long distance to his temple at Sabarimala in Kerala.

"They then took the box, shook it, and reverently placed it in front of Ganesh. Their little girl put her hand in and pulled out a name. When the father unfolded the paper he got a big shock. The name on it was that of the new god *Jesus.* 'Oh it can't be,' he said. So he refolded it and put it back into the box. He gave it another good shake. Again the child, eyes tightly shut, took out a name. Her father opened it and again it was the name of *Jesus.* Once more the whole process was repeated. For the third time the little girl picked the piece of paper with *Jesus* on it.

"Finally they realized something very important and very unexpected had happened. They kept pondering this in their hearts for many days. A friend who came to lunch was told the story and asked if he knew anything about this Jesus god. The friend said he didn't personally know very much but he had the address of a man who knows all about this Jesus god.

"The couple went to visit this man, who turned out to be a believer. He shared all he knew about Jesus. He explained how Jesus, the only begotten Son of God, had come into the world to die for the people and how He loves the people. He told them the whole gospel story. Shortly afterwards Rajiv was sitting in his garden. He wanted to pray to Jesus but he didn't know how. He simply said, 'Lord Jesus, please reveal Yourself to me.' Suddenly, Jesus appeared in the garden walking so majestically toward him. Immediately he was filled with the Holy Spirit and began to loudly praise God in a new language. Then just as quickly as He had materialized, Jesus disappeared.

"The whole household came running when they heard Rajiv's noisy uttering. To their amazement Rajiv couldn't speak in anything else but these strange tongues. This continued the whole day, that night and into the next day. By this time they thought he'd gone mad. They concluded, because he'd left his Hindu gods for this new god Jesus, that the old gods were now punishing him by making him crazy.

"His poor wife was in distress. She was afraid she'd have to put him into the mental hospital. But her sorrow turned to joy when her husband reverted to his native language and explained he'd seen Jesus. He told of how beautiful and gentle Jesus was and of how he'd felt such a great love coming from Him. Now that household are all good believers. They are part of Rajam's church in Karnataka. So you see how the Lord is working in India and how even the very stones have been revealing who the true God really is."

I nodded.

"It's good to see you again Brother Brendan. We'll share plenty of God stories now that I'm back. The Lord has sent you here at this time to record these testimonies of Jesus. But first I must get some sleep."

"Sweet dreams."

As she walked down the hallway Mariamma half turned, "Oh, I nearly forgot. I have a video I've brought back from Australia. It's by a big American preacher called Jesse Duplantis. In it he tells of how he went to heaven and of what he saw there. It's very encouraging. We'll watch it tonight. You'll like it."

Mmmm? I thought to myself, *I'm not so sure about that.*

12

Can I Be A Spirit?

That evening Mariamma's sister Rajam arrived to welcome Mariamma back. She verified the Ganesh story. It transpired Mariamma had in fact brought back two videos from Australia. One was of Jesse Duplantis talking of how he spent five hours and fifteen minutes in heaven. The other was a copy of an Australian television program about problems caused by the dowry system in India. We had no VCR. Instead the video was projected onto the wall by equipment normally used for screening the *Jesus* movie. My bedroom was chosen as the makeshift cinema. Mariamma and Rajam watched enthralled as Jesse described his experience of heaven. They talked about how their recently dead sister, Valsala, would love this or that thing in heaven. There were lots of tears. I watched and listened with a fair degree of Western worldview skepticism until Jesse said something that pierced my shield of cynicism. What he said made me think maybe he was telling the truth. *Maybe he really had been to heaven!*

One Irish Saturday morning in the early 1980s my wife and I were traveling from Coleraine to Belfast for a graduation service. We'd left early so I could collect my graduation gown from a certain Belfast store. We sang and praised as we drove along. Suddenly I was in the Spirit. I saw a vision. In it, I witnessed a host of spirits of unborn babies hovering before the Lord. They were asking Him if they could be born into this generation. I then saw a vision of eggs inside a woman's ovaries. Some of them were circled by light signifying God had chosen them. I then saw, as if under a microscope, the sperm within a man. From the many millions, one became circled by light, signifying God had chosen it. I then saw crowds of people walking toward me. I was able to see inside the wombs of certain pregnant women. The babies in their wombs were again circled with light indicating they were called and chosen from the womb for the purposes of God in their generation.

Then the voice of the Lord said, "So many children want to be born into this generation but My people will not have them." Still in the vision I exclaimed, "Lord, we will have as many of those children as we can." Then the Lord told me to forgo the graduation ceremony and to go instead to a Christian Leader's meeting that was taking place in Bangor, Co. Down. He told me to share this vision with the folk there. Later my wife and I discussed the vision. We decided we'd be obedient to it. The rest is history - our history. That's the reason we have so many children. It has nothing to do with not owning a television.

Here I was, twenty years later, sitting in a dark room in India somewhat begrudgingly listening to an American preacher talking about his trip to heaven. What Jesse said confirmed part of what God had shown me on that graduation morning twenty years earlier. Jesse said in heaven he saw the new lives of little babies singing and flying around the Throne of God. He said these were new souls that emanated from the very thoughts of God. He said he heard them saying to God, "Can I be a spirit? Would You send me to the earth so I can be a spirit? I want to be a redeemed person. Can I be a spirit?"

I was stunned and delighted for Jesse's description was a perfect portrayal of what I had seen in my vision. "Forgive me Jessie for my initial unbelief." On that morning twenty years ago I also struggled with unbelief for I was in two minds as to whether to go to the graduation or to the Christian Leader's meeting as the Lord had instructed me.

Thankfully the Lord helped me make up my mind. When we reached the place in the road where we'd either have to go left to Bangor or straight on to collect the graduation gown the car engine went completely dead. Angela and I had to sit stuck in the middle of Belfast city traffic until I eventually told the Lord I'd be obedient. At that the car immediately burst into life. God has many ways of getting our attention. Jesse's main message from heaven is that the Lord is coming back soon. This is a message readily believed in India. There the Second Coming of Christ is an ever-present expectation. They just hope they'll get enough time to evangelize their 97% non-Christian nation before it happens.

The second video looked at the dowry system and other issues detrimental to females in India. The dowry is the amount the bride's family must pay to the groom's family at the time of marriage. The program contained heartbreaking scenes about baby girls being killed because of the financial burden they cause poor families. An Indian man is incomplete without a wife and children. But there is believed to be a certain type of hell, called *put*, from which only a son, *putra*, can save his parents. It is the son who continues the family line, supports the elderly parents and performs the necessary rituals at the funeral that guarantee their soul's safe journey to the home of the ancestors. The daughter, on the other hand, must be provided with a dowry. She then marries out of her family shifting her allegiance to her husband's family circle.

The television cameras followed the progress of one young pregnant woman from a poor family. She already had a baby girl. She was determined to kill her new child if it turned out to be another female. She had been unable to afford a scan. The disappointment that ensued when she gave birth to healthy twin girls was tangible. The presenter talked of sex discrimination in the selective killing of female fetuses. She claimed there was a 'lust for sons in India.'

The video also related stories about brides being killed by the husband's family over unfulfilled dowry promises. The groom's family often demands cars, refrigerators, televisions and so on as well as money. These demands often escalate long after the wedding itself. When the poor beleaguered bride's family can no longer meet these demands the new bride may well be doused in kerosene and burned alive. Then the husband may try again for that new motorcycle or VCR that comes along with his next bride. The program showed an interview with a young bride who'd been badly burned by her husband. She died the following day.

Mariamma visibly winced. She said, "A beautiful girl. A very educated nice girl. How can they do this? Yet it's happening all the time. Thousands every year. One lady in our Bible School is a similar case. She is the girl who jumped out of the train. Her name is Pushpalatha. She was a Brahmin who converted from Hinduism to Christianity. They persecuted and beat her and took her baby away."

As Mariamma was talking the electricity failed. Total darkness pervaded the room. The night's entertainment was abruptly over. I never heard any more about Pushpalatha or her baby but may God bless them wherever they are.

13

Groaning in the Spirit

In Ireland one night I asked the Lord for a dream. I needed some guidance. There were a few things vying for my attention at this particular point. After a fitful night's sleep I awakened without any dream. Regularly the Lord speaks to us in dreams that we don't recall. He seals it up, as it says in Job, to keep us from pride. I remembered struggling in my sleep but all to no avail. That morning, in our kitchen, my wife was praying with our friend Rosanne. She has a gift of prophecy. Angela asked me to join them. At one point I prayed and prophesied for Rosanne. Then she had a vision for me. Her picture involved the scripture where Jesus is talking to his disciples, saying, "You have labored all night and caught nothing, but throw your net on the other side of the boat and you will catch many fish."

This word immediately struck a chord with me. I felt I'd toiled all night and caught no dream. Through this revelation I sensed the Lord was encouraging me to continue to seek guidance and not to lose heart. Five minutes later the phone rang, "Hello, Brother Brendan, how are you? How is joyful Angela? How is the book coming along?" It was Biju. He was calling from Belfast airport. Like his father he'd just arrived unannounced. The wind blows where it will. We spent a few days together and I was affirmed and stirred up to start work on this book. When God speaks to us faith comes and we receive power for the task at hand.

As we sat at her kitchen table, Mariamma said, "Sometimes Beena and I compliment each other on the spiritual plane. We experience similar things at the same time. As well as the incident of the two Muslims we also had an experience with a 'rubber hand' demon about five years ago. This was the time God was giving me a revelation about groaning in the Spirit. In Romans 8, we read like this, 'The Spirit prays with groaning that cannot be uttered, but Father God sees the heart and He knows the meaning of everything.' When I'd pray in tongues, now and then, I'd groan a little. I had assumed this was the groaning Paul was talking about. Then the Lord began to show me differently.

"All our children were still at home in those days. It began to happen, I'd get a burden but when I'd go into my room to intercede no words would come. For hours the only thing I could do was groan. If the children would come in and ask me something I'd answer them. Then I'd immediately go back to this loud groaning. When the burden of prayer was lifted up I'd put the light on and it might already be 1:30AM. Every night for months this continued. I didn't know the meaning of why I was groaning. Each session would last for five or six hours. Just groaning.

"Around then I was completing a Master of Divinity degree. I had to go to Jaipur in Rajasthan for a week's residential. Jaipur is a very ancient city where the kings lived. This campus was in the middle of the city. A dancer, who was also one of the King's prostitutes, had owned it. It is now a Bible School. It's not a very spiritually alive situation. There is some sort of bondage over the place. I felt so forlorn there. During my stay, God opened my eyes to understand something new about groaning in the Spirit.

"One day at class in the chapel the lecturer stopped taking. Everything became pin-drop silent. All of a sudden I heard this groaning noise above me. It sounded like me groaning in the Spirit. I looked up. I saw a dove, sitting on a beam, high in the ceiling. I'd never heard a dove groaning before. This was a totally new experience. This must be one reason why the dove is compared to the Holy Spirit. It groans the same way He does. It was making the same sound I'd been making. I was so happy. It confirmed to me why I'd been groaning for so many months.

"That night I prayed a long time before going to sleep. I was lying on my side in the bed when suddenly it felt as if someone had put their hand around my waist. I reached down and touched it. It felt just like a rubber hand, fingers but no bones. I was so tense. Then something from inside me rose up. I rebuked this thing in the name of Jesus."

"Beena mentioned she felt numb when it happened. Did you feel numb?"

"No. Numb is when we can't even talk. Numb is when our tongue is paralyzed in our mouths. I wasn't numb. After I rebuked this thing the same experience also happened to Beena at the exact same time."

"Have you ever heard of anyone else experiencing this sort of parallel occurrence?"

"Never. Something in the Spirit world, isn't it?"

"Do you have many dreams yourself?"

"I don't have too many dreams. Beena is the main dreamer in our house. She has even seen Jesus in dreams. Biju used to tease her. He said if she was a Catholic they'd have already declared her a saint. God has got great plans for Beena. She is very dedicated to the Lord. I was pregnant with her the first time Thampy went to America. When he returned Beena was about three months old. He brought back all sorts of things people had given him; clothes, nappies and feeding bottles. She had everything from America. I can still remember the beautiful little frocks the people sent. She was born into blessing. She has never really experienced a bad scarcity.

"It was a big step for her to marry Martin. Martin's father was a powerful man of God, but he died without leaving much financially. Beena told me the morning after her marriage they didn't even have money for toothpaste. From day one they've had to walk by faith. Every day they have all these miracle stories about provision. They work very well together. In a short period the church has really grown strong. Martin is a very good boy. I don't think anybody other than Martin would've been able to build up Beena's confidence so well. He is great at lifting her up and encouraging her.

"Just before their wedding someone discouraged Beena by asking, 'How can you choose the hard life of marrying a pastor and living by faith?' Afterwards Beena had a dream in which an angel came down and talked to her. It talked to her in Malayalam, 'You know, Beena, I am sent from God to tell you not to worry. When you worry, it's a worry to God's heart.' I also was under a lot of pressure at that time. The angel's advice not to worry also brought peace to my heart. Beena's visions often speak to me. One sentence the angel said in English to Beena was, 'Isn't Biju excellent?' That was very encouraging news for me. That was God's comment on my eldest son. God shows me many things before they happen so I can pray about them. Sometimes this is through dreams. Other times I hear a voice. Other times God enlightens me inside to something."

"Do you hear an audible voice?"

"Yes, it's like a man's voice, but from inside of me. Recently there was a battle against Thampy's life. Satan was trying to kill him and cut short his ministry. This was last November I think. I was praying and fasting for that situation. Specifically I was praying, 'Lord give him long life.' On the third night of the fast I heard a voice tell me to read Judges 15:13. When I looked it up it was about Samson. His enemies had tied him up with new cords. The Holy Spirit came upon him and burned the cords up. The bindings dropped from him. The last verse in that chapter says Samson led Israel for twenty years. From this, I felt God was saying Thampy would escape from Satan's attacks to lead God's people for a further twenty years. I never knew these verses were in the Bible. Through them God spoke directly to my heart."

While we are talking, Idy and other intercessors came in and spoke with Mariamma. After they left Mariamma said, "Only because of the prayers of these girls am I able to do what I am doing. They were asking me how the meetings in Australia went. I told them, 'When you pray so much for me how can they not be powerful?' They pray for me using words like, 'Lord use Aunty in a mighty way.' So I am telling them God always answers their prayers. This last time in Australia, people said they could see a new anointing, a more powerful anointing on me. These reports are a real encouragement to the girls. They know their prayers are not in vain."

"So you think prayer is important?"

"Oh, sure. I wouldn't dare go on a missions trip without these girls praying behind me?"

"What would you say to my wife Angela whose endeavors to get Christians to pray are not always successful?"

"Tell her to write to us about her needs. These girls will pray for her. Without prayer, very little happens. It is the key for everything. Here I have my own room to pray in. In Changanacherry, when I prayed in my bedroom, they'd hear me on the main road. Binu used to say, 'Mama I could hear you praying so loudly when I came to the bridge.' My kids grew up hearing constant prayer. When they were young I used to put them on my lap and pray. Maybe I'd put them near me on the mat and pray. When they were in the womb they all had a good nine months in prayer. They were birthed in prayer."

"When did you first really start praying?"

"From the time I got saved the Lord put that burden upon me. I was nineteen then. I was saved at the end of 1968. I received a calling for the ministry when I was twenty."

"How did that happen?"

"Mostly through prophecy. The Lord spoke to me through sixteen different people. Almost everything that has happened to me from then until now was prophesied to me in those days. Things like, 'If you come out for Me and if you are faithful I will send you around the world and you will be My witness.' It's all happening now.

"The leader of the first church I attended in Nagercoil, was a Christian sadhu who wore the traditional saffron clothes. In India, sadhus are holy men who have renounced the world and all its pleasures. They don't marry. He was an elderly man. It was the time of my final year exams. After a chemistry practical I was walking home. I had to pass by *Faith Home*, where this sadhu lived. He happened to be standing outside the house. He was like a father to me. He called me over. He looked straight into my eyes and said, 'The Lord has spoken to me. He said He has called you for the ministry.'

"This was the first time I had ever heard this mentioned. I couldn't hold it in my mind because I'd never ever thought about it. My only desire was that I'd be a good believer. I was doing a BSc then. I thought I'd do a postgraduate degree, get a good job and support the ministry from my wages. When the sadhu told me this I just broke into tears. He told me to kneel down. He put his hand on my head and prayed. That was the first time I had heard God wanted me in the ministry. Then, Bang! Bang! Bang! Within a few months, through another fifteen people, the Lord spoke and said the same thing. Wherever I'd go there would be a prophecy for me from people who'd never seen me before. In the end I was completely sure that God had called me for the ministry. Different people from different places would come and tell me, 'You'll be among many people. There'll be a literature ministry. You'll be going and pioneering churches. So many souls will come forward for salvation. The Lord will use you mightily.' Things were prophesied I could not have imagined for myself. At that time, I thought one couldn't serve the Lord properly if they were married. Some people were very much against my idea of staying single."

Mariamma remembered, "One day a prophet came to our Sunday meeting. He was well known for the accuracy of his words. Before going to the meeting I prayed, 'Lord if You want me to get married then You must speak to me through this prophet.' This fellow normally prophesied, before the preaching, while the people were worshiping. I'd told the Lord, 'The first prophecy must be for me and it must be concerning this issue of marriage only.' Normally this prophet didn't foretell about things like marriage. Then I went to the meeting. I was so thin in those days. I sat behind my mum, on the mat, so as to hide from the prophet. When the worship finished and the prophesying was over I was happy. I thought, *Now I am free. I don't have to get married.* The prophet took his Bible and began to preach. Suddenly he stopped. Like an arrow, he shot straight to the place where I was hiding. He put his hand on my head. 'My dear daughter,' he prophesied, 'I will never leave you to do My work alone. You are going to do My work with My servant.' He also gave me other promises. For the rest of the meeting I sat there and cried. I realized I couldn't escape marriage now because Mum had heard God wanted me to marry a man of God.

"Personally, I couldn't even think about marrying a Pentecostal pastor. I prayed, *Not my will but Yours be done.* Shortly afterwards I first saw Thampy in our church. He'd been standing on a street corner preaching and giving his testimony to a mob of people. My pastor chanced to pass that way and asked him to come and speak at our church. My first impression was that Thampy was a big serious man with a beard. We all thought he must be married. His testimony was so marvelous. He was a man kicked out of his home, going through hardships, persecutions and beatings. He'd been captured and kidnapped. All this testimony he was telling. He was on fire for God. Everyone was saying that he was a man like Paul. They had never seen anyone like him before.

"Dad invited him to our house for Sunday dinner. Dad was so troubled about me. I was the eldest. There were another four girls behind me all to be married. Dad had no money for dowries. Neither did he know what to do about my call for the ministry. He said to Thampy, 'I have a daughter. I don't know what to do with her.' Thampy said he had a friend in America who was looking to marry a graduate. He said he'd write and inform him of me. Dad said, 'I can't tell her that for she doesn't want to get married. She wants to starve and suffer for the Lord in India. But Thampy, if it's a man like you that she married I'd be very happy.' 'Please don't say that,' said Thampy, 'If she married me she would indeed have to starve and suffer. I have nothing. I have nowhere for her to live.'

"My father answered, 'I know you have nothing, but God is with you. So you just please pray and see. If my daughter wants to go into the ministry she must do so with full consecration.' This conversation happened in March 1970 during the Easter convention. On October 26th of that year we were married."

"Would it not be extremely difficult for a female in India, particularly then, to be in the ministry if she weren't married?"

"If I wasn't married I wouldn't be this effective in ministry. Marriage to Thampy has given me an exposure I wouldn't otherwise have. It was all God's plan. God brought along the right person for me to marry. Thampy is totally dedicated and open to God's work. Another pastor would never have allowed me to do the things I am doing. Thampy has given me all the freedom I need. Not many pastors would have allowed the intercessors to live with them in their own home. We never ever had the place to ourselves. Our door was always open. All the time people would be staying. Ours has been like a community life. Sometimes the children would say, 'Mama we want to live in a home, not in a community.' For the sake of the Kingdom, Thampy was willing to sacrifice everything. He gives me freedom but I don't use that freedom to try to boss him. I do everything in a quiet way. I think this is one reason why God has given me acceptance and favor among my people. I don't try and lord it over people. We need to do what we have been called to in a behind-the-scenes kind of way. Only God can give you acceptance before the people. It's all God's grace. We are nothing. We are nobodies."

"Do you remember your marriage interview?"

"I remember it so well. The first thing Thampy asked was, 'Have you ever read Richard Wurmbrand's book?' I answered yes because just a week previously I'd read one of Wurmbrand's books that was doing the rounds in Nagercoil. It told the story of how Wurmbrand and his wife Sabina had been imprisoned and tortured in Communist prisons in their homeland in Romania. He had been sentenced to fourteen years; three of them in solitary confinement, for refusing to compromise his Christian beliefs and say that atheistic communism was good. He had been badly tortured, drugged, brainwashed and degraded. His body was a mass of scars from the cruelty. Sabina was arrested for sharing the gospel. She spent three years as a slave laborer in prison. They tormented her by saying things like, 'Your husband is dead, divorce him.' They even had communists come in to jail disguised as prisoners. They told her they'd seen her husband killed. They both suffered so much for the gospel. Sabina and her little son endured terrible hardships.

"The Nazis had previously murdered her parents and four of their children and five of their adopted children. Despite all this, Sabina was able to forgive her oppressors and to walk in love and faith toward them. Thampy said to me, "If you can be a wife like Sabina Wurmbrand, then you can step forward to marry me. I am called to be a martyr for this nation. I want to give my life for the Lord.' He was deadly serious. He said, 'If you have a calling like that then you can marry me, otherwise no.'

"When he had finished talking I knew this marriage was God's perfect will for me. Suffering unto death was also my calling. I wanted to die for the Lord. Even now that is my whole desire. I prayed, 'I know Lord, You have brought the right person to me.' When we have that commitment then anything else that comes along doesn't matter. Whatever the Lord wants is the only important thing. We started from nothing. Thirty years ago when we got married, we didn't even have a rented home. But right from the beginning, our vision has been to reach the nation; *Christ for India, India for Christ.* We were two fools in the sight of the world. People would say, 'What difference are you going to make in a country, so big and so full of gods, poverty and disease?' We had our calling and we knew that God could do something through us. There was a fire in our hearts. We were totally surrendered in his hands."

"What were those early days like?"

"The first three years of our marriage were a training ground for faith from the Holy Spirit. We had to believe for the next meal otherwise we wouldn't eat. But God was so good for each and every need. For example, in 1971, when I was pregnant with Biju, every Friday very poor people used to come for a meeting at our home. They'd have walked seven or eight kilometers. When the meeting finished, around 2PM, we usually served a simple dish of water and rice with some curry. That Friday when I went to cook the meal I discovered there was no rice in the cupboard. We'd no money to buy any. I went back to the prayer meeting a little depressed at the thought of having to send these poor people home without food.

"During the meeting I left to go to our outside toilet. I saw a taxi standing in front of our house. One man carrying a big sack on his head was walking toward me. A friend waved from the taxi and left. When I opened the sack I couldn't believe my eyes. It was three quarters full of good rice. The rest was made up of coconuts, bananas and vegetables. There was enough to fill the rice box with some left over. I cooked the rice, went back to the meeting and said, 'I have a testimony to share.' I cried as I told the people of our recent provision. If someone had given me 10,000 rupees that day I wouldn't have been happier. It blessed me so much to know my Father in heaven loved me so much to see my rice box was empty and to touch the hearts of others to help.

"Later our friend told us he'd been visiting his parents. They had given him the rice and provisions. When the taxi came in front of our house it stopped. They tried everything but it wouldn't start. As he sat there he realized he was outside Thampy's house. He felt prompted by the Holy Spirit to send the rice across the road to us with a passerby. When the man carrying the sack approached me the car started so our friend just waved to me, afraid to stop in case the car wouldn't start again."

Mariamma said, "So often it was like that for us. We had so much lack and so many needs. We'd kneel down and make our requests known to God. He would supply our needs. The principle to believe for the next meal or for one million dollars is the same principle. From having nothing God has brought us this far. Now we have started around a thousand churches all over India. We have nine Bible Schools, three orphanages and a refugee home for about forty ladies. We have to feed them. Many of them we have to buy clothes for. Some of them we have to help get married – 10,000 rupees for dowry— things like that. There are many different kinds of needs, all on top of the ministry needs. We have about 900 workers altogether, men and women, evangelists and pastors. We have the responsibility of so many pastors and all the time new works are being pioneered.

"Our aim is to make the churches self-sufficient. Many of the older churches are self-supporting, but because new churches are continually being planted, the need continues to grow. For example, in January 2000 we sent out a team of nine people in a jeep equipped with PA systems and the *Jesus* film. Every day they were preaching in the villages. Within one year they preached to about half a million people in about five hundred villages. From this, forty-four new churches were established. This is the kind of work the Lord is giving us now. Like the disciples in the boat, we are hardly able to cope with the growth.

"We were forced to start a Bible school in Andhra in the local Telugu language. It offers a three months course. The need is so great and we don't have time to wait. The harvest is now. In three months we train them. The first batch of thirteen students has graduated. Now the next batch of twenty-five students is there already. We have to pay to train and feed them and pay travel money to their teachers on so on. We must keep the fires burning. In Kolhapur by the end of March we had two days of meetings. It's a big city about ten hours journey from Bombay on the way to Goa. Biju rented a house for the team and found a place to conduct the meetings. We preached on Friday and Saturday and on Sunday we started a church. I was there. We have about twenty-five adults and about thirty children. We sent out another team of six people with a fully equipped jeep and within three months, eight brand new churches were started in eight villages. It's a time of growth in India."

"Things are really moving in India?"

"Now is the time for India. The harvest is ripe and ready. All these people were one hundred percent Hindus. They had never heard about Jesus Christ or Christianity but they are so open to the gospel. The only thing we have to do is go and take the harvest. But who will go? We are equipping the nationals for this great task. In Goa Bible School we have students from nine different states. This is the vision, Biju received when he was in England, coming to pass. That vision is being accomplished now.

"In Andhra we started a Bible school. The dean of the school is a boy called Prasad from the Bible school in Goa. The team members working in Kolhapur are also students from the Goa Bible School. Like in the vision the compass circles are reaching ever outwards. This growth is occurring through the ministry of our Bible School graduates. We have to train, equip and support them. We must also visit and encourage them every now and then but they are the ones doing the job. To date 99% of our Bible School graduates are all in the ministry.

"We want to impart our vision of *Christ for India* to these capable local leaders. We could never speak all these languages. India is a very complex and diverse nation. All of this creates financial needs. But just like I knew what to do with the bag of rice when I got it, if we had one million dollars we would also know how to spend it. We would use it quickly to harvest the souls of this present generation."

132

"I also hear a lot of talk about orphanages and AIDS victims. What's your opinion on these things?"

"In the past we've never had a vision or burden for orphanages. Our primary directive is to reach the nation with the Gospel. We are always wary of being trapped in social work. Bini and Beena are the ones in our family who have always wanted to help the poor and homeless. Beena also has a growing desire to help people with AIDS and their children. But when we went to the villages in Andhra Pradesh we were staggered by the tremendous needs there.

"Many parents are killing their baby girls because of the dowry system. Every year in India around five thousand ladies are killed on the basis of dowry alone. From the time a baby girl is born the parents have to save for her dowry. But these poor people don't have any money to save. They go to far off villages to work from morning to evening. They might only receive ten to fifteen rupees wages. That is enough for just one meal. If they have a boy they can send him to the field at age seven to work. Economically, a male child is a blessing and a female child is a liability.

"About six weeks back, there were regular articles in a national newspaper telling of how some parents are killing their little girls. Some were destroyed by stuffing rice and sand down their throats. Others were burnt or buried alive. Some were drowned. Some were stabbed to death. Some parents were asked why they did it. They replied if they had money they'd never have killed their children. It's all down to economics. 'Our girls will have to suffer,' they said. 'Why should they go through so much pain? Better to kill them now and prevent all their suffering.' Poor parents they have no hope in the world.

"One day two of our lady missionaries, Elcy and Marykutty went into a village in Andhra. A very old lady with three young girls came up to them. She said, 'You preach Jesus loves everyone, but what is your answer for these little children?' This lady told them, 'These girl's mum, aged thirty-three, died a few days ago from cancer. Their father had already left them.' This old grandmother had nothing. She couldn't look after the children. She said, 'You say Jesus loves everyone, but what is his answer for these children?' That really struck me. There is no point in preaching alone and ignoring needy people. In the book of James we are warned not to say to the hungry, 'God bless you, keep warm and well fed.' James tells us faith without works is dead. I don't want dead faith. I told our ladies to go and rent a house and help these little girls. I was sure that God would provide.

"That's how that orphanage started. Last time I visited there were seventeen children in that three-bedroom house. Others came asking us to take their baby girls but we didn't have the room. The need is so great. When we see this hardship we can't keep quiet. In Isaiah 58 it is so clear, 'What is the real fast; ... breaking the yolk and feeding the hungry, clothing the naked and giving shelter to the wanderer. Then you will call and the Lord will answer.'

"Over the years, we have done much prayer and fasting. Now God is also asking us to do the kind of fasting He talks about in Isaiah 58. In the past we concentrated on getting the people saved, but now as we are growing older the Lord is taking us a bit deeper. I think our children's vision is bigger than mine in this area. Recently I was scolding Beena for keeping the AIDS lady in her house. She spoke, 'Mama you have been helping needy people all these years. Why are you now scolding me for helping people?' 'But I didn't have AIDS patients,' I told her."

Mariamma went into kinks of laughter at this memory. I love the way she is able to see the funny side of very serious issues; a good woman laughing in the face of the impossible task.

She said, "Beena has such a heart of compassion for people. She wants to see them saved and cared for. She wants to bring them all to heaven to meet Jesus. She doesn't want anyone to go to the hell-fire she saw in her dream. When people heard she was helping AIDS people so many wanted to come because they are rejected everywhere else. I wish I had the money to give her to have a home for these poor people. At least they should die peacefully, knowing Jesus.

"The need is so great, but God is our help. He has never let us down. That is our courage. He will never put us to shame. We kneel down. We shed tears. We cry, 'God, speak to the hearts of somebody somewhere to help.' We are still operating the same principle as believing for the next meal. First faith for little things, then faith for bigger things."

Mariamma thought of Biju. She said, "It's the same principle for our children too. They all have that faith. When Biju was in England he didn't have any money of his own. For everything he believed – from razor blades to his fees. For three years we just threw him into the sky like the

134

mother eagle that throws her little eaglets out of the nest so they might learn to fly. Now he can soar in faith himself.

"I'll never forget a dream the Lord gave me in 1981. I was doing a six-month leadership-training course in Australia in order to gain the confidence to start the ladies Bible School here. I had a BSc and B.Ed but no degree in Theology. Thampy used to write to me about the financial crisis in the ministry. I was very upset by all this. I was praying, *Lord, please open some doors for us.* Our dedication was we would not tell our needs to anyone. I can tell people like you when you ask, but we don't want to go around begging from people. God knows our needs and God has to speak to people's hearts. Only then will it come from a heart of faith.

"I was staying with Pastor Bob and Kath Mc Gregor in their home in Adelaide. That night I had a dream in which Thampy and I were standing on the seashore. We were standing near our car on a beach. I saw two pure white ships, many stories high, standing out at sea. We had to go in little country boats and unload the cargo. Somebody in the dream said, 'Everything in these two ships is for you. It's all for you. When the need comes all you have to do is to go and unload it and take it by faith.' I shared this dream with Kath McGregor. I thought the two ships signified the spiritual blessing the Lord has for us. Kath said, 'You saw two ships. Perhaps one is spiritual blessing and the other is material blessing.'

"That dream was a great encouragement to believe the Lord can supply all our needs, spiritually and physically. We only need our small boats of faith to go and receive it. By faith we receive from God. All these years God has been providing in marvelous, marvelous ways. Sthothram!"

"So instead of the taxi with the bag of rice that stopped outside your house, there are now two ships from the nations waiting? Maybe one is from America and one from Australia."

"I'm believing God will speak to the hearts of people who have the wealth to help the nation of India receive the gospel. Not many people have the vision to send money and not come themselves. If someone would send the price of an airfare to us, we could do so much with it. Its good for people to come and gain an understanding of what is really happening. A sacrificial vision to give to the work is rare among many people from the West. Nowadays young inexperienced people don't come to do the work in India – that is done by the trained indigenous leaders.

"The one obvious resource the West has is money. If people could get a vision to help like Chester Bieson they could be so effective in taking the work forward. Finance without strings attached is a great blessing. We really put ourselves out for the teams from the West that come. One sad thing is that the vast majority of them never even think of writing a letter to us after that. Most come, go, and forget all about us.

"But always in the crowd there are some people whose heart God touches to help. Many have caught the vision and have become faithful friends over the years. They have grasped the reality that times have changed. In the days of Evangeline Booth things were different. Colonialism was at its peak when my grandfather got saved through the young Salvation Army girl's kindness. Chester Bieson understood the changing times by supporting Thampy and putting him forward. Nowadays it is indigenous leaders that are equipping the indigenous saints for the work of the ministry.

"The government of India is so much against foreign missionaries. If they see a big team from the West coming and ministering they get all stirred up. They can stop us and ban the meetings. There is too much danger now for big teams to come here. However, unless people come and see how it is here they won't get a vision either. Some need to be here to understand. You can't just say, 'Please stay at home and send the money.'

"In most cases that might be the most effective way but it hardly seems appropriate. It takes real maturity and love like that of parents for their children to do something like that. All of this is a delicate matter that needs to be handled with love and grace. Perhaps people don't really know what's happening here in India. Maybe God wants you to tell them Brendan."

I saw the twinkle in Mariamma's eye and kept silent. Next one to speak loses. These are delicate issues with a great potential for cross-cultural misunderstanding. Yet, I think I understand something of what she's trying to say. I have had similar experiences with many overseas Christians that have come to Ireland. Over this last twenty-five years, I have worked with numerous individuals, ministries and teams that have come to visit. Like Thampy and Mariamma, my wife and I have put ourselves out to help facilitate these people. We too have been saddened by the lack of any future contact from most of them.

For our part we shared our home, lives, time and contacts that we had so painstakingly and carefully cultivated over the years. God has called us to work across the Catholic/Protestant divide in Ireland. All this requires special sensitivity and a careful understanding of certain cross-cultural issues.

I have often felt that these outside Christian brothers and sisters have marched over our well-tended lawns with their great big hobnailed boots completely unaware of the mess they were making or of the devastation they were causing. Often it seemed they were not so much concerned about what the Spirit was doing in Ireland as in carrying out their own agenda. Often there has been a great lack of understanding and maturity among the folks that have come. Regularly proper spiritual protocol has been totally ignored. I personally have spent far too much time in sorting out situations where visiting ministries have transgressed procedure by bypassing the indigenous leadership and using contacts of mine and others so as to promote their own ministries. Many of the best indigenous leadership in Ireland are so burned out with this "Colonial Christianity" that they refuse to be involved with it any longer. This is a tragic loss for all involved.

Often outside teams are terribly naive as to the real issues involved. Some haughtily claim they can't understand why Catholics and Protestants don't live in harmony in Ireland. They say this without as much as a backward glance over their own shoulders at the massive injustices in their own backyards caused by their blind ethnocentric attitudes.

I too have been dismayed at how much it costs to keep foreign missionaries in the field in Ireland. Often they have their own stuff shipped over. They need cars, computers, holidays, friends to come visit and a host of other requirements. Nearly all will have disappeared within two or three years merely having muddied the water for the indigenous leadership. This keeps happening year after year.

Some teams come over with numerous prophecies of revival in Celtic Ireland but when their traveling road show has moved on the local people are no better off. It would be something akin to a bunch of Irish Christians dressing up like cowboys and going over to Texas and prophesying revival for the lone star state. Year after year, clouds without rain.

If only they'd use some of their resources to help support indigenous leaders involved in spiritual change and innovation it could all be so much more effective.

But as Mariamma said there is always one in the crowd that is touched by God to genuinely help. Lionel Batke, a teacher-prophet from Vancouver,

Canada has been such a person to me. He has come alongside and helped. He was the first to open the door to Thampy's ministry in India for me. Without Lionel's input I wouldn't be writing and you wouldn't be reading this book right now. Lionel's purpose has always been the furtherance of the kingdom of God and not self-promotion.

Chris Van Gorder, a missionary from Pittsburgh in America is another who genuinely tried to help and grapple with the real issues involved. He has opened doors for me in America, Morocco and China. We have also led a number of cross-cultural courses in Ireland with Christian college students from America. He has had a heart to try to work with indigenous leadership. Cross-cultural communication and partnership can be extremely difficult, but when it works it can really work well.

For my little lesson on cross-cultural-partnership let's look at the issues of the Irish, the Americans, the moon and *Riverdance*. Let's take the moon first.

The Irish have written love songs:

'The pale moon was rising above the green mountain. The sun was declining beneath the blue sea . . .'

And rebel songs:

'I've got orders from the captain; get you ready quick and soon
For the pikes must be together at the rising of the moon . . .'

We have written reams of song and poetry about the moon, but what did the Americans do? *They went to the moon. Americans went to the moon.* No Irishman in his right mind would ever have remotely considered spending all that money and effort to actually go to the moon. Why would you want to go to the moon? There's nobody there. But Americans, *God bless them*, went to the moon.

Different worldviews - planets apart. An issue like this could well cause cross-cultural problems. Picture an American, proud that his nation was the first to walk on the moon and picture an Irishman scratching his head unable to understand why anyone would spend all that money on such a venture when there is so much social need in the ghettos back in the good old USA. Lots of room for misunderstanding.

Now, let's take the instance of *Riverdance,* the show that propelled Irish dancing onto the world stage delighting international audiences with its great music and spectacular footwork. A second generation Irish American from Chicago, Illinois, called Michael Flatley, was the principal choreographer and dancer.

With that marvelous American capacity for reinvention he spiced up and freed the old Irish dancing from its limiting restraints. He gave it a more international flavor creating in the process a new form of Irish dancing that astonished the world. I well remember seeing the very first performance of *Riverdance*, when it was only a seven-minute, interval filler during the 1994 Eurovision Song Contest. It took my breath away. I felt like crying.

Here was one instance of America and Ireland in partnership, producing a synergy that created a real magic far and beyond the sum of its parts. So there you have it, on a bad day total misunderstandings about the moon and each other, on a good day *Riverdance*. I'm totally convinced it's well worth persisting and struggling for the breakthrough and new life that *Riverdance* brings.

Please don't get me wrong here. I'm not having a go at America or its people. America is well respected both in Ireland and in my life personally. It was America that opened its doors to the Irish over the years, especially during what has been euphemistically called the Great Famine. Millions of Irish have great cause to thank God for America. America is also appreciated for its sacrificial implementation of the Marshall Plan that helped Europe survive financially after the Second World War. America's real interest in fostering peace and justice in Northern Ireland in recent years is also to be commended.

On a personal level, Americans have brought great encouragement to my family and myself over the years. They have visited us often. Others have had some of our children over to the US to holiday in their own homes. The American prophet John Paul Jackson came on the basis of a dream to Ireland in 1987. He stayed in our home during which time he prophesied significantly for all my family, much of which has come to pass. He even prophesied the Lord would bring me to India. He sure got that one right. I appreciate and regularly pray for America and Americans.

When I was in India writing this book a young American girl called

Sheila Henson from Boston came and helped my wife cook and look after our children.

My goal is not to knock America or any other nation but rather to point out that we must be very careful when we approach another country and its people. God will have been there before us. He will have been working already. Our part is to slot in with that work and not to come with our own agenda.

We must not think our way is the only way or even the best way. Let us ask how we can be of help to the indigenous leaders that God has raised up in that nation. Let us exercise proper spiritual protocol. The fact that there have been problems with some Americans probably springs from the fact, that by and large, it has been Americans that have put their money where their mouth is and, have traveled into the world in order to share the gospel. So let us put our heads together and help create a synergy that propels the Great Commission forward.

Let's hasten the Lord's return. Lets *Riverdance,* but let's also remember it takes two to tango.

Does that help Mariamma? De de de de de de diddle de la de de de de de de diddle de la de de de de...

14

Padma's Story

This morning I was far too tired for the Kottayam crows to fully waken me. *Crows, crows go away and come again another day.* I lay half asleep in the cool of the day thinking about nothing in particular when suddenly I heard it. In the quietness left behind by the departing crows it sounded crystal clear and as large as life. A few days previously Angela had phoned and asked, "Have you heard it yet?"

"Not yet." I said, *"Perhaps it was only our imagination."*

"Don't say that," she scolded, "it was real and you know it."

Now here it was in sharp clear bursts. *"Stottt - ramm, Stottt - ramm,"* it intoned. The little Sthothram bird was back. Each time I've stayed at Mariamma and Thampy's home I've heard this little prophetic minstrel of the morning. Initially I thought I was hearing things. I was "over the moon" that a wild bird was actually flying around praising the Lord. When Angela was here she loved listening to this little bird. She said creation is always praising the Lord. The problem is with our ability to hear and not with creations ability to praise. For a full five minutes I listened to this little worshiper, as it soared outside, leaving the signature of its music tangled all through the leaves of the rubber trees, *Sthothram, Sthothram, Sthothram.*

At breakfast Mariamma is still replenishing her Omega 3 oils. She starts to talk about her family line. She said, "Mum and Dad were not in the ministry. Yet all six of their children ended up as full-time Christian workers. We five girls, Anna, Valsala, Sheela, Usha and I, all married pastors. My brother Abraham became a pastor and married Joyce who was a pastor's daughter. I believe this happened because our forefathers had poured out their lives for the Lord. God was keeping His promise in Exodus 20 that says He shows love to a thousand generations of those who love Him and keep His commandments. It's all part of a much larger picture. We didn't choose

Him. He chose us. Both of Mum's grandfathers were men of God. They were pioneers in the evangelical movement in India called the Marthomites. They suffered many trials and rejections.

"Mum's paternal grandfather, Varkey Aasan (Aasan means 'the teacher'), was a poet and a songwriter. He wrote over half the songs in the present Marthomite songbook. Maramon is the name of the biggest Christian convention in the whole of India. It is held yearly on a riverbank in Kerala. It started over a hundred years ago with granddad, Varkey Aasan as its first worship leader.

"Mum's other grandfather was also a well-known Christian songwriter. Today, all over the world, Malayalam speakers of all denominations still sing their songs. These are Indian Christian classic hymns similar to, *Amazing Grace, The Old Rugged Cross* and *Abide With Me*; well-known songs that are part of the lives of millions of people.

"Mum's maternal grandfather P. V. Thommy died at the young age of thirty-three. Ten of his eleven children also died young. Only my grandmother survived. Out of these painful experiences he wrote his songs. Perhaps that's why they still speak to us today. When I read the words of my great grandfather's songs, I am amazed at the depth of the revelation they had. Great-granddad, P.V. Tommy died from cholera as he helped nurse the people in his village. Recently, I was thinking, *Lord what am I doing comparative to my great granddad*. Within his short lifetime he was able to leave behind such a legacy of blessing in his songs. Both great grandfathers were good friends. They gave their children in marriage to each other.

"My father's father was also a dedicated man of God. He is the one who was saved through the Salvation Army girl's kindness. He loved me like anything. He died in 1961. He had four sons. My father was the only one to survive. It was all the choosing of God. My father was the least of his brothers. The others were so handsome and intelligent. My father was nothing beside them. That's what the people were saying. In the normal course of events there'd have been no chance of Dad and Mum ever meeting. She came from the northern part of Kerala while he came from Tamil Nadu. Dad, who was a postmaster, happened to get a job near her place. He also happened to become friendly with my mum's father who arranged for him to live in his home. He also arranged the marriage to Mum who was only sixteen. God was putting something together.

"Dad's father was also a songwriter. He wrote a lot of the songs in the Tamil Christian hymnal. I recently discovered that many of the songs written by my mum's side of the family were translated from Malayalam to Tamil by dad's father. Small world, isn't it? From Thampy's background there is no Godly heritage that we know of. Like Elijah he just appeared on the scene causing trouble to the status quo. Dad's father was very special. He stood up for very poor people that were being persecuted by the higher castes. Like a lawyer he would go and argue for them in the court. He had a great command of the English language. He was high up in the Salvation Army. He has built so many churches. He used to tell me stories about his life. Once he went to pioneer a church in a place where the whole caste was robbers. Their job was to steal from people. Grandfather was like a character from the Old Testament.

"Nowadays, when we go to a place to plant a church we do spiritual warfare so as to break the hold of the powers and principalities in the heavenlies. When grandfather went to plant a church he would literally break all the idols and statues into little pieces with a sledgehammer. Imagine breaking the gods of these notorious robber castes. How will they feel? One day he was conducting a service. As he left the meeting he found the whole church was surrounded by a big mob of robbers who'd come to kill him. He took a stick and drew a circle around himself and shouted, 'Anybody who has the nerve to kill me, I dare him to come inside this circle.' No one moved. That's the kind of man he was. Fearless!

"He was also involved in much social service for the poor and the needy. He had a covered bullock cart in which he traveled from place to place. In those days the roads were very bad. The whole area was like a forest. One night he heard a woman screaming. He stopped the cart and found her in the bushes. She had been raped and stabbed. Her stomach was slashed. All her intestines were hanging out. He replaced her insides and wrapped her up with his turban. Then he took her to the hospital where they sewed her up. Miraculously she survived.

"He was eighty-four when he died. His wife and three of his sons had died before him. One of his sons called Jaba Thurai was a beautiful musician who played the flute and violin. In those days the kings ruled Kerala. Once the king invited all the top musicians, to play at an eight-day marriage celebration in Trivandrum. Uncle Jaba Thurai was also invited to perform.

Like his father he joined the Salvation Army and worked with the poor people of the slums. One day an old lady gave him something to eat. He didn't like to refuse her kindness. He was about twenty-three. He got dysentery from the food. Grandfather managed to see him in the hospital. 'Appa, please pray for me,' he said, just before he died.

"Another son was so handsome people used to say that even looking at him was a big sin. Yet the three of them died between the ages of twenty-one and twenty-eight. The only son left was my father who in everyone's sight was the black sheep. He was a heavy drinker who wouldn't go to church. He was also a very worried man. In India they say if you have five daughters you're a pauper. How will you find the dowries for five girls? He was in big trouble. He tried to forget his problems by drinking. Really Granddad was more like our father. Only now is Dad our father.

"Granddad would gather us around him and tell us so many stories. His name was Nalla Thampy, (Nalla means good. Thampy means younger brother). He did everything for us. Mathematics was a hard subject for me so he appointed a teacher to help me in the early morning. As the teacher was a man it was not appropriate for him to sit with me alone. Every morning, granddad would arise early and sit with us. Each day at 5:30AM he'd wake us for prayers.

"I can still see us, sitting half asleep, wrapped in our blankets and sheets. He was very adamant that we pray each morning and evening. He'd especially written for us most of the songs we sang. If we didn't rise on his first calling he'd sprinkle water on us. He also took us for picnics. He was such a good grandpa. His wife was named Karuna. She died in her sixties, when Mum was pregnant with me. I was called Karuna after her. Mariamma is my official name. At home they call me by my pet name Karuna, which means mercy. Everybody back in Nagercoil knows me as Karuna."

While Mariamma was talking, an elderly woman, dressed entirely in white, appeared at the backdoor. She stood motionless until she caught Mariamma's eye. Then she sat down and whispered quietly for a few minutes. When she left Mariamma said, "Just now you saw a lady talking to me? She is over eighty years old. For two and a half years, she and three daughters have been homeless. They're from a good family but they lost everything. They were reduced to begging for food in the street. One daughter called Gracie is helping Biju and Secu at the moment. Another daughter is a very

144

good prayer warrior in our prayer tower. "The mother was telling me just now, she has another daughter whose husband has abandoned her and her three little girls. Now they are also on the street. She was asking me. 'Can I also bring them here. Please find a place for them.' Brendan, it's like this every day. My heart melts when I hear these terrible stories. Idy and the intercessors sometimes tease me. They say, 'Aunty you are called Karuna and you act like Karuna. You can't refuse mercy to anyone.'

"Everything on our campus is called Bethesda, which means, *The House of Mercy*. Initially we called our Bible School, *Bethesda Training School* because Thampy received financial support for it, from Bethesda Church in Adelaide, Australia. We didn't think about the meaning of Bethesda then but God is involved in all the small details of our lives. His fingerprints are everywhere. He knew that someday we would have mercy ministries. Our God is a God of mercy. Wherever God is, there is also mercy. If there is no mercy in any situation then God is not there. There is no mercy in hell.

Mariamma's thoughts returned to her ancestors. She said, "Dad's grandmother was from a Sikh family in the Punjab. They worship at the Golden Temple in Amritsar. They are the ones who killed Indira Gandhi, the Indian prime minister. My grandmother was a very beautiful lady but like many women in our refuge, she had to leave her home when she believed in Jesus. Her conversion was a great shame to her family. A Christian missionary doctor adopted her and took her to South India. Granddad used to describe her to us children; very tall, slim, beautiful body shape, very fair skin with long shiny hair. He made her sound like a fairy princess. She named my father Ranjit Singh after her own dad.

"On Granddad's last birthday he was so much worried about my father. He wondered what would happen to us when he died. Then my father was an unbeliever and a drunkard. Grandfather loved us all. I felt he especially loved me because I was his first grandchild and I was named after his wife. On his last birthday morning, he woke us all early as usual. We were sitting sleepily, wrapped in our blankets. He said to my dad, 'Ranjit my son, I have a great burden for you. I have no peace. I have been concerned for your salvation. Yesterday I was praying for you and breaking my heart. Last night God gave me a dream. In it I saw you standing with a bright face. The darkness had left you. Your face was shining. You were so happy. Six healthy lion cubs were circling around your feet. When I woke

145

up I knew God was going to save you and take all your six children for his ministry. These are not ordinary children. They are not just little kittens. They are lion cubs chosen for God's ministry. They will be as bold as lions in the future.'

"I was just fourteen at the time. We were giggling. We laughed and sniggered unable to understand the symbolism of granddad's dream. 'You are a lion, not a pussycat,' we joked with each other. Nowadays we understand much better. God saved my parents and called all six of us children into full time ministry. This was God's promise to my grandfather on his eighty-fourth birthday.

"I cried for two years after granddad died. Not being a believer I'd no hope for eternity in my heart. I only felt the pain of loss. I could only think of him being put into the grave. Even before his death, I used to cry, thinking about that. I'd been the one responsible for looking after him in his old age. He gave me a blessing before he died. He called everyone and he blessed us. I remember his words so clearly. He said, 'Karuna, you are the one who has got the love. You are a person with the grace of God. You must be like this always. No matter what happens, you must never lose the reality of love and grace of God in your life.' His eldest sister lived with us when she was old. I looked after her. From a little girl I've always had compassion for people. When poor people came begging I always loved to help them. God has put his love for the outcast and the homeless into me. In India there is a great need for compassion.

. "Shortly after he blessed us, granddad died. There were thousands of people at his funeral. There were big obituaries in the newspaper and in Christian magazines. One article said the reporter had gone to granddad's office and saw that he'd kept large stones on his desk. These were some of the rocks that'd hit granddad when he'd been preaching. He kept them as souvenirs. Granddad was a good singer and violinist. He was an all-round figure. He was a man of prayer whose prayers are still being answered.

"Hebrews 11 talks about people who were still living by faith when they died. It says they didn't receive the things promised by God. They only saw them and welcomed them from a distance. They were highly praised for believing like this. Grandfather was one of these people of faith. He died believing in the dream God had given him. There was nothing in the physical realm to give him any hope at all, with Dad still drinking heavily and none of us saved. Granddad died in faith because like the prophets of old he'd seen what God was going to do and he died believing that God would do it. Now we see God has kept his promise to granddad. Mum and Dad are beautiful believers and the lion cubs are all in the ministry. Grandfather's death was the turning point for our whole family. We were all so broken-hearted when he died. I remember the memorial service. They were singing songs he'd written. My Dad also spoke at it. His father's death was the thing that got my dad back to the church."

Mariamma said, "It was at this time the evangelist Nataraja Mudaliar came to our town. We were good soil for the gospel by then. Our hard hearts had been turned over up by the plough of grief. Nataraja Mudaliar was an Indian born and brought up in South Africa. He was a great singer and an accordion player. After he became a Christian the Lord said to him, 'India is your nation. It's a heathen country. Go and tell them about Me.' Nataraja said, 'How can I do it God?' The Lord spoke to him and said, 'Moses went with a rod. Your accordion will be your rod. It will be your sign.' He used to draw crowds of up to twenty thousand to hear his singing. He came to our town in 1968.

"I was the only person from that area at Holy Cross College. The sadhu who first called me to the ministry was organizing these meetings. This was the first time he stepped into our home. He asked me, 'You study in the Holy Cross College?' Then he handed me a bunch of posters that had a picture of Nataraja Mudaliar on them. He asked me to pin them up on the college notice boards. I took them because he was a man of God, but I was ashamed at the thought of being seen putting up notices for Christian meetings. I couldn't imagine myself doing that.

"There was a girl called Padma at our College. She was a Christian. She was the first person I'd ever seen handing out Gospel tracts. At college I belonged to a group of five naughty girls. We were good students but we were very worldly and very fashionable. Padma was a Hindu convert. She used to ask, 'Mariamma, are you saved?' I'd answer, 'Padma, that's only for you Hindus. I am a Christian. I was born into a Christian family. I don't need salvation. You need it.' She was always talking about the love of God. In my heart I knew I didn't have what she had. One day Padma showed me her badly bruised back. Her brother had beaten her.

'He beat you for what?' I asked.

'Because I was praying to Jesus, he belted me,' Padma replied.

'What did you say?'

Padma answered, 'I said, *Praise the Lord!'*

"She told me she'd read her Bible and that God would speak to her through it. All these things were unknown to my experience. I'd never heard God's voice at that time. My friends used to tease, 'She won't leave you alone until you too become saved.' She was trying to win me with her life. If the ink would run out in my pen she'd give me her pen and she'd write with a pencil. She showed many kindnesses like this to me.

"When the sadhu gave me the job of distributing the posters I immediately knew whom I could pass the work onto. One day, when everyone else had left the classroom, I said, 'Padma, I have something for you.' She looked at me suspiciously, 'What is it Mariamma?' When I produced the posters she read one and shouted, 'Sthothram, Sthothram, Sthothram.' I can still picture her. She was so excited. She told me, 'I will do it on the condition you agree to attend this meeting also.' In order to escape putting up the posters I consented to go to the meeting. Mum and Dad also came along to hear the accordion-playing preacher. Nataraja Mudaliar had such an anointing. His songs could move you so much. They came straight from his heart. I got saved through one song. Everything I've gone through was contained in that song's lyrics. It was a song of commitment. It was so meaningful for me. Recently I translated it from Tamil into Malayalam for Biju to sing on his cassette. The meaning in English is:

> *Are you willing to walk Jesus' path of loss*
> *And share the suffering of the Cross.*

The chorus is:

> *Yes Lord.*
> *I will cling to the cross*
> *I will never leave it.*
> *I will never leave it.*

"That song has been like a prophecy to me. During those meetings, Mum, Dad and the four eldest of our family – the others were too young – all got saved together. We were baptized at Cape Comorin in Tamil Nadu where the three oceans meet: the Indian Ocean, the Arabian Sea and the Bay of Bengal. We traveled in Nataraja Mudaliar's van and had a picnic in his mission tent. It was a fantastic time. I remember him saying, 'This day we will rejoice and enjoy ourselves. Persecutions are coming, many obstacles are coming but today we will rejoice.' This was the beginning of a new life for our family. Granddad's prayers were beginning to be answered.

"After lunch Nataraja took me aside and whispered, 'Did you ask Padma?'"

Mariamma smiled at the memory. She said, "Previously Nataraja had mentioned he felt a certain leading towards asking Padma to marry him. He'd asked me to sound out her feelings towards such a match. This hadn't been easy. At first Padma appeared to be attracted to him. Then one day she said, 'I don't like Nataraja anymore. I thought he was a nice man. Now I hear he is going to get married.' She said this as if marriage was a sin. Wherever Nataraja went mothers would come along and give him proposals of marriage for their daughters. Padma had overheard talk of such a proposal. She had mistakenly thought a marriage had been arranged.

"This was my very first attempt at matchmaking. I invited her to our home so I'd get a good chance to talk to her. I asked her what she wanted to do with her life. She said, 'At fourteen I dedicated my life to the Lord. Now I want to be full-time in ministry.' I asked her how could she do full-time Christian ministry in India as a woman. I suggested she should marry a man of God. 'If the Lord has a man of God for me, I will marry him,' she replied. 'If it was Nataraja Mudaliar would you have any objections?' 'No objections whatsoever, but isn't his marriage already arranged?' she asked. 'It's just being arranged as we speak,' I said. I explained the situation to her. She was overjoyed. When I told Nataraja, of her willingness to marry him, he too was very happy.

"My next big obstacle was how to approach her family. Not only might they not want her to get married to a man aged thirty-eight, but they mightn't want her to marry a Christian preacher. As Hindus they didn't even want Padma, who was only eighteen at the time, to be a Christian at all. Padma's brother, Prasad, sensed that something was happening. Very tactfully he asked her a few questions. She let slip about the marriage proposal. He became angry and beat her until she lost consciousness. She was near death.

Each day our school bus stopped outside her house. I'd always save a seat for her. That morning I was so shocked when I saw her running out from her house. She looked like a mad woman. Her hair was disheveled and her tear stained face was black and blue. She gave me a letter and ran back inside. The letter explained how Prasad, had lost control and knocked her senseless. He thought he'd killed her. It was all too much for him. Their father had died and their mum wasn't well. Prasad was responsible for Padma's welfare. They were both studying in the city. He loved Padma but he couldn't cope with her marrying outside of Hinduism. He decided to commit suicide. As Padma drifted in and out of consciousness she asked the Lord to keep her alive. God revived her. When he realized she was still alive Prasad didn't hang himself.

"Because I was Padma's best friend Prasad came to ask help from my father. He told Dad, 'Please advise my sister not to do this terrible thing for then she will have no future.' Dad said if it was God's will for the marriage to take place then he couldn't advise against it. Prasad was not pleased with this answer but as my younger sisters were friendly towards him he calmed down. As time went on and there was no change in the situation Prasad decided to kill my father because he thought Dad was the one responsible for keeping the problem going. He took a knife and hid behind a tree on a lonely road my father had to pass through on his way home from work. As Prasad got ready to attack he saw a vision of my younger sisters coming before him. This image stopped him from killing Dad. He put the knife away and walked after my father. Dad tried to ignore him. He followed Dad on to the bus. He said, 'Do you know I nearly killed my sister and committed suicide.' 'What is that to me,' said Dad, 'you have the right to do both.' He followed Dad home. He came inside and sat down without talking. Soon it was time for our family prayers. Our prayer times were a bit like revival meetings in those days. We would be singing and praying. Heaven would come down.

"Dad said, 'Prasad, we are going to have prayer. Do you want to join us?' That day, the portion of scripture read was about the conversion of Saint Paul on the Damascus road. Afterwards Prasad said he wanted to tell us something. He put his knife on the table. He said to Dad, 'I'd wanted to kill you.' He then told us of how he'd seen the vision of my sisters, as he was about to lunge at Dad. The scripture reading had convicted him. He gave his heart to the Lord in our living room. Next day, at college, Padma was so happy. It had been her constant prayer Prasad should come to know and love Jesus. Now that her prayer was answered she was full of joy. It was decided Nataraja should baptize him. Back we went to Cape Comorin for another day of victory. These were dramatic times for us. Finally the doors were opened and they were married. After this Padma moved into a new realm with the Lord. She and her husband have been used powerfully over the years. That was the first marriage I arranged. They were married in Madras, which was too far away for me so I never got to the wedding. Nataraja became responsible for hundreds of churches and many orphanages in India. He was also made president of World Missionary Evangelism. Padma was raised up to a big position of responsibility. She is a powerful preacher."

I asked, *"Do you ever see her nowadays?"*

"Occasionally I invite her to preach at our annual conference. She preaches in Tamil and I translate in Malayalam. At school our campus was fifty acres on land covered by cashew trees. Padma used to conduct lunchtime prayer meetings out in the open. One day one of my friends said, 'Mariamma look at those girls sitting under the cashew trees. There are about forty of them. They are crying and covering their heads. They are talking to God just like you'd talk to a person.' This impressed my four Hindu friends but I said it was all humbug, 'Why do they have to pray out in public. Why could they not pray at home?' But they began to pray for me and I eventually joined them under the cashew trees. We were just young girls of eighteen and nineteen praying for the salvation of the people of India. We didn't know very much but are hearts were on fire to see God move on our friends. A couple of years ago, Padma told me everyone in that prayer group is now working for the Lord. Some of them married pastors. They are all in some sort of ministry all over India. I remember the first time Padma met Nataraja. He'd shown a film about Pandita Ramabai in one of his meetings. Afterwards, at the altar, he laid his hands upon Padma and prayed, 'Lord make her like Pandita Ramabai.' It was a powerful prayer."

"Who was Pandita Ramabai?"

"Pandita Ramabai was an Indian lady who believed in the uplift of women. She was a convert from a Hindu background. Along with a Methodist missionary called Minnie Abrams she had a home for widows and orphans at Mukti Mission in Poona. There were hundreds of people there. Her father was a Sanskrit scholar who believed in educating women. She herself became

151

a famous teacher. That's how she got the title 'Pandita'. She cared for and educated women and orphans. She was against the caste system and child marriage. Her own mum had been a child bride, married at eight years old to a man aged forty-one. In 1905 the Holy Spirit fell upon this orphanage and revival broke out. People were saved and baptized in the Holy Spirit. There was speaking in tongues, prophecy, dreams, visions, repentance and lots of prayer. Some people actually saw 'tongues of fire' on the heads of believers. There were many signs and wonders including the miraculous provision of food. Food just appeared to feed the crowds of people that came. That's a good miracle for India. The Holy Spirit fell in powerful ways in many places in India in those days. This was the lady Nataraja prayed that Padma should be like."

"But in your case you wanted to be like Sabina Wurmbrand."

"I also want to be like Pandita Ramabai. She cared for widows and orphans. She taught the people to pray for revival. The Bible says caring for widows and orphans is pure religion. God calls Himself the God of widows and orphans. My heart is to help widows and orphans just like Pandita Ramabai. Her church and the orphanage are still there in Mukti. That church was completely built by ladies manpower."

"Women power!"

"All the stones of that huge church were put in place by women. I couldn't believe it when I saw it. Pandita Ramabai was a woman to encourage the ladies. She would say to them, 'Rise up, you can make it. Things can be better.' She gave them a vision and a destiny. She encouraged them to have a go. I like to do the same thing."

"Do you know of many people from Muslim backgrounds that have become Christians?"

"Sure. Have I not told you about my good friend Fibi?"

"I didn't even know you had a good friend called Fibi."

Mariamma smiled. "We'll talk later. You'll love Fibi's story."

15

Daily Facing Death

Over dinner our talk was about the increased harassment and persecution of Christians in India especially since some in high places and antagonistic to the gospel had come to power. There were stories about meetings being wrecked, musical instruments destroyed, Christians beaten, believers jailed, churches being torched and so on. Mariamma talked about the death of a Christian worker from Australia who was burned to death in Orissa. She said several pastors had been killed in that State. She told how her brother Pastor Abraham had personally witnessed the total destruction of two hundred and sixty houses by fire in a Christian village there. Militant religious fanatics were doing everything in their power to stamp out Christianity. The Christian worker burned to death in Orissa was Graham Staines. His wife was called Gladys. They had three children, Esther, Timothy and Phillip. Evil extremists burnt Graham and his two sons aged seven and nine to death on the night of 22-23 of January 1999.

Mariamma said, "Before eight months went past, like God's wrath, a Super Cyclone came to Orissa. All the trees were just torn up by the roots. So many villages were wiped away. In many places not even a sign of human life survived. It was massive. Thousands and thousands of people died and millions lost their homes. Orissa and Gujarat are the states in India in which the worst persecution of Christians has happened. Many Christians have been beaten and many churches have been burned. In the past, Gujarati leaders said they wanted no help whatsoever from any Christian country. Then within a few weeks a massive earthquake hit them. Thousands died and millions were left homeless. This happened early this year. My brother Abraham visited after the earthquake. He said no man can believe what has happened there. Four or five story buildings were swallowed up in the earth. So many people were buried alive.

"One government minister from Karnataka State spoke publicly about these two disasters. He said, 'This is nothing but the judgment of God on Gujarat and Orissa because there are the two states that have persecuted the most Christians.' He lost his job for saying this. He had to resign. But he did a good thing in telling the truth.

"Graham Staines, who first came here in 1965, had spent most of his life sacrificially working among India's lepers. They had a great love and respect for him. Through his work he was showing the love of Christ to the people. His enemies grew envious of his influence, so they decided to kill him. That night Graham and his sons were sleeping outside in a jeep while all the others were sleeping inside in the hall. The mob of fanatics gathered around the jeep and set it on fire. Graham tried to open the door but was prevented. He grasped his two boys in his arms. Together they burned to death charred beyond all recognition.

"Afterwards Gladys was interviewed for television. She said, 'I don't hold any grievance against the people who killed my husband and children. I loved Graham and Timothy and Phillip. I miss them very much but my Jesus has taught me to forgive and love my enemies. So I forgive them.' This was a very powerful statement she made. It went out all over India. It really shook the people. She is still working in India. She is determined to finish the course God has set for her. She wants to work with the lepers until the end of her life. All over India people were aware of the murder of Graham Staines. When the Super Cyclone hit Orissa they made the connection. They realized the Christian God is more powerful than their gods and understood He was displeased with their actions. Indian people understand these things."

I said, *"Many Christians in the West might say God is a God of love and wouldn't do such a thing. How would you answer them?"*

"God has many characteristics. He is love on one side, but He is also a jealous God. The word of God says that if anyone touches His people then they are touching the apple of His eye. The 'apple' is the small vulnerable pupil within the eye that one unconsciously protects. People cannot fool around with the living God. He is a God who is just. People must understand. There is a sowing and reaping that happens. These people sowed to the wind and reaped a whirlwind. There are consequences for persecuting the Lord's people. Ask Pharaoh."

Daily Facing Death

I said, *"You promised to tell me about the Muslim girl Fibi."*

Mariamma said, "India has over a hundred million Muslims; one of the biggest Muslim populations in the world. Many Hindu and Muslim girls have been saved and gone through our Bible school. Fibi is one example. Her previous name was Jameela. She was the daughter of a wealthy Muslim who was a Hajji and a Muslim league president. He owned a fifteen-acre campus. He had two wives and ten children. Fibi was his fifth child. She was studying at the university. She had a friend, in the next room, whose name was Sally. Sally's father was a drunkard. She and her mother had become Christians. Fibi was into dance and drama. She was totally indifferent when Sally tried to share the gospel with her. From childhood Muslims are taught, for every little wrong they do in this life they have to pay a big price in the after life.

"They all have this terrible prospect of severe punishment after death. Fibi had been told as soon as the mourners take seven steps from the grave then the punishment for every single sin starts. One day she opened Sally's Bible and flicked through it. Her eyes landed on Romans 8:1, 'Therefore there is no condemnation for those who are in Christ Jesus.' This was a revelation for her. All her life she heard nothing but talk of condemnation and the likelihood of an awful future punishment. Now she was reading that one could live with no condemnation. She couldn't believe this. She asked Sally, 'How can you have no condemnation?'

"Sally explained, 'It's not because of one's own righteousness but by the blood of Jesus that a person can be saved from condemnation and hell.' She also read Fibi the scripture where Jesus said, 'I am the Way and the Truth and the Life. No one comes to the Father except through Me.' Sally witnessed and Fibi believed that Jesus had died for her sins. She gave her heart to the Lord. Sally loaned her two books - comparing Islam and Christianity - written by a converted Muslim. During the holidays Fibi brought one home. She hid it under her bed. Previously her Dad had put a letter, from his son in the Gulf, in the same hiding place.

One day he went to retrieve his letter. To his horror he discovered the Christian book. He roared, 'Who has brought this poisonous seed into my home?' Fibi was caught and warned never to read such a book again. Sally was also banned from coming near their house and Fibi was forbidden to ever speak to her again. Sometimes at the university Fibi would sneak to

155

a prayer meeting. Whenever she was found out, she was beaten. Once she was thrashed so badly they thought they'd killed her. They locked her inside a room. When she regained consciousness she heard them tell her little brother, who was seven at the time, to go and see if she was dead or not. 'How will I know if she's dead?' he asked. 'Put your finger to her nose. If she's not breathing then she's dead,' they said.

"Despite the beatings Fibi's faith grew strong through the prayer she shared with Sally. After her graduation she was not allowed out of the house, but she devised a way to keep in touch with Sally. In her home everyone would be asleep around 2AM at night. Fibi would dress like a man in lungi and shirt. She'd then walk through the snake-infested jungle to Sally's house by the light of her pen torch. If she ran into any strangers she'd whistle and try to sound like a man. Sally slept with her window open. Fibi would awaken Sally by shining her torch onto her face. Then together with Sally's mum they'd go and pray near a little rock under a certain mango tree. They also exchanged letters with each other using the rock under the mango tree as a secret mailbox. These meetings were a lifeline for Fibi. She'd tell of her persecutions and thoughts throughout the day and Sally would encourage her from the word of God. That is how she kept going. Once when things got to be too much for Fibi, she and Sally ran off to a certain pastor's house about forty kilometers away. She was found and given a very severe beating. Her face and body were very badly bruised. She was left in a room, for many days, with only water to drink. Her home now became her prison. When Fibi's sister was married over fifty guests stayed in her house for eight days. The family's security system was so efficient the guests never knew Fibi was in the house.

"She was very grieved. She thought, *These people don't love me.* Her little brother used to steal food for her. She'd say, 'I don't want anything from them.' Her little brother was heartbroken, 'If you don't eat you will die. If you die I too will die because I love you.' She also had a little sister. None of her family would talk to her, except the little children. Her elder sister was a lawyer, a very determined and strict lady. She lived nearby. She took Fibi to her home and kept her in solitary confinement. They sent away the servants and forced her to do all the work. Then when she made a mistake they'd kick her like a dog. They beat her often trying to force her to give up her Christian faith and return to Islam. Their abuse only made her more determined to follow Jesus.

"Finally they decided the only remedy was to marry her off to her cousin who had a good job in Bangalore. She said, 'He will never put the Thaali on my neck. He will put it only on my dead body.' (A Thaali is a necklace that symbolizes the marriage union much as the wedding ring does in the West). They replied, 'If you don't marry a Muslim boy we will kill you. That's your only alternative.' Fibi knew she was facing death. She managed to place a letter under the mango tree rock. She wrote, 'Sally, please save me from this situation. Otherwise I'll be dead, because I won't live as the wife of a Muslim.' A week later, she managed to go to the mango tree. Her letter was gone but there was no reply. Things seemed very dark. She became very distressed and oppressed. She decided to kill herself with some weed killer she'd got hold of. After everyone was asleep she drank a mouthful of it. Immediately she heard a thunderous voice. 'If anyone puts their hand to the plough and turns back then they are not worthy for the Kingdom of God.' Loudly the voice kept repeating, 'Not worthy of the Kingdom of God. Not worthy of the Kingdom of God.' She was bewildered. She'd never heard this verse of scripture before nor had she ever experienced a voice speaking like this. She thought the whole household would be awakened by it. Then a gentle voice from within her said, 'Before you do anything worse give God a chance to work on your behalf.'

"When she heard this she knew the loud voice must have been sent from heaven. She began to vomit and convulse, then she passed out. She awoke a few hours later in a pool of vomit. She cleaned herself up. Later that day she went to the stone under the mango tree. To her great relief there was a letter from Sally. Sally wrote she'd been able to contact a Muslim convert, now a pastor, who'd agreed to help them escape.

"On the eighteenth of that month there was a festival called Bakreed. The plan was that Fibi should act as if she was reconciled to the wedding so she'd be allowed to go shopping on that day. She was to go to a certain bus station at 11AM where she'd meet two people. They'd be a husband and wife. The husband would be wearing a white shirt on the back of which would be written the words, 'Rejoice in the Lord Always.' The lady would be wearing a white sari and a blouse. Fibi was to join them and travel on the same bus.

"From the moment she read this letter Fibi began to act as if she was

157

willing to go along with the wedding plans. Sally packed up and went to the Muslim pastor's house. The news spread she'd got a job in Rajasthan. She collected some of Fibi's clothes that Fibi had left under the mango tree, then she went to the pastor's house. When they heard the news that Sally had left Fibi's family were very pleased. The Christian girl who'd caused all their trouble was gone. Happy because Fibi was about to get married, they began to talk to her again.

"On the morning of the eighteenth, Fibi was awfully nervous. There was only three more days until her wedding. All the arrangements had been made. A large pandhal had been constructed, jewelry and clothing had been purchased, people invited, food had been paid for and so on. Such a big fuss had been made. The previous evening Fibi had told her mum and dad she wanted to go into town to buy some personal things. They said a girl who is engaged shouldn't even think of going out of the house before the wedding. Everywhere the news had spread that she'd become a Nazrani; a Christian. This was a great shame for her whole family. They didn't want her to be seen out in the community but neither did they want to upset her so near to her marriage. When she continued to plead and get distressed her father eventually gave in. He told her, 'You may go in the morning but I cannot let you out alone. Your sister will meet you at nine o'clock.' It was arranged her little brother would accompany her to meet her sister. That morning she knew she was leaving her home and family forever. Her sadness was tinged with anxiety. She was to meet her sister at nine o'clock and she wasn't to meet the couple that'd help her escape until eleven o'clock. She had no idea how things would turn out. She was scared.

"It was drizzling rain outside. She told her little brother, 'You walk and I'll take the bus to protect my clothes.' Her brother protested, 'Papa will scold me if I send you alone.' She said, 'I won't tell Papa if you don't.' She gave him five rupees for the Muslim festival day and soon the bus came. She kissed her little brother and boarded the bus. As she sat down her heart raced with relief. Two seats in front of her was the man wearing the 'Rejoice in the Lord Always' shirt. Sally and her friends were on this bus on their way to meet her. They were all encouraged by this divine appointment. They traveled, two hundred kilometers, to a Hindu convert, a doctor, who'd agreed to help them. The 'Rejoice in the Lord Always' pastor took them to a meeting where they gave their testimony. Then he and his wife left for the long journey home. Someone else was to take them to the doctor's home. However, when they eventually arrived at the doctor's house it was locked. No one was there.

"They were then taken to the home of a believer, whose wife happened to be out shopping. He refused to take them in. He said his wife had too many doubts. They were brought back to the church where they stayed praying and crying all night. The next morning they saw a lady coming towards them. She was smiling. Her name was Sumam. She was a lecturer in a local College. She had heard Sally and Fibi's testimony at the previous evening's meeting and couldn't sleep thinking of them. God had been speaking to her heart, 'If they'd been your girls would you've left them alone there?' She looked after Fibi and Sally until a more permanent place could be found.

"At that time our Ladies Bible School was in it's first year. Somehow Sumam managed to get into contact with us. She phoned asking us to take the girls. It was a big step for us to say yes because we were living in a Muslim area, next door to a Mosque. The vast majority of the people around us were Muslims. When we heard Fibi's dad was a Hajji and a Muslim League President we were anxious because the Muslims are so close. They'll die for one another. If they should find out we were harboring a runaway Muslim girl they'd set fire to our place. It could've ruined everything.

"We had to really think about it. But when we heard their stories I said, 'Yes, we will take them, for these girls have lost everything for the sake of Christ.' I remember so well the morning they arrived. Young girls in skirts and blouses, looking very scared. Everywhere people were searching for them. You can only imagine the confusion and misery of Fibi's family. They knew nothing about Christianity or Jesus. They only felt shame and confusion at their daughter's desertion of their way of life and traditions. They couldn't even place an ad in the newspapers to report she was missing because of the awful disgrace involved.

"These girls had to pay a high cost for the sake of following Jesus. When Fibi first came to us, all of a sudden her teeth would clench together and she'd pass out. After these seizures she looked as if she was dead. The beatings had taken their toll on her. I believe her family were also doing witchcraft against her."

I asked, *"Do Muslims really practice witchcraft?"*

"Oh yes. They are the biggest witchcraft practitioners. There were constant attacks against Fibi. We had to continually pray. Shortly after she came to us she was baptized in water but she still needed a lot of deliverance. Whatever sickness was about she would take it; jaundice, pneumonia, you name it. The doctors said her lungs and liver were in very bad shape. They told us to inform her family of how sick she really was. We were fighting life and death all the time, one sickness after another. After one year our female Bible students normally go into the field as missionaries. If they are not fit for this hard work they return home. During their year at Bible School, Sally and Fibi remained indoors the entire time for fear of detection. By this time we'd grown so close. They were just like our own children. I prayed, *Lord, what are we going to do with these girls? How long will we keep them? You know the dowry problem here. We have no money. We can't marry them.*

"Sumam, the lecturer from Quilon, came to their rescue again. She told a Christian graduate from her university about these girls. He came and chose Sally and married her at our church. I had to buy everything for the occasion; wedding saris, other saris, all the clothes, inside, outside, handbag, footwear, everything. We conducted the wedding party in a good way. Everything was done properly.

"Sally went to live with her husband's people, and Fibi was left with us. Then we heard of a good boy, a Muslim convert, called Nooruddin Mulla. He was studying in another Bible College. He is from northern Karnataka. He'd also been kicked out of his home for believing in Jesus. We sent word we'd a good Muslim girl with us. If he was interested he should come and see her. We told him, 'She is a very talented girl, a beautiful singer with a powerful testimony.' We said she was an excellent capable girl. He came. He saw. He liked her. We gave them fifteen minutes to talk, while we all sat and chatted over tea. Then I gave them half an hour to talk together on their own. Usually they'll only be allowed ten minutes on their own but I really wanted this situation to work out. After the wedding, because they'd nowhere else to go, I'd to prepare the marriage bed in our home; something nice for their first night. Since then I have done this so many times. In the morning I'll carry coffee and tea to their room. Normally mothers will do this for their children. Before I did it for my own children I'd done it many times for others."

Mariamma chuckles. Her face lights up like sunshine through clouds on a soft Irish day. "Plenty of practice," she says. "Fibi stayed with us until

Nooruddin finished Bible School. He'd visit on weekends. They were like our own children. After his studies we put them into a church in Thalayar about 10 kilometers away. Although Fibi had no contact with her home, Sally still managed to get the local news from her mother. Fibi's family were all very mad at Sally. They were sending witchcraft against her also. She suffered very much in her life because of this."

"Mariamma, that's very hard for people in the West to believe."

"Is that right? Oh Brother Brendan, I know Muslim witchcraft so well. I can feel it in my fingers and lips. For me it is easily discerned. I remember waking up to a Muslim witchcraft attack early one morning. I jumped out of bed, clenched my fists and immediately began rebuking the attack in the name of Jesus. I ran out of the room, out of the house and around the campus all the time rebuking the demons sent against us. It was such a fierce attack. These assaults were sent against Fibi who was staying here so they also came and hit us. It was so difficult at times that my mother used to say, 'Why are you suffering like this just to save one person? Why go through all this for just one girl?' It really was very testing. We had to endure a lot for Fibi.

"One day the news came from Sally that Fibi's little brother had drowned in a local river. This was heavy stuff. When I heard this I thought, *How can we tell her this terrible thing?* Nooruddin asked me to break the news to Fibi, 'Aunty I can't tell her this. You must tell her.' Fibi loved her brother so much. She missed him. She was always talking about him.

"I invited her over for lunch. We went into my bedroom and talked about the suffering she'd gone through in serving Jesus. Then gradually I broke the news her little brother had died. When she heard this she immediately fainted. I began to pray. After a while she opened her eyes, screamed and fainted again. This happened three times. Then she remained unconscious for over an hour. I kept interceding during this. When she came around the Lord gave me the right words to say. With authority and love I said, 'Fibi, you must understand that God loves you. The Lord loves you so much He wants you and your little brother to spend eternity in heaven together. If he'd grown up as a Muslim you'd never have seen him there. But the Lord is so good. He has remembered all your suffering for Him and has honored your prayers. He has taken your little brother home to heaven. Boys and girls that die young go straight to heaven. The Lord has taken him because he wants him to be with you for all eternity.' This is the way I talked. My words just seemed to go inside her. Her face grew brighter and brighter. Some bondage was broken. She prayed and thanked the Lord. All mourning left her as she looked forward to seeing her beloved brother in heaven. It was amazing. I've never seen such a transformation before.

"Fibi and her husband have worked with many churches. Nooruddin is a very good preacher and convention speaker. He was also in charge of our Bible School for a time. For six years he helped us around here in the ministry. Within this time Fibi had two children called Praisy and Prince, both born by caesarean section. I was there at their births. They were both placed into my hands. They were our first grandchildren. Our children loved them so much. Now they are both excellent singers and musicians. In 1990 they decided to bring the gospel to Belgaum, Pastor Nooruddin's native place. Their leaving was so tearful and painful for us but the Lord is using them in a wonderful way. As well as pioneering a new mother church in Belgaum, they now have four or five outreaches. Last year they got a jeep with a PA system. With other pastors they reach around ten new villages everyday.

"Fibi hasn't seen anyone from her family for nearly twenty years. All are grown up. Some are in America. Last year Fibi, Nooruddin and the children came to stay with us for a two-week break. A couple of years ago she called home. Her dad answered the phone. 'Papa,' she said. 'Who is Papa?' he screamed. 'We don't have a daughter like that. Our daughter Jameela is dead. We cursed her.' Fibi fell sick after that. She cried and cried for such a long time. Her mum is a kind lady but is in a situation where she cannot contradict her husband.

"Last time Fibi came I encouraged her to again try and contact her mum. It was near 11:30 at night when she rang. Her mother answered. She said, 'I'm going to call Papa and give the phone to him.' 'Oh, please Mama, don't do that,' pleaded Fibi. 'Please talk to me. I want to hear your voice. Please, I'm your daughter.' I was sitting here praying and listening. Slowly her mum began to melt. They talked for a short while. Fibi was asking questions about her family, 'How is he doing? Where is she now?' 'Mama, I'm married. I have two children,' she said. She rang again before she left for Belgaum but her mother couldn't speak because other family members were present. To them she is as a dead person. This is part of the price converts have to pay. It's very difficult for them."

Mariamma fell silent for a time. She then said, "There have been so many stories over the years. So many Hindu and Muslim girls have passed through our Bible Schools. We are the ones who've had to take the place of their parents and look out for husbands for them. They have nobody else. We know the girls and we know the boys at the Bible School. We know who will match whom. I have arranged at least seventy of these matches over the years. The first one was Padma's marriage with Nataraja Mudaliar. I'm arranging another marriage at the moment between one of our Bible School girls and a boy from Goa. We sent him one of her photos. The boy has said yes. This marriage will take place within the month."

"What practical responsibility do you have towards these girls."

Mariamma said, "The dowry is the main thing. We have to give at least 5,000 or 10,000. These boys could easily get 100,000 rupees elsewhere for a dowry but they'll drop the figure because the girls are called for the ministry. They must have some money to start their married life with. These dowries are a big burden for me yet these girls are great assets to the Kingdom of God. They are totally dedicated to Jesus. In this culture some sort of a dowry is necessary."

"What do you think of the dowry system?"

"I don't agree with it. Thampy didn't get any dowry for me. We didn't give any dowry for our daughters' marriages. We didn't get any dowry for our son's marriage. We are totally against this system. We've taken no part in it in our own family but it's very hard to get this through to the people. The dowry has been part of our culture and history for so long. Many people go into terrible debt in order to comply with this custom. It's a very difficult tradition to break. In order to help our Hindu and Muslim Bible School girls we have to supply some amount of dowry and money for the wedding.

"They have no one else to help them. I try to get some support from Thampy but he says it's my job to believe for my girls. That causes big fights. People in the West don't realize this dowry burden that is caused by conversion to Christianity. There is such a great need for financial backing towards the female workers and their needs. Always since the Garden of Eden, when God put enmity between the woman's seed and the serpent's seed, women have had a very hard time. There are so many demons against them. Perhaps that's why life here is very difficult for women. When we send our female workers out to pioneer a new work we have to rent a house

163

and also feed them. In going into new areas they don't have the support of a local church. They are the pioneers starting a new church. We pray and hear from the Lord where they should go. It's only the really needy areas that we send them to. There are so many villages not reached yet with the gospel. Over the years we have been sending them to the coastal and seaside villages. These are poor villages with very little work for the people. In all of these places we have churches now, most of them being pioneered by our girls. These girls are doing a great work for the lord. But they need support. The harvest is plentiful and the laborers are there. Pray for God to touch people's hearts to partner with us in this vital work. Pray He will especially bless and provide for the faithful praying women of India."

16

All Hell Broke Loose

"Within six years of first meeting, Thampy and I had four children and twelve churches. We were married on October 26, 1970. Biju was born on August 21, 1971, Bini on July 7, 1973, Beena on October 2, 1974 and Binu on April 30, 1976. I was only twenty-seven years old by then. These were difficult times looking after the children and the churches. Thankfully many of the believers helped with the babies; my sister Usha came and stayed for one year. In reality my priority was for the ministry though this is not the popular teaching nowadays. The popular teaching is that we are to put our family before ministry. When other people's children were having two or three curries for their dinner our children were having just one. We lived simply. I didn't spend all day cooking and making nice things for the home. I only did the most basic things. I also did the ministry. My parents used to get angry with me, 'How can you do this? Look at other pastor's families. They are spending time with their children. How can you do this? In the morning you take a Bible and bag and go running here and there praying and casting out demons. You are going to this church and that church. Stay at home and look after your children.'

"I heard this kind of talk from the people who loved me the most. I'd get guilty and stay at home for one week. I'd cook for the children, pamper them and do all the things they wanted. But when I'd stay at home, the children would be sick the whole time. That was my experience. When I'd go out and about in the ministry they'd be as healthy and happy as wild salmon. Every evening I'd play and pray with them and put them to bed. My brother Abraham used to warn me, 'You'll save the whole world and you'll lose your own children. They will give up on God and leave you.' Sometimes I'd help them with their homework. Unlike other mothers I didn't spend all my time trying to educate my children to achieve the first rank. In

India, academic achievement is highly sought-after because the competition is so intense. Most mothers are more anxious than their children about their education. I was always very relaxed about this. I clung to the words that said, 'If you look after My business I'll look after your business. Seek first the Kingdom of God.'

"I know so many ladies who started out with me in ministry but who got caught up looking after their husbands and their children. They got into cooking so many different curries and other dishes. To this day they are still locked up in their kitchens. Now I have something to tell the ladies. Whenever I go anywhere I always say, 'Don't be cheated, don't be trapped.' I have lived my life now. Others used to tell us our children would be gone from God and not educated, but this is not true. Our children must realize being called to serve the Lord is a very precious thing. Many are called but few are chosen. They must see that what we preach, we mean. They need to know we are not just fooling around.

"Our children have watched Thampy and I giving our time, money and lives to the ministry. They understand it is something very important. We not only talk about the gospel. We live it daily before them. As the years went on all of our children got a university education. They all love the Lord. In fact, sometimes I tell Thampy they are a bit more ahead of us in spiritual things. Like us they all have the same vision of reaching the nation of India for Christ. They have the same burden to reach the lost souls. All these years, I prayed they'd serve God not because of us but through them hearing directly from God for themselves. They must get their love and vision from God. That has been my earnest prayer and God has answered it.

"Every Wednesday I used to fast and pray for the family. Even when they were in the womb I'd lay my hands on them and pray, *Lord we dedicate this child to You.* I believe if we fast and pray for our children they will never go astray. God has given us ladies a great responsibility to intercede for our families. We should be like the prayerful lady in Proverbs 31 whose candle doesn't go out even in the night. To me the candle represents prayer. The scripture says such a lady's family need not be fearful of the snow for every one of them gets a red cardigan. These cardigans or blankets for me represent robes of salvation. A prayerful lady's children will be blessed.

"One day, when Bini and Beena were seven or eight, I shared the gospel with them. As they prayed the prayer of salvation they both saw a vision of Jesus. They said, 'Mama, Mama, Jesus is standing here.' Both of them saw Jesus at the same time. Then I prayed for them and both of them got baptized with the Holy Spirit. They were speaking in tongues and tears were rolling down my cheeks. After that they used to see all these dreams. One morning Bini came into the kitchen. She said, 'Mama, I saw Jesus appear to me.' I asked, 'What did He tell you?' She said, 'I saw a hand with a scar on it.' Then I heard a voice saying, 'This is My right hand. I will lead you with this hand.' I said, 'Oh, this is Jesus talking to you.' I was so excited. I'm always delighted when Jesus talks to my children. Another time when they were eight or nine they both had the exact same dream about the Second Coming of the Lord. That morning they were so animated as they talked of what they'd seen. Beena would say she saw such and such and Bini would clap her hands and say she'd also saw that. From the time they were little the Lord was doing something special in their lives.

"God was moving on Binu also. One day there were around twenty children in the church aged between eight and fifteen. They were all sitting together. I said I'd pray for them to receive the Holy Spirit. Binu was about eight at the time. I prayed for them. They all began to speak in tongues.

"Biju is the only one of my children who was not filled by the Holy Spirit by me alone praying for him. He was about thirteen when I felt he needed to be baptized in the Holy Spirit. Bob and Kath McGregor from Australia were staying with us then. One day when Biju was home from school for lunch we prayed and he was baptized in the Holy Spirit. It was shortly after this that he cut his first singing album. There were many songs on that album I wrote myself.

"Bob and Kath also helped me pray for a girl called Vasantha. She was a convert from Hinduism as well as a beautiful singer. She'd been on the radio chanting songs to various Hindu gods. She was paralyzed from her hips down. She was possessed by many demons. She'd become a Christian through a neighbor witnessing to her. After Vasantha became a believer her people wouldn't allow her to leave the house or to go to Christian meetings. She was from Trichur where I was born. The name Trichur is an anglicized version of the Malayalam word Trissivaperur meaning the 'Town with the name of Lord Shiva.' It is the cultural capital of Kerala. One day Thampy and I went to a seminar there. Some pastors told us about Vasantha. They pressed upon us to take her to stay at our place. Reluctantly I agreed for we had so little space. I'd nearly forgotten all about our promise when one evening a couple of weeks later our door opened and four men appeared carrying Vasantha. 'Where will we put her?' they asked. We put her into a room with a toilet attached.

"You won't believe this, Brendan. There were over one hundred demons in her. We wrote down the names of eighty-five of them. They were all different names of false religious spirits. I used to sit and pray for hours with her. One day I started praying in the afternoon and went on until 3AM the next morning. I had to pray for these long periods of time because I couldn't leave her when the spirits were stirred up and manifesting. They were all telling their names and leaving. On another occasion I spent forty-eight hours praying for her. It was a hard job. Now that I'm older I don't think I'd be able for such a long stretches of prayer. Bob and Kath were a great help. We three were praying. It was so glorious. I will never forget that scene when Vasantha finally got free. When the last demon left she was immediately filled with the Holy Spirit. Her face was shining. She began to sing in the Spirit. I have never ever heard anyone singing so beautifully.

"After this Vasantha began to write many Christian songs. A converted Muslim girl called Phoebe who was living with us also began to write songs in Arabic. She was able to write songs in the Muslim genre with Christian words. We had never heard songs like that before. I also translated many Tamil songs into Malayalam. On Biju's first cassette, Biju, Vasantha and Phoebe all sang. Vasantha lived with us for three years. Although her health returned she was never able to walk. Because she couldn't move or go out she became a great intercessor and support to me. If she needed a glass of water it had to be put into her hand. All her primary duties had to be done by someone else. Even though we had to pay a price for looking after her she turned out to be a great blessing.

"Some local ladies got saved and we had a powerful prayer group going. Every Tuesday we used to pray and fast for India. Vasantha was always in her room. She was always willing to pray. So many deliverances were done in that room. This was in 1986. This is when the real prayer ministry started to grow. We had to go through lots of trials. In the next room people would come to visit Thampy and discuss church matters. Suddenly we'd be shouting in tongues and doing spiritual warfare. Students would come running from the Bible College asking what all the fuss was about. Their teachers claimed we were praying so loudly they couldn't hear to teach. Thampy would come in and tell us to slow down and pray quietly. We began to pray the Lord would give us a place just for prayer alone; a place where nobody would come to tell us to shut up.

"After we came here to Chingavanam the first building we built was the prayer tower. Since then our prayer ministry has gone on non-stop with no one to tell us to keep quiet. In 1989, when we moved to Chingavanam, Vasantha became very insistent on returning home and visiting her family. I knew if she went we wouldn't be able to get her back. I felt if she left, the girls who were attending her would not want to resume caring for her. For six months I battled with her not to leave but in the end she was adamant. Sadly I let her go. And that was it. Afterwards I received many letters from her asking us to take her back, but by then it was impossible.

"In those years our house was so full of people our children didn't have any space for themselves. They have played a big role in our ministry. They've coped so well. They've co-operated with us. They might start off sleeping in their bedrooms and wake up in the lounge. On Sundays we'd feed all the people first. The kids would have to wait until everyone else was fed. They'd just eat whatever was made for the Bible School students. That was a big sacrifice for them. No other church leaders children ate like this. Our meals would usually be simple dishes like samba and rice. We were very particular we should be an example of fairness for everyone and that no one should get special privileges above another. Because the house was so full we had to put our three youngest children in a boarding school. They came home once a month. We'd also go and see them throughout the month.

"In 1980 when we had the major breakthrough in Changanacherry all our children had to go through a lot of trouble. Everyday we were getting threats and telephone calls. People said they were going to get a petition against us because too many people were living in the one house. Some of the believing women's husbands would come and shout threats and abuse. Once a man came with a big knife to kill us. He stood outside and demonstrated to the people how he was going to stab Thampy and I.

"One night we had a knock on the door around 2AM. It was a lady called Marykutty and her friend called Chinnamma. They'd walked three miles in pitch darkness to get to our house. Earlier that day they'd been baptized in water. When their husbands heard of this they were both severely beaten. In Changanacherry denominational people had never heard of adult baptism. They were afraid of it. Marykutty's husband continued to beat her regularly. He would stick his two fingers up her nose and then thump her on the head. She would bleed very badly from the nose. He'd also take her out in front of the whole community and beat her. During this, the people would be cheering and approving of his cruelty. He'd be shouting, 'You have gone with Thampy. You have gone with Thampy.' Then he'd jump on her stomach and kick her.

"We heard she'd been admitted to hospital. She couldn't stop passing urine. Our house was like a funeral home. Nobody was cooking anything. People were crying and praying. We realized at any moment these ladies could be killed. It was so bad. When I heard Mary was in the hospital I decided to go and visit her although some of our friends warned me not to because her husband had threatened to kill me. He was a big man. Without telling Thampy I went. In the hospital she was lying on an iron bed without any covering. We hugged each other and cried. Instead of me comforting her she started to console me. She said, 'Aunty, even with all the beatings I don't feel any pain. My Jesus was having all those beatings for me.' She told me her husband had just left only minutes before I'd arrived. I gave her a New Testament and went home. Mary was in her thirties at this time. She had four young children. The hospital staff thought she had done something dreadful for her husband to abuse her in this way. When they asked her what bad thing she'd done, she'd preach to them and say, 'What is happening to me is all in the word of God.'

"One day her husband threatened, 'Tonight I am going to kill you.' When Marykutty's sister heard this she decided to take Marykutty home for protection. Marykutty's husband followed her to the sister's home and began to beat her. Again he stuck his fingers up her nose and battered her about the head. Some young men came and said they wouldn't allow him to kill her. They asked her what she had done wrong. Like the apostle Paul she opened the Bible and began to preach, 'Look it is written in the word of God, you must be saved and baptized. That is all I did. I obeyed the word of God.' They asked who taught her all these things. She told them of us.

"The next day a big crowd came to our place to find out what was going on. Thampy went out and shared the gospel with them. They all gave their hearts to the Lord. Eventually her husband came and took her home.

All this happened in 1980. After about one month Mary sent a note asking me to visit her. Without telling Thampy I went to her house. When she saw me she was very afraid. We embraced each other and cried. She asked me to leave. Her husband was asleep in the next room. I said, 'No, I'm going to face this once and for all.' He awoke and came in shouting at the top of his voice. He began beating her in front of me. He told me, 'I'm going to make you eat her dead body.' I didn't know what to do. He was running in and out. In the end I had to leave. The whole thing was like a nightmare. For an entire year he continued to beat Marykutty so that she'd give up her belief in Jesus. Initially when Marykutty had come to faith I'd gone to her home and shared the gospel with her and her husband. It was only after she got baptized that the whole community turned against her. When the new converts took baptism the whole city got stirred up. It's one thing to pray for revival but it will always cost you something when it comes. It's one thing to have a crusade but the hard work starts afterwards. Making disciples is not an easy job. But to cut a long story short, one day Mary's husband give his life to the Lord. Eventually all their four children were saved and now they all come along to church. The love of God won through in the end but it was a long, hard road."

Mariamma said, "Another lady called Marykutty was also converted that year. One day a lady from Alleppey and her sixteen-year old daughter came to visit this Marykutty. She was their only daughter. She had been possessed by demons for six years. The family had become very poor in trying to get her set free. They'd sold their property in order to pay hospital bills and buy medicines. They were denominational people who took her to shrines. She used to break out at night. She'd jump into water to try and drown herself. Eventually her mother couldn't cope any more and tried to drown herself in the ocean at Alleppey. When she came to Marykutty's house she said, 'I'm at my wit's end. As a last attempt I'm going to do some witchcraft to try and free my daughter. There are some Muslims in Changanacherry who'll I'll pay do this for me.' Marykutty told her there was a place nearby where people prayed for healing without charging money. At this point Marykutty was not a believer. She'd been at our big crusade in Changanacherry. That's how she knew about us. She'd also attended some of our daily prayer and fasting meetings. She told her friend she'd seen people getting delivered from demons at our meetings. 'Why don't you take your daughter there?' she said, 'what have you got to lose?'

"This girl's name was Kunjumol. I remember when she was first brought to us. We'd been praying from early morning. Immediately we opened our mouths to pray for her she began manifesting. She'd roll and writhe on the ground. Sometimes she'd stiffen out as if she were on a cross. All the time she'd be screaming at the top of her voice. During the days we prayed for her she couldn't eat or sleep. Our home was like a hospital. Every room was filled with the sick and the demon possessed. Those were revival days. Neil Milne was teaching in one room, Thampy was preaching in another room, I was praying for deliverance and someone else would be cooking the food. On top of all this Kunjumol required constant attention and twenty-four hour prayer. After a few days everybody was fed up. Thampy said to me, 'Mariamma, that's enough. You can't be giving all your time to this one young girl. You have so many other things to do.'

"When we were praying for Kunjumol the demons were talking through her, telling their names and this and that. As the days went on everybody got depressed and discouraged. Our people told me, 'Enough, enough, enough, Mariamma, you have done your part.' Eventually I realized I couldn't keep this up. I asked Kunjumol's parents and brothers to come and be prayed for. They all gave their hearts to the Lord. Then I fasted for three days. On the third night around 2AM another lady and I were in the church hall praying quietly for Kunjumol. There was a curtain down the middle of the hall. On the other side the Bible School girls were sleeping. As soon as we began to pray Kunjumol passed out. I continued singing in the Spirit and worshipping. I didn't want to waste my time."

"Were the students asleep during all of this?"

"Yes. I was singing quietly. Then I thought to myself, *This is a very cunning demon. It never does what it says.* All the time it was cheating us. There was a window behind me. I told the demon, 'That's it. I've had enough. Tonight you are going to leave. You must show a sign and depart. You are going to leave through this window. You must open this window and go. That's it!' I commanded it to leave in the name of Jesus. I continued to worship in the Spirit. All of a sudden, like lightening, Kunjumol rose up, rushed to the window and slapped it open and shut three times. Then she fell like a tree cut down. The Bible students woke up. They asked, 'What was that noise? What's going on?' For twenty minutes Kunjumol lay perfectly still. Then she opened her eyes and smiled. This was the first time I'd ever seen her smiling. She'd been so horribly tormented by the demons. 'Kunjumol, what happened? Did you see anything?' I asked. 'I saw a lady with a white sari, white blouse and very long hair. The lady slipped through that window,' she said. She pointed to the window she'd slammed open and shut. The demon she described is much feared in India. It is an exceptionally vicious demon that constantly demands blood. Sometimes it is depicted with a white sari, white blouse and long black hair. The moment Kunjumol saw that thing leaving through the window she was immediately set free. Her family were delighted.

"Marykutty had said to herself that if Kunjumol got delivered then she'd join us because then she'd know what we were saying about Jesus was true. Soon after this, Kunjumol's family and Marykutty got baptized together. Immediately all hell broke loose. Oh, those were such good days. Blessings and persecutions. Great days.

"News of this deliverance spread everywhere. Because of it people were coming to the Lord, getting saved and baptized. Then some denominational people organized a big rally in the center of the town near their church. Every day preachers from their denomination would speak against believer's baptism. At the close of each meeting they'd say, 'How dare Thampy come and take our people away. Young men where is your courage? Why do you allow this to happen?' One leader made them take an oath, 'Hereafter we will never allow anybody to come here and convert our people. If anybody comes we will count their bones.' They had a big procession around the town chanting slogans like, 'We'll never allow those people to come here. Converts, this is your last opportunity to come back and rejoin us.'

"Most of the people who came to our church were women whose husbands were not believers. The denominational people were giving their husbands free alcohol and encouraging them to beat their wives. They raised a petition against Marykutty. She was arrested and taken to the police station. She walked through the jeering crowd clutching her Bible to her chest. She had six children; the youngest was only two and a half. The police inspector, who was a Hindu, said he heard she'd left home. She answered, 'No sir, I haven't gone anywhere. I'm still at my home.' He said, 'I heard you have left your faith.' 'No sir, I have the same faith. In the past I didn't know what

173

my faith was about. Now I read the Bible and learn more about my faith.' The inspector said, 'I don't want to hear anymore talk. If you forget what you believe now and go back to what you used to believe then you will still have your husband and children. If you continue to believe in this new way then you will have to leave your home and family.'

"While he was talking three phone calls came from influential people in the city. They told him to put her in jail. They wanted to make an example of her so others wouldn't get saved and leave their church. Mary said she'd not give up her new faith in Jesus. The inspector said, in that case, she must leave her home and family. Outside the police station people were standing with sticks to beat her if she didn't go home and obey her husband.

"Someway or another she escaped them and made it to our place. Every day her drunken husband would come. He'd shout abusive things about Marykutty and bad things about Thampy and me. There were also lots of threatening phone calls promising to kill us. Mary wasn't officially allowed to see her children. Sometimes, during their lunch break, they'd sneak round to our home. Their hair would be disheveled. I remember us cutting the knots and brushing out their hair. Not being able to look after her children was very hard on Mary. 'I love my husband and my children but not more than my Lord,' she'd say.

"Sometimes her husband would come and interrupt our services. Then one day the news came he'd had been admitted to hospital. His system had collapsed from too much free drink. He was only forty-two at that time. Mary and I went to visit him in the hospital. He was sitting all alone and his friends had deserted him. We began to share the love of God with him. Before her conversion Mary and her husband had a very loving relationship. The problems started when she was baptized. I told him all that Mary believed was in the word of God. He said if that was the case then why weren't all the Christian leaders doing it? He rarely went to church and wasn't at all concerned about the spiritual side of things. He was just being pressured by his community to behave like this. In the hospital they found out he had T.B. Everyday we sent him food from our home. I encouraged Marykutty to stay and look after him. 'You must nurse and love him,' I told her. He got liver fry, mutton curry and all the goodies. Breakfast, lunch and dinner. He said to Marykutty, 'How can they love me like this after all the bad things I've done to you and them?' Marykutty said, 'That is the love of Christ. The Bible tells us we should love even our enemies. That's all they're doing.' One day, during a ladies meeting, Marykutty and her husband arrived from the hospital. We were all so happy. Thampy prayed for them. It was a great day. Within two weeks Marykutty's husband vomited some blood and died. This was a big shock to the whole city because everybody had known what he'd done. That really caused fear among our enemies.

Mariamma said, "Then something else happened. Just opposite from where our new believers lived the denominational people put a group of young men in a building. They named them *The True Christian Fellowship*. The main purpose of this group was to beat and persecute us. For about two months the Holy Spirit warned us not to go near that area. He told us to stay at home and pray. Daily we interceded that the Lord would reveal Himself in the city. Shortly after Marykutty's husband's burial, the leader of *The True Christian Fellowship* stabbed a nineteen-year old member of the group to death. He was an only son. The knives intended for use against us ended up being used against them. Again the whole city was shocked.

"Then the Lord told us to go again and pray with the ladies in that area. When I went they were so afraid. They warned me to watch out for *The True Christian Fellowship*. Once, during those days, I traveled to a place, about a hundred miles away, to pray with a prophet. He is no more now. He had no knowledge of what was happening in our situation. He prophesied, 'The Lord says, *My daughter, I was looking after you. They were planning to kidnap and kill you and put your body down a well but My hand protected you.*' The old prophet even knew the location of the well. When I came back I inquired about this well and discovered that many people had been drowned in it. Every morning, after that, the ladies would come and we'd hold Bible studies and prayer and fasting meetings. We started evangelizing again. Throughout the day we'd visit various houses and we'd have meetings in the evenings.

"One night we were praising the Lord when a crowd of over a hundred people surrounded the house. They began to shout and scream through the bars of the glassless windows. Stones were coming through the openings. They were shouting, 'Get him out! Get him out! Where is that Blackbeard? Get him out so we can hang him!' They were looking for Thampy who was coming later to the meeting. I couldn't warn him. There were no mobile phones in those days. We continued to praise and sing as if nothing was happening. Thrown stones were hitting the fan and shooting around the room like bullets. Suddenly the crowd went silent. A voice cried out, 'Here he comes! Let's kill the Blackbeard.'

"Thampy had parked his car some distance away. Normally he never took the children but this night for some reason he brought three-year-old Binu along. This whole mob surrounded Thampy. He held Binu in his arms. They began to accuse him of stealing people from the community for his church. One man lunged forward to strike Thampy. As he did so, Binu reached out and grabbed him by the beard. The crowd started to laugh. Binu held on tightly. This funny incident diffused the mob's anger. Thampy took the opportunity and spoke to them calmly. They allowed him through to the meeting. A couple of days later a group from that crowd came to our house. They showed us a knife. Their leader said, 'The other night, we came with this knife to stab you but we weren't able to. Something was preventing us. What was that force that stopped us?'

"Thampy laughed. He told them it must have been the angels of God. 'Angels from heaven protect God's people,' he said. He shared the gospel with them. They all became believers. Many times people come to persecute us and end up giving their lives to Jesus. So even though we were going through all these things we were not really too upset. We were so happy these things were happening. It was like in the Bible. In Matthew 10 Jesus said, 'I am sending you like lambs amongst wolves. They will take you before the authorities.' Those verses also said even though they kill you, you don't have to worry. Your reward will be great in heaven.

"One day Biju came home from school. He told me the principal had made him stand on a bench all day. She told the rest of the students not to talk with Biju because his father was an antichrist. The whole city had named him 'Thampy Christo' which means,'Thampy Christ the antichrist.' This teacher told Biju, 'Don't worry. Your father will be killed soon because he is cheating and deceiving us.' When I heard this I was broken. The next morning I went to the school. I waited in the parlor. People were peeping round the door at me. They knew why I was there. When the principal appeared I said, 'I thought you were people with some common sense. Don't you have any common sense? If you wanted to complain you could have sent word to me. You should talk to me and not to that little child. Don't you even have that much common sense?'

"She replied, 'What are you doing here? You are confusing our people. I warned the Bishop not to encourage this Charismatic business but he wouldn't listen to me. Now look at all the trouble we're having. How dare you come to our city? We've never even allowed the Communists to come and work in this city. You Pentecostals, how dare you come here! Can't you go to the heathen? We are all good Christians here.'

"I said, 'I don't think you are any better than the heathens. You told our son you are going to kill us. We are not fearful of death. We're quite prepared to give our lives for Jesus. We've come with the gospel to reach the people who are doing sinful things. Everything one sees in the heathen world we also see in Changanacherry amongst you good Christians. The Hindus might make the alcohol, but it is you good Christians that drink it!' She said, 'How dare you speak against our True Holy Church?'

"I said, *'True Holy church?* Every day I have been casting demons out of your *True Holy Church* people. They may go to your church to pray but they go to the Muslims to do the witchcraft. In this *True Holy Church* they are all demon possessed.' This was only a short time after the girl, Kunjumol, from her church had been delivered from the many demons.

"Our children suffered a lot of persecution because the only good schools in our area were Christian denominational ones. As they got older we sent them to a boarding school run by Pentecostals. Even there, Binu had to suffer harassment from a teacher who was not a believer. She harbored a grievance against Thampy for baptizing her cousin. She took this out on Binu. He was a clever child but she kept asking him hard questions until eventually he couldn't answer. Then she'd pull his ears and call him stupid. She'd tell the class that Binu's father was a pastor and a hypocrite. All the children would laugh and jeer, 'Hypocrite pastor's son, hypocrite pastor's son.' Binu kept all this to himself. He never told us. He didn't want to worry us. I heard it for the first time when he gave his testimony in Australia recently. He told of how he'd come home from school with his ears swollen from the teachers pulling them.

"He was nine years old when he sat on his bed and asked, 'Lord, why am I born to a pastor? Why am I a pastor's son?' He cried himself to sleep. In the night a voice called his name. Three times it called, 'Binu, Binu, Binu.' He woke up. The Lord asked, 'Binu when I call you for My ministry, will you come forward?' He had a vision also. He saw a martyr

177

having his head chopped off. Then the Lord told him to read Psalm 116, part of which is, 'Precious in the sight of the Lord is the death of His saints.' At that time there was a white patch coming up on Binu's chest that I was very worried about. In Psalm 116 the call of death had come but the Lord delivered the psalmist from everything. Binu ran to me and said God had spoken to him. I was so happy he was hearing God's voice. It's my constant prayer that all my children hear the voice of God for themselves. He was having a stone in his bladder at that time. When he prayed and went to the toilet the stone just came out. From that day on the white patch also began to disappear."

Mariamma said, "In 1978 we moved to Changanacherry. We were there for ten years. In those ten years God increased the number of our churches from twenty to two hundred. When we arrived I said to a friend, 'What are we going to do? This place is too big.' Yet in ten years it had become too small. Every room was packed. One year a team of twenty Australians came and stayed with us. I couldn't count the thousands who have eaten at our dining table there. My father can never stand to come to our homes. He won't stay for more than a day. He says we have a public railway station instead of a home. People are everywhere, eating, praying, sleeping, and going through the bedrooms.

"That's the sort of environment our children grew up in. They never had a private home. It was always a community way of life. That was a big sacrifice on their part. In someway or another I always found time to spend with them. Everyday we always prayed together. But if we wanted to have time alone as a family we had to go elsewhere to do that. In order to have a meal together we had to escape from our house to a restaurant. In 1989 we moved to our house in Chingavanam. Only then did our children have a room of their own; one for the girls and one for the boys. We were all together in that house for five years. There were even separate gates for the church and the house. It shows you how much the Lord cares for us.

"In September of 1989 the Lord showed me a vision of a huge temple and a huge church. *Huge* doesn't refer to the size of the building but to the power behind it. Later I found out there is a temple three or four kilometers from us. It is the only Saraswathi temple in the whole of South India. Within one kilometer there are also six orthodox churches. I was asking the Lord how we were going to overcome all this stuff when two girls from the Trivandrum area came and said, 'Auntie the Lord has told us to fast and pray for twenty-one days here in the headquarters.' I replied they had surely heard from God.

"At that time we hadn't yet built the prayer tower. On the platform where we have the convention hall nowadays we made a little covering from coconut leaves. This was our place for prayer. Each day until 1PM we prayed in the Spirit. We knew we were not wrestling with flesh and blood but with the powers of darkness. Only after one o'clock would we start praying in our own language. When these girls had finished their fast two other girls arrived from the north of Kerala. They said the Lord had told them to come here to fast and pray for twenty-one days. In November two more girls came. After that I prayed and fasted for twenty-one days. Up to February 1990 people came without knowledge of each other to pray and fast for twenty-one day periods. That was six months of prayer and fasting led entirely by the Holy Spirit. From the month of March 1990 we began to see a breakthrough. Prayer and fasting has under girded this ministry from the very beginning. That's the only way for India."

17

The Mad Trumpet Man

This morning Mariamma and I were talking about money. Earlier I'd read from 2 Corinthians, "We are not like so many others, who handle God's message as if it were cheap merchandise; but because God has sent us, we speak with sincerity in His presence as servants of Christ." I'd also read somewhere that 13% of Christians lived in the prosperous developed world while the remaining 87% were in the financially strapped third world. We discussed the implications of these things.

Mariamma said, "From the very beginning money has been a constant giant that has tried to stop us entering our promised land. In the early days we'd go street preaching at 4 o'clock in the morning when it was still dark. I'd a good voice and would sing to draw a crowd. Thampy would preach. Everywhere was so hard against the gospel. We rented a room here in Chingavanam for twenty-two rupees per month. That is less than half an American dollar. A few months after we were married we went to live in this room. We called it, *The Good News Tract Society*. It had shelves for all of our gospel tracts. Gospel literature was a big part of our ministry. Thampy calls a tract a mobile missionary. He wrote many of the tracts himself such as, *I am Coming Soon*, *Who is Jesus?* and *The Big Salvation*. I remember once he sold his watch so we could print more tracts. With the tracts we'd go to a street corner and start witnessing. We didn't see much fruit in those days.

"One day, our landlady started shouting. She was using very bad words. She told Thampy, 'You'll have to leave this place. You are a mad man and a bad man. Get out of here.' I asked Thampy why she was so angry. He said it was because he wasn't able to pay the rent. I asked him how much it was. He said twenty-two rupees. I thought, *Dear Lord, I've married a man who can't even afford twenty-two rupees a month rent.* All this was quite new to me. Mum and Dad were government officers. We weren't rich but we never owed money. Nobody ever came and shouted at us. The life of faith was a different matter.

"Thampy put a sign up outside this rented room. It said, 'Christ is the Answer'. One day a Christian backslider was on a bus going past our place. He'd run away from God and his family. He glanced out the bus window and noticed our sign, 'Christ is the Answer,' and it really struck him. He said, 'Lord You saved me but I went away from You. That's the reason I'm having all these troubles.' He decided to fast and pray for three days. The words, 'Christ is the Answer' spurred him on. After the three days of prayer and fasting he went back to his wife and family. He was reconciled to his wife. Some time afterwards he thought, *I want to see who put that sign up. It really spoke to me and turned me around.* He went in search of the person responsible, so he came to our room. It turned out he already knew Thampy. He sat down and told us the whole story. We prayed for him and as he left he put an envelope into Thampy's hand. It was enough money to pay the rent.

"The next month there were no more financial miracles so the landlady kicked us out. A denominational bishop had influenced her against us. She had been looking for a chance to please this bishop. That's how we came to be in Changanacherry. The Bible says if they kick you out of one town you should go to the next town.

"Before we were married Thampy had a falling out with a bishop who was from the same denomination. It was a big struggle for Thampy to leave this very controlling church. They don't marry or permit marriage from outside their own community. Thampy couldn't go back to that church now because he's married to me, an outsider. After he was saved Thampy really struggled against the idea of believer's baptism. He knew if he got water baptized they'd kick him out. He wanted to remain in the church and evangelize his own people. One day he argued with a believer from Alleppey, called George, about adult baptism. They searched the scriptures until three o'clock in the night. It was then Thampy became convinced that water baptism was for believers. So the next day he was baptized in the backwaters at Alleppey. The news spread. When he came home his dad and mum were waiting for him. They said, 'You can't stay any longer in this home. You don't have any place here. You have to get out.' Kurien, his older brother said. 'We are going to see you as a beggar on the streets.' They were ashamed of him so they put him out.

"Early morning at the rooster's cry, Thampy would go among the backwater villages, climb up a coconut tree, and through his megaphone he'd preach all the scriptures he knew, 'Unless you are saved you and your household will perish. You drunkard, you will not enter the Kingdom of God.' In that area all the people knew about this coconut tree ministry. One evening he was preaching on a street corner in Chingavanam when a Canadian missionary, called Alice, passed by in a car. She couldn't believe her eyes: a young Indian man, standing alone preaching the gospel. When the crowd dispersed she approached Thampy. She asked, 'What are you doing?'

'I'm preaching Jesus.'

'What is this?'

'It's a homemade megaphone.'

"This incident really touched her. Back in Canada, she told the story of their encounter; 'I met a young Indian on fire for the Lord. Nothing stopped him. He was preaching through a megaphone made from a kerosene can.' One twelve-year old boy in the congregation ran home. He fetched a beautiful Italian-made megaphone he'd been given for Christmas. He handed it to Alice. He said, 'Please give this to that young man in India on your return.' When Thampy got that megaphone he was really touched. He treasured it. Like the little boy's lunch given to Jesus that ended up feeding a multitude this little Canadian boy's gift of a megaphone allowed multitudes in India to be fed with the word of God.

"After Thampy left his job in the rubber plantation he got a letter from a man called Rajan inviting him to come and testify in a meeting at Ranni. There was a four-rupee money order in it. This was the first money Thampy ever made from preaching the gospel. Until then his ministry had been confined to coconut trees. This shows me if a person is truly called to the ministry, he doesn't need a pulpit or a platform for everywhere is the mission field. The whole world is his mission field. Recently we started our second church in Thampy's home place. It's a very remote place; water, paddy fields and no roads. When I think about Thampy's early days of ministry I am really stirred up. Even when he was starving he'd never give up!

"Recently an influential man from that area invited Biju and I for breakfast. He told us, 'Only now do we understand what Thampy was doing in those days.' It can take a long time for gospel seed to grow. Thirty-five years ago Thampy would go, and stand in front of each house and roar, 'Hallelujah,' through his megaphone. People had never heard 'Hallelujah' before. They didn't know what it meant. Then he'd preach. Some people would swear at him and some would listen. When he shouted 'Hallelujah' through his megaphone some said it sounded like a trumpet. They named him, 'The Trumpet Man.' Children ran before him shouting, 'The Trumpet Man is coming, the Trumpet Man is coming.' At breakfast, this believer also said, 'We didn't know what the Trumpet Man was talking about in those days. Now we see the gospel seeds he planted bearing good fruit in our lives.' Thampy never imagined so many churches would grow out of his ministry. All he wanted to do was share the gospel in his own area amongst his own people. A few years back, one lady asked me whom I was married to. When I explained I'd married Thampy, she exclaimed, 'You're married to *The Trumpet Man* but he's a bit mad, isn't he?' She felt sorry for me. In those days he was considered to be crazy. Now when he drives through that area all the men drop the hems of their dhotis as a mark of respect. Times have changed.

Mariamma said, "At that time, at Ranni, they wanted him to become their pastor. Although he was only twenty-one they began calling him, *Thampy Upadesi*. In Malayalam, the *Upadesi* is the one who gives advice or counsel. Jesus is called the wonderful *Upadesi* in Isaiah. In Ranni, until today, they still call him *Thampy Upadesi*. His friend Abraham began to join him on his preaching missions. Every evening they witnessed on the street corners. They also hired a hall in the center of town for meetings. Those times were like in the days of the Apostles. They met from morning till night and everyone shared whatever they had. Those were revival days. People were getting saved, healed, delivered and baptized. These new converts had no tradition of giving or tithing and Thampy had no background in the ministry so he never asked for anything. He was just learning as he went. He didn't know the people should share some of their money with him. As he walked from Ranni to Chingavanam he'd hold meetings wherever there were people. Like the Holy Spirit, he just blew where he willed and he took his own time.

"One day he met his mum. She said, 'My son come home. Stop this preaching business and we will feed you.' The previous Sunday the Bishop had come to their local church. He warned, 'There is a boy from this very place who has become a Pentecostal. He is converting all our people. His parents are in this congregation. Our people have had enough. They have decided to kill him. His parents need to know he has to be stopped from this preaching. Otherwise he will soon be dead.' The Bishop was just like St. Paul who thought he was doing God's work when he hunted the early Christians. Thampy's mum was so scared. When Thampy heard these threats he got angry. He walked all the way through the paddy fields to the Bishop's town. Across the road from the Bishop's residence was a huge banyan tree. Thampy sat under it until four in the morning. Then he climbed it. Hidden by its leaves he began to preach. 'Pharaoh, Pharaoh!' he blared through the megaphone, 'you who don't know my God. Moses told Pharaoh to let his people go. Pharaoh said, 'No.' What happened to him? My God made him drink the salty waters of the Dead Sea.' He preached about all the plagues that came upon Pharaoh and Egypt. He proclaimed, 'You are holding the people back from worshipping the living God. Repent Pharaoh. Let the Lord's people go! Repent and worship the living God.'

"The palace lights come on. The Bishop appeared on the balcony. With folded arms he stood looking defiantly towards the banyan tree. He couldn't see Thampy but Thampy saw him, 'Pharaoh, I see you with your folded arms defying the living God. Repent while you still have time!'"

As Mariamma related this part of the story she melted into infectious kinks of laughter. Leelamma and some girls from the laundry came rushing in to see what was happening. Holy laughter rolled through the hallways and rooms. Mariamma was the good woman of Proverbs 31 laughing at the days to come. It was like medicine to me. She said, "There was a man, who helped the Bishop. He also knew Thampy. He said, 'Thampy, what is wrong with you? You can't play with that bishop? You know what he is like. If he decides to do something he won't be stopped. He asked me, "Who was that bloody guy who shouted in the early morning from the treetop? Can it be anyone other than that Blackbeard Thampy? Just go and break his legs. Will you do that please?" 'If you want to break my legs, you better do it now,' said Thampy, 'Otherwise I'll walk all over India preaching this gospel.'"

Mariamma said, "There was a famous priest among this denomination called Father Thengelil. He was a powerful preacher, baptized in the Holy Spirit. He was a prayerful, unmarried man. There was a revival in his church. Whole families used to walk from over ten miles away to get to his meetings. There were many miracles happening. Many people gave their lives to Jesus. Thampy and Thengelil were both kicked out of that denomination at the same time. They began to work together. They became very good friends. They ate together. They traveled together. They preached together. They regularly held twenty-one and forty day fasting prayer meetings. Hundreds of people were being saved and baptized in water and the Holy Spirit. They were traveling all over the place. This was in 1968/69.

"The Bishop was not at all happy about this for he was losing his position of control. Thampy and Thengelil thought they'd make a new Pentecost among their own people. This was the extent of their vision. One day they were preaching outside the church Thengelil had been evicted from. A huge crowd had gathered. An angry mob arrived on the scene. Some had knives. A big fight broke. One of the mob members was stabbed in the ensuing fracas. He put his bloody hands on Thampy's head. He shouted, 'Blackbeard, you drink this blood for you have turned this town upside down.' The blood streamed over Thampy's head and face. It ran all over his clothes. He and Thengelil knelt down in front of the church. They lifted their hands and cried out, 'God Almighty, see what is happening. Lord, You help us. You come down.' Some people held hands and made a circle around them. They escorted them to the highway and stopped a bus so they could escape. Next year the assistant priest of that place hanged himself inside the church. Shortly after we were married, we were street preaching. A lady approached me and said, 'You know something? I'm the one who washed your husband's clothes when they were soaked with blood from that riot on Thengelil's church steps.'

"Another time they were going to have a big public meeting of all the people who'd got saved. This was the first meeting of this kind in that area. The denominational people became so angry. Hundreds from their church were taking baptism. They thought a revolution had started. They went to the Mayor of Alleppey and demanded that he declare a 144 curfew. They said two religious parties were going to have a commotion. They wanted to stop the meeting. The Mayor sent the Police Inspector to Thampy to find out the facts. The inspector asked, 'Are you Thampy?'

'Yes sir.'

'Are you the one who is going to make some commotions here?'

'Oh, no sir. We are children of the Lord Jesus. Our principle is if they beat us on one side of the cheek, then we must turn the other side. We

185

will never fight or make a commotion.'

'If this is the truth, and if you promise me that no trouble will come from your people, then you can have your meeting,' said the Inspector. 'If you have a prayer hall, then you please have it there and I will give you the protection.'

"Thousands of people came to this gathering. They were curious to know what would happen. Initially the meeting was planned for three days but in the end it went on for five days. On the fifth day, Thampy climbed onto the platform and said, 'All the evil powers and all the people with the evil powers got together. They proclaimed a 144 against this Gospel meeting. But my God in heaven has proclaimed a 145 taking the meetings to the fifth day.' The people were overjoyed. I remember one normally quiet and wise leader throwing his chair up in the air. People were shouting and whooping. Exciting days. Breakthrough on one hand. Opposition on the other. One day Father Thengelil failed to turn up for a meeting. The people were waiting for him – 6 o'clock, 7 o'clock. At 8 o'clock they got the news he'd been kidnapped. Some denominational people bungled him into a taxi. Nobody knew where they took him. Later we learned he was under custody in a big church, set in many acres of ground. He was kept there for two years. They brainwashed him. Thampy used to go and hide at the church but he never managed to contact him. After two years Father Thengelil came back as a puppet priest. We don't know what they'd done to him. It was very sad. Whenever anyone tried to approach him he was very nervous and guilty. They'd broken him. He was not the same man. All the fire and zeal had gone. He died recently. Many people who persecuted Thampy in those days came to him before their deaths to apologize.

"One man who had badly beaten him suffered a terrible death. He called for Thampy just before he died, but unfortunately Thampy was in America at the time. Those who persecuted Thampy either got saved or became a pastor or something. Otherwise they died a very pathetic death. That is what we have been seeing all these years.

"After Father Thengelil's kidnapping the whole responsibility for the new believers fell upon Thampy. He was only a young man. The people who'd kidnapped Thengelil decided to kill Thampy. The word went out, 'Kill the Blackbeard.' In those days it was only the ladies that were getting saved so Thampy couldn't stay in their homes. He'd walk through the paddy fields after the meetings. He'd wait by the highway until daybreak when the bus would come. Often his enemies were lying in wait for him. They might be in a certain place but the Spirit of the Lord would prompt him to go another way. One time they nearly caught him. He was with another believer. They chased them with sticks and knives. They both jumped into the river and managed to escape by swimming under water. In preaching to these people Thampy was risking his life yet there was such a love amongst these new believers, that it didn't seem too great a sacrifice to make. He was living the life of an itinerant evangelist. Over time, many doors opened for him into all sorts of churches though he himself was of no particular denomination. Everyone loved him. Everyone wanted him to preach in their churches. 'Why can't you come and work with us,' they'd say. Thampy just smiled. In his heart, he knew God had called him to a bigger vision. He knew India was full of places where the name of Jesus has never been whispered. So he began to travel outside of Kerala as the Spirit led him. That's how he came to Tamil Nadu where we met."

Mariamma said, "Those first three years we lived at Changanacherry, after we were kicked out of Chingavanam, was the time the Lord taught us how to live by faith. Before we left Changanacherry we sat down and remembered all the ways the Lord had blessed us. We were amazed at the number of conventions we'd been able to host. God had supplied all our needs. Even our small needs. I remember once going into my kitchen. There wasn't a spice left in the whole house. This is a disaster for an Indian woman. I said, 'Lord what am I going to do?' I was standing there when I heard shouts of, 'Hallelujah! Hallelujah!' Changanacherry was a difficult place. It was the headquarters of the Muslims and the high caste Hindus. There was no Pentecostal or believers witness in that city. Anyone who began a work there was persecuted out of it. This was the challenge before us. In Changanacherry there are many universities for boys and girls. We began to work among the students. I was around the same age as them. In one college they gave us use of a big room that held over one hundred people. We had a prayer and worship meeting going there every Thursday. A postgraduate student called Elsie used to help me. It was awesome. Every Thursday we'd all sing, preach and give testimonies. A revival was happening. Girls and boys were getting saved all the time.

"One of the boys named Matthew George got first rank for four subjects in the whole state of Kerala. There was also James and Raju. James is a professor of a university in Hyderabad now and has been awarded by the British as an inventor. We also ran many student conferences in which hundreds would come during a vacation day. Once I invited Nataraja Mudaliar and Padma to minister at a meeting of over three thousand students. Prior to this there had been no work among these students. We saw that as a breakthrough. In those days I was so fresh and full of enthusiasm. Many of the students were baptized in water. At that time we weren't seeing many baptized in the Holy Spirit. I was only sharing the love of God and getting them saved.

"In 1973 I studied for a B.Ed. Our heart was always in North India. Each year before we were married Thampy used to travel to the North evangelizing in Pakistan. Our hearts desire has always been to start works where no work exists. We really wanted to go to the North but we couldn't imagine who would support us. Where would our provision come from? With our natural thinking we thought it would be a good idea for me to do a B.Ed. degree, so I could earn enough money to support us. Our plan was to go to Rajasthan the hottest place in India. I'd work during the day and Thampy would work in the cool of the evening. We had planned to buy a generator and a movie projector so as to show the *Jesus* film. That was the reason why I did the B.Ed. The college was very close to were we lived in Changanacherry. I graduated in 1973. As a student I had access to other students. They looked to me like their own sister.

"That particular day as I stood in my kitchen, praying for spices, in waltzed James the inventor shouting, 'Hallelujah.' He had a big bag over his shoulder. He told me he'd been renting a house for a few weeks during his exams so he'd have some peace to study. He had to buy all the stuff to cook with. Now the exams were over he was leaving. When I opened the bag I couldn't believe my eyes: black pepper, cardamom, cinnamon, cloves, ginger, turmeric, nutmeg, chili, cumin and much more. Isn't it wonderful how the Lord provides our need to the last detail? He knows us so well."

18

Intercession

Mariamma said, "In a nation like India, the work can never go forth, without prayer and intercession. The spiritual forces we have to deal with in this country are very strong. Remember more than 97 percent of India is non-Christian. We can't just be caught up in evangelism alone. First, there is always warfare so we can break through in the spiritual realm. Only then can our outreach be successful. We had no theological education when we started. We only had a total dedication to Jesus. I knew nothing about intercession. I spent lots of time in prayer because I knew only the Lord could help us. I was praying in tongues and in the Spirit. I would sing for a long time and then pray. Singing would encourage my spirit and strengthen me. As I gave myself to hours and hours of prayer the Lord taught me more and more about intercession. He took me a little deeper day by day.

"Early 1974, was the first time I cast out a demon. I didn't know anything about deliverance. One day, when Thampy was in America, a demon-possessed lady was brought to me. I just cast it out. I remember little Bini was about seven months old then. This was the first time Thampy had gone to America. I was staying with church people. There was a pastor who'd come to minister on the weekends. He was having a twenty-one day fast; all day the whole congregation would be fasting and praying in the church hall. I was also pregnant with Beena. I had to go through a lot then. Each night Bini would awaken and cry. I didn't know why. Later, some visiting prophets discovered the place where we'd built the church had been the site of two temples side by side. The gods had got used to traveling up and down between the temples. They still came through our house. That's what the prophets said. It may have been that Bini was disturbed because of this. For whole nights she'd be crying. I'd have to walk with her on my shoulder trying to comfort her. Often she'd just fall asleep as the first people arrived for the prayer and fasting meetings. Many demon-possessed people were brought along to these sessions. Although I didn't know much about deliverance I was able to jump into this ministry because I did know about the power of the Lord and the name of Jesus Christ. Because Thampy was away I had to learn to depend on the Lord totally. It was very hard but a very good training. It also helped me to understand what our new pastors and wives go through. Nowadays I can understand and encourage our pastors and their wives because I went through the same thing. I was in a position where I had to pray to get answers from the Lord. There was no other way.

"After Thampy returned from America we went to Nagercoil to start a Bible School to train young men to take with us to North India. During this time we were asked to go to Ranni to help the church there. There were many prophecies that told there'd be a testing of our faith. They said this testing could only be overcome by prayer. Soon afterwards we were thrown into situations where only God could help us. We had to cling and pray to him alone. I was compelled by the Lord to sit and pray for hours. Every day I'd to pray and believe and receive from the Lord."

"How did you pray?"

"I'd sit and sing some songs that were apt for my situation. I'd get encouraged through the songs. Then I'd pray in tongues. Then I'd pray for all the other various needs that I knew of in my own language."

"Did you pray for long in tongues?"

"Yes. It was getting better and better as the years went on."

"Better and better means longer and longer?"

"Yes," she smiled. "Then in 1977 we went again to Changanacherry. The ministry was expanding and more workers were staying with us. The needs were growing so more and more we had to stand in faith for provision and answers to prayer. In June of 1979 the Lord gave me a heavy burden that lasted for six months. I was really doing well in prayer then. I could pray for hours and hours. Neil and Joy Milne were staying with us. My brother Abraham only came to see us once after his marriage. He said, 'I'm not going to put my wife with Mariamma because she might learn from her. Then Joyce too will sit and pray all the time. I don't want this.' Everybody was giving me a hard time. They were making fun of me for my long bouts of prayer. People were not pleased I was praying so much but I couldn't do anything else. The burden was there."

190

"You mentioned you feel the burden in your head."

"Yes, it started over twenty-five years ago. I feel it in my head. God must show us the burden some way or other. With me it's feelings in my head. I always intercede until the burden is lifted and I have a sense of breakthrough. This is how I always pray. In 1983, when we started our women's Bible School, I was able to teach them the things the Lord taught me. How to pray. How to intercede. How to breakthrough. How to pray until the burden is lifted. Intercession is an urgent call. If a house is on fire we can't wait until the morning to put it out. We have to do it right away. Similarly, when God gives us a burden we can't just put it off. The need will be urgent. We must pray there and then. For example, if someone is in danger of death God may give us a burden. We cannot put such a responsibility off until it suits us otherwise the person will have died. In intercession we must be instantly obedient to the leading of the Lord. It's a very serious business. When God calls us to come to our knees we can't read a book or visit a friend instead. It's vitally important we obey instantly.

"God shows intercessors many things before they happen. Sometimes he will show me things up to a year before they occur. Since 1985 we've had prayer times in our home. God will normally show one of us what is happening. He will often show us what Satan is planning. For example, Shoba came recently and told us that an attack was coming against Thampy. We will fast and pray and somebody will take and carry the burden.

"Another example occurred in 1993. A girl called Karen from Australia was staying with us. She is a very good girl who'd go and intercede in the prayer tower. One day she opened a window and the glass broke and cut her. We rushed her to hospital. The doctor said the cut was dangerously near an artery. It was a narrow escape. A few days later on April 19th Karen said, 'Mariamma, will you please get me out of this place. I feel so bad. I sense this whole campus is in danger.' I said, 'It's alright Karen. Last year God told us about this attack.' I went and got my diary. I showed her the entry of the previous year on April 19th. It told of how exactly one year later the enemy would have an out and out attack against us. In order to counteract this attack I'd been fasting for twenty-one days timed so my fast would end on the 20th of April. I was forewarned. I said to Karen, 'Running away is no good. Satan will come after you in a more vigorous way if he knows you are frightened of him. You have to resist the devil and it is the devil that has to run from you'.

"Prior to Karen's visit a prophetess from our church had told me, 'Aunty, I saw a dream in which we were both standing near a big tree. You told me to go and pluck a fruit from it. When I went near I saw a huge snake, twelve inches thick, coiled around this tree. This snake had seventeen eyes.' (Someone told me seventeen is the number of fullness.) 'These seventeen eyes were looking at you. Then after some time I saw only the skin. The snake had gone. You told me to cut the skin from the tree. That was the end of the dream.' This dream weighed heavily upon my heart. In the past many demons had come to harass us but this time we felt that Lucifer himself had come to attack. There were so many assaults from all directions. Everyday I was praying for four or five hours against this snake. When Karen told me her forebodings I went into my room, and sat on the bed.

"As the burden came I looked at the clock. I started groaning in the Spirit and tears started rolling from my eyes. This lasted for exactly one hour. Then the burden was lifted. I knew something was accomplished in the heavenlies. That evening the intercessors came to our usual Monday all-night prayer meeting. They said they sensed something big was happening. For two hours everybody, with full heart, mind and body was lost in prayer. After that I could feel the presence of the Lord. Then Shoba said, 'Aunty I see a vision. Can I tell it? I see a ladder. The angels are climbing up and down the ladder. Jesus is standing in our midst. He is smiling. He is saying, 'I have given you the power to overcome the enemy.' At that point we knew Satan's plans had been broken.

"I think of it like this. Satan comes to us carrying a big bundle of hay, but the Lord shows us this beforehand. So, we pray and woosssh, it is burned up before it even comes near us. During this time we saw lots of churches being birthed. Before every victory and every breakthrough we've had to go through situations like this but the Lord warns us beforehand. That is his grace. Without that we could never succeed. There is always a testing. Satan always comes to test. Without the test there is no victory.

"Another example occurred in 1995. A girl called Ramany came to me. She studied at our Bible School and is married to a pastor, She said, 'Aunty I had a vision. It was in two parts. In the first part I saw confusion and trouble among all the pastors. A group of them were standing against Thampy and attacking him. This was an inside attack.' Then she saw the morning newspaper coming. On the front page was a picture of Thampy being arrested and taken to a police station. In the second part of the vision she saw herself running to tell me of these awful happenings. When she came here the whole place was empty and locked up. She saw Thampy lying on a bed in a cell. She asked him, 'Where is Mariamma?' He told her I was away at some meeting. In the vision, the police had locked up our headquarters. Everything was closed down. Ramany was very grieved in her spirit. When I hear things like this I know the enemy is planning an attack. At that time I had to leave for the USA. Some girls came and said, 'Aunty the Lord has put it upon our hearts to fast for twenty-one days.' "

"When you say fasting does that mean you skip a meal or two?"

"It means we just drink some water. In America, I was staying in Tulsa, Oklahoma in a pastor's house. Each morning before I came back to India, I heard a voice telling me, 'Soon after you get home you must fast for seven days.'"

"A voice? Was it inside or outside of you?"

Mariamma said, "It was God's voice. After I arrived back I started fasting and praying. In the Spirit I could see the bondage being broken. I could see all those who were coming against us. I could see the problem with the pastors being sorted out. The power of disunity was being broken.

"I was praying, 'Lord what is going to happen next?' One day I went to visit some friends. Shortly after I arrived there, a phone call came saying, 'Please come home immediately.' Had I been here I would've fainted at what took place. During the heavy monsoons of 1995, one of our deep wells completely filled with water. A Hindu girl had been brought to us. She was recently saved but still demon possessed. Her Hindu parents had left her here against my protests. I'd told them to take her home. I said we'd pray for her when we found time but they wouldn't listen."

"How did she get saved?"

"I don't know. She just ended up here. At that time we were having a pastor's seminar. This girl also attended the meetings. The morning session was over and the Bible School girls went for lunch. One of them went to fetch a bucket of water from the well. When she looked down she saw this demonized girl at the bottom of the well looking up. You can imagine how deep that well is. The girl with the bucket screamed and ran for help. A big crowd gathered. Nobody knew how long she'd been down there. A man was lowered into the well with a rope to try and rescue her. He grabbed her by the hair and they hoisted her up. Everybody was frightened for her. What condition would she be in?

""To everyone's amazement not one pleat of her sari was out of place. Not one scratch was on her body. How can somebody in such deep water not drown? Thampy asked her publicly, 'Why did you jump?' She told us she saw a big light and from the light a voice said, 'There is a beautiful flower at the bottom of the well. Go and pluck it and give it to your mother.' That is why she jumped. I believe, because of our intercession, the angels of God kept her from drowning. Drowning was Satan's plan. If she'd drowned there is no doubt Thampy and our ministry would've been blamed. In another place a nun drowned in a well. The government closed that whole place down. If this girl had drowned there would have been big headlines in the newspapers. You can only imagine what they would have written. The whole place would have been closed down and all the meetings stopped."

I said, *"In part, Ramany's dream was a warning against legalism amongst the leadership. The pastors were acting out of the law of God as opposed to the grace of God. They were judging Thampy for something. The law brings death while the Spirit brings life. They were judging instead of loving. Had this continued it would have finally manifested in the 'Law of the Land,' the police, being able to close the whole ministry down. Spiritual transgression will always have a physical manifestation."*

Mariamma said, "In Nehemiah 4, God allowed Nehemiah to know things that were being planned against the people of God. Satan never wants us to know what he is scheming against us, but God always wants to expose his plans. Nehemiah responded to his enemy's hostility with warfare and with direct action. The people worked with tools in one hand and weapons in the other. This shows that spiritual warfare was as necessary in building the wall, as was physical work. Day and night they had to be alert. That is how we are in India. When you are trying to build something for the Lord the enemy will always come against you. You can never relax or sit back. Since the beginning of our ministry all breakthroughs have only been achieved by prayer and fasting. In 1977, through prayer we got Changanacherry. In 1987 we got Chingavanam and in 1997 God gave us Goa in the same way. As we look back we can see every ten years God was expanding us. Because our vision is 'Christ for India' we can never accomplish this by being only in

Kerala. Now we have a center in Goa, in the middle of India, where we can train the nationals from all different states. We train them in English and then send them back to their own states where they can teach their own people in their own language.

"When we bought our place in Goa another battle started. There was a huge mango tree, well over one hundred years old, with a little shrine underneath it. Local people used to come and worship there. Not a single Christian lived there. After we took possession of the property I had a vision in which I saw a group of demons coming to attack Biju. I saw a force from Ponda coming against him saying, 'I will make him mad.' This was a face-to-face attack. This particular demonic strongman is always depicted alongside a serpent. That year Beena was in Australia having her baby. When I came back from visiting her I lay down on my bed in Chingavanam. While I was praying I could feel a snake coiling itself around my hand. I jumped up and shook my hand. I couldn't see it but I could definitely feel it. We had an all out fight with this demon for months. Biju had to go through a lot of problems in those days. Oh the pain, the hurt and the tears we all went through. I could write a book about it. Satan resists every advance of the kingdom of God. He contests every period of growth and expansion in the ministry. From the outside people see only the blessing. They don't see the continual prayer and intercession that goes on behind the scenes. They don't know the pain, the praying, the fasting and the groaning.

"Six years after we moved into our present headquarters I had to fight death all the time, as it constantly attacked Thampy and the children. There is one denominational leader who does witchcraft and sends it against us. He is very big into this. He has a Hindu who does his spells for him."

"This leader is not a Christian?"

"Not born again. In 1986, after the crippled girl Vasantha came to live with us, our intercession really began in earnest. We got a group of ladies together and we used to pray for India every Tuesday. We'd pray and intercede for all of India's states. We'd spend twenty to thirty minutes on each state. We'd pray the power of the spirits, holding back the progress of the gospel, would be broken."

"Aren't there quite a few states in India?"

"Yes. In the 1950s India was reorganized into new states according to eighteen officially recognized languages - Assamese, Bengali, Gugarati, Hindi, Kannada, Kashmiri, Konkani, Malayalam, Manipuri, Marathi, Nepali, Oriya, Punjabi, Sanskrit, Sindhi, Tamil, Telugu, and Urdu."

"That list sounds a bit like speaking in tongues to me."

"There are lots of languages in India. As well as these eighteen official languages there are as many as 1,600 dialects that vary from state to state and village to village. Would you like me to name them?"

"Mariamma, please! Leave the jokes to Biju."

"These many languages are the reason we take in students who can speak English plus a local language. We teach in English and they can teach their own people in their own language. Otherwise how could we do it?"

"So the Tuesday prayer meeting for India could last for eight or nine hours?"

"Sometimes longer if we got excited. One day, shortly after we started interceding for India, a demon-possessed girl was brought to me for deliverance. It was a long session that lasted all night. Towards morning all the demons had left except one that manifested all the characteristics of a well-known demonic strongman. This particular demonic being claims to be the main principality and power over India. It proudly boasts that all of India lies under its rulership and authority.

'Why are you remaining?' I asked this demon. 'All your friends have gone. You must go too.'

"The demon said, 'Why are you praying and fasting for India every Tuesday? India is ours. It belongs to us. Leave it to us.'

"I said, 'What have you done for India? My Jesus has shed his last drop of blood for India. So you go right now in Jesus name.'

"It left but this experience was a real eye opener. Here we were, a few praying ladies in one small room in Kerala. This principality had come all this way to personally tell us to stop. He was afraid of the intercessors that pray and fast. His kingdom was being shaken. We were so encouraged by this, that since then, every Tuesday, all the Bible School students also pray and fast for India. Instead of stopping, we have multiplied our spiritual warfare. I know very well it is because of this prayer the Lord has expanded us and taken us to all the states of India. In those days we'd never been out of Kerala. We just stayed and prayed. First we have to go by faith and break things in the heavenlies and only then will the Lord open ways for us to go there and do the ministry. Now we see churches being quickly established all over India."

Mariamma said, "Since we built our prayer tower twelve years ago somebody is always praying and fasting. On this campus you can hear the voice of prayer all the time. It is the power behind the ministry. It is the secret of our power. Without prayer we could never do what we are doing. It is the key for our success. We will never see revival without prayer. Jesus is looking for people to stand in the gap and pray for God's will be done on earth as it is in heaven."

"He looked for a man to stand in the gap and he found Mariamma Thampy."

"Oh no, our girls are interceding much more than me now."

"Why do you think ladies intercede more than men?"

"Maybe its because women have more concentration and patience than men. Like having a baby, intercession takes time. Think of your wife Angela. In carrying your fourteen children she has been pregnant for well over ten years. Men could never do that. They have so many distractions. They cannot be in one place for too long.

"Thampy could never do it. His mind is filled with so many things. He has to go here and there to do this and that. I am here at home. Although things are busy around here, once I lock my room I am alone with God. No matter what else is going on, the moment I lock that door, I am in the presence of God. I always find time for prayer. When I get the chance I sneak away and pray. I should pray more."

"You think you should pray more while everybody else including India's main principality and power thinks you should pray less?"

We laugh, loud and long, our joy blending with the prayer from the intercessors in the next room.

Gaenor Hall, Thampy's English secretary, strides into the kitchen. There is a look of total exasperation on her face.

"I've lost them," she declares, her eyes wide with disbelief, "I don't know where they are."

"What have you lost, my little English rose?"

"I've lost Cliff and John Beard somewhere in Bombay. I was arranging their itinerary. They've gone and checked out of their hotel without telling anyone. I can't contact them anymore. Nobody knows where they are."

"Don't worry," said Mariamma, "God knows where they are."

I was amazed. *"Is this the Cliff Beard from Australia that I've been hearing about? The Cliff Beard who introduced Chester Bieson to India? The Cliff Beard of the big evangelism Crusades?"*

"Yes," said Mariamma.

"Dear Lord," I exclaimed to Gaenor. *"You've lost the Beards? My ancestors were right. You can't trust the English."*

Gaenor smiled.

What are we going to do now? How are we going to find two Australians in a land of over one billion people?" I said.

"No worries mate," said Gaenor, "they'll be the ones wearing the Crocodile Dundee hats."

"How long is it since Cliff has been in India," I asked.

"Must be over twenty years," said Mariamma.

"I can't believe he's coming at this time. It's a divine appointment."

"Of course it is," said Mariamma. "God wants you to meet him. It was God who told you to write the book. He will help you with the content."

She sounded like my wife. Her simple faith stopped any further questions. I bit my tongue and looked forward with anticipation to meeting Cliff Beard. What tales would this old warrior tell?

19

Spiritual Breakthrough

Tea was called for. Gaenor calmed down after a few sips of the English national beverage. The burden of sorting out Australia and India subsided for the time being. She told us Thampy and Binu were arriving on an afternoon flight from Goa. In India many things are learned on a need-to-know basis. Regularly information is shared only minutes before an important event occurs. This creates a very real sense of living in the moment. I was excited by the news that Cliff Beard was coming to visit. I asked Mariamma, *"How did Thampy first meet Cliff?"*

She said, "We were staying in Changanacherry working amongst the college students. Thampy was traveling working as an evangelist. Those were hard times. Our good friend Pastor K. C. John was organizing an evangelistic meeting in Kottayam for Cliff. He invited Thampy to go and meet Cliff who was staying at a local hotel. Later, Cliff told us the Lord had spoken to him and said, 'This man Thampy is My apostle.' Later Cliff told Thampy, 'Last night the Lord told me to take you to America.'

"We thought going to America was a sinful thing. So many anointed leaders from here have gone there, got money, bought property and lost their vision. They have sold out their dreams for a comfortable life. Some even went and never came back. India has lost so many of its Christian leaders in this way. In our case God had told us to leave everything for the sake of the Gospel. Thampy had left his job and I was not permitted to teach. We have been wary of losing our vision, *Christ for India and India for Christ*. For this we have sacrificed everything. When Thampy told me he'd been invited to America I was very upset. I warned him, 'This is the trap of the enemy. Satan is trying to steal our vision.' Thampy said, 'I don't want to go if it's not God's will. Let us pray. He will make things plain.' He didn't even have a passport. I was earnestly praying, *Lord if this is not Your perfect will please close all doors.* But the opposite happened. Doors quickly opened. Within a couple of weeks all the necessary documentation was ready.

"We felt we should proceed though we didn't have any money. In the end Thampy borrowed 10,000 rupees from a friend to buy a ticket. This was the first time we'd ever borrowed money. We didn't like doing it but we felt it was God's will. Before he left for America we prayed, *Lord, whatever You put into our hands we will put into the ministry. We will never take the money for ourselves. We will use everything for Your work.* That was the dedication that we took. His flight arrived in Montreal, Canada. There were twenty-nine Indians onboard. Unknown to us the law had changed. For a person to alight in Canada they had to have either, three hundred dollars on their possession or to have a blood relative in Canada. All twenty-nine Indians had neither. They were told that they'd be returned to India on the next available flight.

"Now Thampy had a big problem. Many friends from India were against him going to America. They feared he'd lost his vision. If he came back to India unable to enter America they'd taunt, 'He went away from God's will. Now he is in debt for 10,000 rupees. God has punished him.' Thoughts like these ran through his mind. His enemies were laughing at him. 'What will you do now?' they jeered. Next day, customs sent the other twenty-eight Indians back home. Thampy refused to leave. They held him in custody in a cell at the airport. For three days he prayed and fasted. He prayed, *Lord, I didn't ask to come to Canada and America. You told the man of God, Cliff Beard, to bring me here. We prayed to know Your will. You said, 'Go.' Now look at me. What can I do?*

"During those three days he made certain decisions. In his heart, he decided, 'If I ever go to another country, I will never remain there. I will always go back to my nation of India. I will never keep money to bless myself. I will always give it for Your Kingdom.' All these promises he made to the Lord. On the third day he was called before a tribunal. He could hardly speak English and he had great difficulty understanding the Canadian accent.

"One officer said, 'Why are you coming to Canada?'

'To preach the Gospel,'

'Why should you preach in Canada? Canada is a Christian country.'

Thampy had a Canadian newspaper with some headlines of recent murders and robberies. He showed it to them. He said, 'I am going to preach against things like this.'

'If you preach, what is your reward?'

'My reward is in heaven.'

'Who will look after you?'

'My Jesus will look after me.'

"After some time they got very annoyed with him. They said, 'Young man, Canadian immigration is not spiritual. So please forget your Jesus, your heaven and your reward in heaven. Forget all that nonsense and answer our questions plainly.' When they said that Thampy got mad. 'Forget my Jesus and my reward in heaven? No. Never. I don't want to go to your country if it means I have to forget my Jesus and my reward in heaven. Those are the only things I have. I don't have three hundred dollars, but I have a wonderful Savior. Him I will never forget. Please send me back to my country now.' He stood up and walked back to his cell. The Chief Officer went after him. He said, 'Young man, we have decided to allow you into Canada. God be with you.'

"Thampy flew to Vancouver where he met Cliff Beard. From there he went on to Seattle. Years later, people told me even though Thampy could hardly speak any English they could easily understand the passion in his spirit for the lost in India. They said they were blessed by his testifying because of the anointing on him.

"God knitted his heart with so many people in Seattle, Washington. Don and Peggy Cundiff and their two children. Another couple called McKee. And the Garners. Don Cundiff was such a good friend to Thampy. I used to get pictures of them standing together, looking just like David and Jonathan. One day some believers said, 'Thampy, please stay here and be our pastor. We will bring Mariamma and the children over. We will look after you.' That night Thampy packed his bags to leave. 'Where are you going?' they asked. 'I have to go,' said Thampy, 'You will compel me to stay here, but I can't. My vision is for my nation. I must go back to my own people. My vision is *Christ for India*. If you talk about me remaining in America then I cannot stay in your home any longer.' Residing in America was never mentioned again.

"There was a sixty-year old widow, Irene Albrow, living in Seattle. She was an atheist who saw an advertisement in a newspaper about four men from India testifying about spiritual things. She decided to go along and listen. Their message really touched Irene. She invited them home for supper and she was so happy. She gave them $1,000 dollars each. This was worth around 10,000 rupees in those days. Thampy's flights were paid for. After Seattle, he went to Michigan, 3,000 miles away. While there he had a terrible headache that persisted for days. He never used to take any medicine. The pastor with whom he was staying said, 'Even though you don't take medicine I insist on bringing you to a doctor. I must know what is happening to you.' Eventually he persuaded Thampy to go for a check up. The doctor said, 'Because you are a missionary I am going to tell you the truth. According to medical science you don't have more than thirty days to live. Both of your ears are badly infested by bacteria. The bacteria has spread into your skull. As soon as it touches your brain you will die.'

"Can you imagine this situation? Thampy was only thirty-two years old. I was pregnant with Beena. Biju was two and a half and Bini was only seven months. Now my husband was about to die.

"Thampy locked himself in his room. He began to fast and pray, *Lord You have brought me here, away from my wife and children. Now they tell me that I am going to die. Help me Lord.* On the third day he got a telephone call from Irene.

"The first thing she said was, 'Thampy, what's wrong with you?'

'Why do you ask?' he said.

"She said, 'I've been praying for you. These last few days I've felt so worried about you. You are in some sort of trouble. Is it your wife or children?'

"The doctor had told Thampy his only possible hope was in an operation. This was only available in either New York or Seattle. This operation cost $9,000. In his wildest dreams Thampy could not imagine having that amount of money. When Irene rang he told her the whole story.

"When he finished she said, 'Thampy, you don't need to worry about anything. I have that much money in my bank account. Take the next available flight to Seattle. I'll pick you up from the airport. I'll make all the arrangements with the doctor here.'

"Thampy didn't know what to do. He never went to doctors. Pastor William began to reason with him. He said, 'Thampy, a woman, who until recently was an atheist, says that God has put a burden for you upon her heart. Without knowing anything about your situation she telephones from 3,000 miles away and is willing and able to pay the $9,000 for the operation. She is also from one of the two places where the operation can be done. Thampy this is God working for you. You must never limit God by your theology. He must be allowed to do things in His own perfect way. We must have teachable spirits and not be stubborn. Please don't test God any further in this matter. Just receive His provision.' Thampy listened to Pastor William's advice and flew to Seattle. The doctor turned out to be a friend of Irene's. The operation took eight hours. Each ear was operated on.

"Don and Peggy looked after Thampy when he was discharged from hospital. Peggy used to write me long letters and send photographs. They were so kind. The doctor told Thampy the operation would save his life. He said he didn't expect he'd ever get his hearing back. But, 'Praise the Lord,' after a few days the hearing also came back. Later the doctor arranged a meeting, for all his friends, in his home. Like Irene, he too had been an atheist. He had Thampy testify. When Thampy finished the doctor stood up. He said, 'I never believed in God. But after seeing this man and what has been done in his life I am now a believer. If Thampy was still in India he would definitely be dead by now and no one would have known what had happened to him. He would be dead and buried. But his God has taken him all the way to America and spoke to Irene here to help him. I am amazed by these circumstances. Now his life is saved and his hearing is perfect.' He then gave Thampy a gift towards the work in India.

"Like that, wherever Thampy went, God was confirming His word through signs and wonders. People were being blessed and touched. It was Irene and Don and Peggy that founded, *Christ for India* in America in 1974. Irene was the Treasurer and Don was the President. After that Mickey and Martin Garner took over followed by Hank and Fay Smith. They were all working out of love for India. They didn't take a penny for themselves. They collected money and sent out newsletters. From 1974 to 1998, the Garners and the Smiths have been looking after *Christ for India* in America. Now a man called John Sims has taken over. These people were all so dedicated and faithful to the work. I thank God for them every day. We couldn't have done it without them."

Mariamma reflected, "I was in my childhood home in Nagercoil when Thampy came back from America. I'd gone there for the delivery of

Beena who was now two and a half months old. Before he returned he wrote, 'We'll have to rent a house in Nagercoil.' He and K.C. John planned to start a Bible School to train indigenous missionaries for the harvest fields of North India. The money from America was earmarked for this ministry. The plan was for K.C. John to stay in Kerala while the Thampy family would go and evangelize in the North. Within a few months we had forty students in training. At this time the church in Ranni experienced some relational trouble. They wrote, 'Please come and help us, please come immediately.' We didn't want to get involved because we didn't want anything to hinder us from going to the North. They eventually sent an elder, called Samuel, to us. He said, 'By all means you must go to North India. We won't hold you back. But first you must sort out these troubles in the church. We have no pastor. You must help us. You can't just leave us like this. Please help us. Then you can go.' So, we went back to Ranni to sort out the church problems. K.C. John continued with the Bible school.

"It was the beginning of 1975 when we received lots of prophecies saying before the year was out we would face many ordeals. They said, 'Trials and testings of your faith are coming. If you stand firm and overcome then everything you've done until now will only be the foundation for the real building.' Many people, through dreams and visions and prophecies, confirmed this word about trials and testings.

"In November we rented a house in Ranni. By then, we were experiencing a lot of spiritual attack. For example, I used to see things. At times, Thampy might have gone somewhere to preach when I'd suddenly see him returning again. *Why was he back so soon?* He'd come and sit on the bed and look at me. Then the Lord would reveal to me that this was a demon. I'd rebuke it. It would disappear. I had never met such demonic attack until that time."

With my Western mindset I probed Mariamma for exact details. In the Bible, in Acts 10, we read about Peter falling into a trance, seeing a vision and hearing a voice. In the same chapter we read about Cornelius' encounter with an angel but in the main we don't really expect similar things to happen to ourselves. Our Aristotelian educational system and resultant mindset is the culprit. Mariamma said the phenomena of a demon masquerading as Thampy happened three or four times in that house. They occurred while she was awake. She was always cognitive, "I could see with my naked eye.

These were mysterious experiences. Something in the Spirit realm, isn't it?"

She said, "We were the only Believer's church in Ranni district at that time and gradually peace was restored to the people. Every evening the men would come visit, talk, and pray. I met with the ladies and we'd also share and pray. Love and unity came back. We also had two new breakthroughs. In November we built a new church in Ranni. We also started an outreach called *Soul Clinic,* in a rented room in the middle of the city. A worship team, led by our good friends Raju and Eliyamma, and J. V. Peter attracted a good crowd on the opening night. *Soul Clinic* opened on Friday. The church inauguration was on Saturday. Up to then I was so active and so happy.

"We'd been cooking for housefuls of people. We were all so loving and close. During the opening of *Soul Clinic* a small pain started in my legs. It gradually spread into my back. Before the inauguration meeting was over I'd come home, unable to stand. Next day I had very severe fever and diarrhea. Forewarned this attack was from the enemy I decided not to take any medicine. They found out it was diarrhea and typhoid. I was also pregnant. The news spread throughout the whole area that Thampy's wife was going to die because she wouldn't take any medicine. Crowds of people from all over came to see me, *the person who was going to die.* Even Mum and Dad came. It was such a miserable time. I could see little Beena. She was maybe one and a half years old. She had a big abscess on her neck full of puss, the poor little thing. She'd climb up to the window and look in at me. I felt so helpless. One day Thampy went to a man called Samuel. 'What am I going to do if she dies?' he asked. It was a life and death struggle. Day and night, church people were praying and singing in our home. One day as Shibu's Mum got off the bus she heard the people singing a song that is only sung at funerals. She burst into tears. *Poor Mariamma is gone,* she thought. This was a Thursday. By God's grace I felt the presence of the Lord. That day God delivered me. I was instantly healed but still very tired. Scariah and Annamma, Shibu's Dad and Mum helped us. They said, 'You must come home to our home. We will look after you until your strength comes back.'

"These attacks started in November 1975 and lasted until February 1976. One day Thampy and I were traveling by scooter. I wanted to be dropped off at a certain lady's house. Going through her gate I tripped and fell on my mouth. I chipped some teeth and burst my lips. Thampy took me to hospital on his scooter where I had to have stitches. There was one attack after another. Biju took a very high temperature. He was in bed sweating. He told us, 'I see the high heaven. It is open. Jesus is standing there.' Still tired from my sickness, I was upset to hear him talk like this. For five days he had this temperature. Then it turned into measles. Then one after another all the children got measles. They were all so skinny. Bini cried throughout the night for no apparent reason. We couldn't sleep for her howling. Every night I had to put her on my shoulder and walk about the room. Bini and Beena had bad chest infections. We were aware that measles could lead to pneumonia, so we took the children to hospital.

"Two ladies, Ammal and Sosamma, used to help me. They had to cook a huge pot of rice because lots of people were visiting. Ammal was emptying off the boiling rice water when the entire contents fell on her body. This happened while we were bringing the children to hospital. As I sat in the hospital I was shocked to see Ammal being carried in. I thought, *What next?*

"I didn't have to wait too long to find out. The day they all got discharged, Thampy had an accident. This was during the time when millions of pilgrims converged upon Sabarimala, a hill near Ranni. Thampy was getting off a crowded bus. The vehicle's bumper hit him and gashed his leg. Oh, the tears we had to shed. We thought he might lose his leg. The infection was so severe it went into the first layer of the bone. He was bedridden for two months.

"That year we started working in a place called Kattodu where there was a breakthrough. God touched many souls. We also started a work in Chingavanam, where we are now. With support from America we were able to conduct crusades in different places and to quickly move forward. Wherever we went the Lord was confirming his word through signs and wonders. Chester Bieson was helping us then. He was such a wise man. He was a very gentle person sitting behind and carefully watching everything. He was a silent listener who caught the vision for what was needed in India. He was a real strength to us. He was God's blessing to India.

"In 1976 the need for government registration came, so we could marry and bury and be allowed to receive foreign financial support. A handful of us had a three-day fasting prayer at Joseph Chacko's house in Changanacherry. It was there we received the name, *New India Church of*

God, for our ministry. At the beginning of 1976, my brother Abraham was studying at the university. He was a very smart student and an excellent sportsman. He was offered a good job as the representative of a medical company. While he was praying about this the Lord said, 'Come out for the full-time ministry.' He was so scared to tell my Dad. Out of five girls only Rajam and I were married. My parents' salaries were not enough to give a dowry to these girls. All my parents' hopes were on their only son to improve their financial position. This was a big responsibility on Abraham's shoulders. After marriage, Thampy became very close to all my family. Abraham told him about his dilemma concerning the job. Thampy advised him, 'You don't worry about that. If God is calling you just be bold and tell Papa. When God tells us to do something we must be obedient. Be scared of no one.'

"Abraham took courage and told Papa. Dad said, 'Even if I have to starve I am happy you are going to do God's work. I release you for the ministry. Go ahead. Just do it.' Abraham joined us and lived with us. He was like a right hand for Thampy. He was a capable, quick learner. Thampy made him testify at every opportunity. Neither of them has ever been to Bible school. They learned their way from reading the scriptures, being led by the Holy Spirit and from experience.

"J. V. Peter, who was a good singer, came to join us around then. He had nowhere to live. He sold his watch to get the bus fare to us. He was so broken-hearted. I could hear him praying and crying the whole nightlong. I used to tell Thampy, 'You know, that poor boy doesn't have anybody? Why can't you take him?' One day we told him, 'You can stay here and work with us if you like.' Afterwards Thampy took him along wherever he went. Peter would pay the guitar and sing. He is a boy that God healed from bone cancer. His testimony is so powerful. He wrote his own songs. Having a minstrel with us was a great help. He could draw a big crowd by his beautiful singing. He could bring the presence of the Lord into a meeting.

"T. M. Kuruvilla who is also called Rajan came and worked with us around that time as well. He has been with us ever since. He has been a very faithful godly man. He has held many responsible positions in *New India Church of God*. It is dependable, capable men like him that has helped keep the vision going.

"Abraham, Rajan and Peter were all young men sleeping out on our veranda at night. They had nothing in the natural but everything in the Spirit.

207

They shone as bright as the stars above them. As the churches grew so did our need for pastors. Boys from our own congregations were ready to do the ministry but we had nowhere to train them. We began praying. Joseph Chacko heard of a suitable place. It had half an acre of land and three buildings. It was in an excellent location, in the center of the city. We asked the owner if it was available for rent. 'Why can't you buy it,' he said. 'It's yours for one lakh.' (Lakh; one hundred thousand, usually rupees or people, written 1,00,000). 'If you give it to us for 80,000 rupees we will buy it.' He took the 80,000 rupees, with an immediate 10,000 deposit and the rest of the money payable within three months. We put our car up for sale. That week it sold for 10,000 rupees. Same week, Thampy got an invitation to preach in America. During that trip the Lord provided the rest of the money for the property.

"In 1978 Thampy was invited to Australia. The previous year he'd been in America. Twice, totally unexpectedly, he'd bumped into Cliff Beard. Cliff said, 'Thampy, God is doing something otherwise we wouldn't meet like this. Why don't you come to Australia?' So Thampy went for the Easter convention. It was held in a large tent in Mildura. Neil Milne, who later came to India with his wife and family, was a young man helping with that crusade. Cliff arranged meetings for Thampy in different parts of Australia. He went to Adelaide to the *Bethesda Christian Centre* where he met Bob and Kath and Esma and Bill. They've been great friends to us over the years. Pastor Peter Vacca is also from there. That church really blessed us financially. With that money we started our Bible school. We named it *Bethesda,* after the church that loved us so much."

Mariamma said, "In 1979, Cliff Beard brought a team of twenty-four people among who were Neil and Joy Milne, Bob and Kath Mc Gregor and Esma and Bill. We had a crusade in Vellarada, near Trivandrum. There were around 50,000 people at each meeting. Demons, healings, many miracles and conversions. Very noisy. Within a few weeks of the team going home, we received a letter from Neil Milne. He said he felt a strong call to work amongst the unreached of India. 'What can I do to help?' he asked. Thampy wrote back, 'Neil, my home is always open for you. Whenever you feel like it, just pack up and come work with us. We are always here to receive you.' In 1979, my brother Abraham went to Australia for the first time. He met up with Neil and Joy and they became very good friends. When he returned to India he was accompanied by Neil and Joy and their three children, Clifford,

Judson and Vanessa and another couple Kailine and Roy and their children, Brad, Candy, Topy, Elsa, Helen and Alida. They all came to live and work in India.

"Doctor Phillips who'd just finished a course of study at Bethesda Centre also came back with this Gideon's army. Dr. Phillips went to pastor in Ranni. The others stayed with us. We were about twenty people in the same house: cooking together, eating together, washing up together and praying together. Amongst us there were only two toilets. Neil and Joy and their three children stayed in one small room. We had to go through that room to the toilet. They had to suffer many sacrifices in coming to India.

"Thampy and I were praying for guidance. Although our burden was for the unreached peoples in North India we found ourselves with growing responsibilities in South India. When 1979 came Thampy and I were restless. We decided to take our children and just go to North India. Then my brother Abraham came and spoke with us. Abraham never had a burden for North India. He told us, 'I am a bachelor without any ties. I will take your burden and vision and I will go to the North.'

"In January 1980, Cliff Beard brought a large team of seventy-four people to Kerala. We divided them up into five groups. They went to various places for crusades and outreaches. The last crusade was at the Municipal Stadium in Changanacherry. That was a big crusade in which the whole city was shaken with the Gospel. Special classes had to be arranged to teach the people. Thousands of sick folk were brought from distant places. There were so many healings and deliverances. Our enemies tried hard to disrupt us. On the final day they destroyed most of our equipment but they still couldn't stop the move of the Lord. Over 50,000 people were saved in that meeting. Many cripples were healed.

"This was a tremendous time of spiritual breakthrough. It was also a very miserable time for me personally. It was then that Abraham, Neil and Joy, Kailine and Roy and the rest of the team decided to move to North India. Thampy, Neil and Abraham went to look at many cities to see where God wanted us based. At last they felt it was to be Delhi. It was a heartbreaking departure. Abraham had been with us all these years and our children really loved him. He was part of our family. When he moved to Delhi it was a great sacrifice for us. I was sad. The children were sad. We cried for many days. At the airport our eyes were red and swollen from tears. Then just like that they were gone. For us who were left it felt like a death. I'd been praying for six months non-stop. I had just seen my prayers successfully answered beyond my wildest dreams yet I was so sad. Isn't life strange?"

Mariamma said, "In those days, my usual routine, after I delivered the children to school, was to visit one of our twenty churches. I'd take a few ladies with me. We'd go to people's houses and intercede for the whole area. By the time the children got out of school I'd be back home again. By the middle of 1979 all this changed. Such a heavy burden came upon me. I couldn't do anything but pray. After I sent the children to school I'd go to my room and I'd start praying. Most days I'd only move from there when the children would return home. I was lost in prayer in those days. I began to feel guilty about praying so much. As the weeks went on I started to think something was wrong with me. I had no desire for anything but prayer. If anyone would call to see me, they also would have to sit and pray. I prayed like this for six months solid until the group came in January 1980. Later on I understood that God was using me to prepare the hard ground for revival and breakthrough.

"Changanacherry was a satanic stronghold against the gospel. We hadn't known what to expect at the crusade. We'd booked the Municipal Stadium that held tens of thousands of people. Maybe only a few people would turn up? We advertised that a Charismatic team would be ministering. The Charismatic wave had just then come to India. We also got the Catholic assistant bishop to inaugurate the meetings. This was so the Catholics would feel free to come to the meetings. A whole crowd of people, including nuns and priests, all came. Nightly, thousands upon thousands accepted the Lord, many were filled by the Holy Spirit. Demons were shrieking. People were being healed. I stood on the stage. All I could see were thousands and thousands of faces. I thought, *Lord, even if I die tonight I'll be happy*. For ten years from 1970 to 1980, we'd been praying and interceding and doing everything we could for that area. When I saw the whole city in front of me listening to the gospel I was so happy. I knew then why the Lord had me on my knees for the previous six months.

"There'd been so many prophecies about breakthrough in Changanacherry. One said, 'A band around the city will be broken. A river will flow. There will be so many fish in that water.' We believed these prophecies and they came to pass. For nearly two thousand years Satan had been holding back the advance of God's Kingdom in Changanacherry. There'd never been a spiritual breakthrough in that city. This was the first real advance against the powers of darkness in that area. So many miracles happened that it turned into a revival.

"From morning to night there would be something happening. Neil would be having a Bible study. I would be casting out demons. Thampy would be preaching. It was just like in the days of the early apostles. It was a season of harvest, with plenty of work for everybody to do. We'd work and eat together as in a harvest field when somebody brings the food. There was also much persecution. When the ladies came to faith they were usually beaten and kicked out of their homes. Without a place to stay they had to live with us for many months. Blessings with persecutions. That crusade in Changanacherry resulted in five new churches being established. Now from the coastal and backwater villages around that area we have over eighty churches.

"In 1981 I went to Australia to study for five months. This was a big thing for me. I hated leaving Thampy and our children. Binu was only three years old. In Australia I stayed with Bob and Kath McGregor. I was so homesick. I'd intercede and breakthrough and leave them in God's hands. Only then I'd be peaceful. Those were wonderful days. I could pray for hours on end without disturbance. The studies helped me a lot and they gave me the confidence to start the Ladies Bible School.

"Women's ministry has always been a huge concern for me. I know what it's like for a woman in India to have a calling to the ministry; nobody to encourage, nobody to support. I also know there are many women who are called by God. I prayed, *Lord, I am available if you open the way for me.* So when the chance to study in Australia came I jumped at it, even though it was personally a big sacrifice. It was also a very difficult time financially. I was constantly burdened about money. I prayed, *Please Lord, open a way for Thampy to come here and take some meetings.* Every month I'd fast and pray for three days. I wrote down sixteen prayer requests I was believing for. One was for an open door into Australia for Thampy. Clarke Taylor came to stay at Bob and Kath's for a few days. When I first met him he said, 'Why can't your husband come and preach in Australia? I'll bring him over. He can preach in my circle of churches.' Clarke was an answer to prayer. He opened a door that was a very rich source of blessing. In 1983, Clarke Taylor came to us in India for some crusades. That was the first time we'd ever seen the phenomena of being slain in the Spirit. There was such a powerful anointing on him. Rajan who interpreted for him used to be slain in the Spirit as he translated.

"Bob and Kath started Christ for India in Australia. They were very faithful people, working sacrificially. They started a shop called, *Anything and Everything*. *Bethesda* church people donated things to this shop and the money was forwarded to us. That was our main income. *Bethesda* in Australia was like my home church. They were so good and loving.

"In 1983, we started the Ladies Bible School with sixteen girls in the first batch. We taught them from 9AM to 1PM. After lunch we sent half for door knocking ministry while the rest stayed back and supported them in prayer. We had all night prayer chains and three days of fasting prayer each month. After one year's training we sent them to the mission field. We'd have a crusade. Then we'd put these ladies into a rented house in that area. They'd follow up on the decision cards. They'd visit the people who had responded at the crusades. First they'd share the Gospel and get the ladies saved. Then they'd pray for the family and God would save the whole family. In so many coastal villages, these girls have pioneered the work. When there are enough believers to form a church we send in a pastor. Then we move the girls on to their next mission. This is how the ladies' missionary work has been going on since 1983.

"We have trained hundreds of these women. We have only one Bible School for ladies at present but we are praying for a new place where both men and women can be trained. It's very much on Biju's heart to include women in the three-year, full-time, Bible School Courses. It's our hearts desire to continue to pioneer new works for all those whom God has called, both male and female. We want to equip and release the saints into the work that God has called them to do. It's the way forward in India."

20

Cliff Beard's Story

I awaken hot and sticky. My ankles are stinging from insect bites. Thankfully there is water and the shower is working. The cold water as usual is lukewarm. Then suddenly a clouding over and a slight drop in temperature alongside a noise like a huge electric kettle beginning to boil. It is the quick rush of rain on the rubber trees outside my window; God's air conditioning courtesy of the monsoon. Coming downstairs I hear the whispered talk of women in the kitchen then the unmistakable sound of an Australian voice from the veranda, "No worries, mate". The Beards have found their way here. Cliff and John are sitting chatting and drinking coca cola with Mariamma and Thampy. They stand up to greet me. I feel like a hobbit. They are both well over six feet. John as big as a basketball player extends his hand. "G'day blue," I say as I shake it, adding, "Fair dinkum," thereby using up most of my Australian vocabulary in one go. "I hear you're from Ireland," he says. "You guys used to get free tickets to my country." He is referring to the time when England used to deport thousands of Irish to Australia for *crimes* such as stealing bread or potatoes. He knows some of my history. I like him straight off.

Soon lunch is announced. Cliff is glad to be back in India after twenty years. He and Thampy, two old apostles, reminisce about times past. Crusades and revivals are the order of the day. Mariamma chips in occasionally clarifying a point here and there. The phone rings and Thampy is called away. He's his old self again full of energy and purpose. I met with him briefly after we'd left the hotel. It transpired the doctor had given him a course of antibiotics. He'd stopped taking them after he started to feel better. I'd prayed and prophesied, "Finish the course to finish the course." He liked the pithiness of it. Prayer, medicine and rest had finished their course. He was as right as rain and back at the helm. Cliff is holding court and is full of chat. I say, *"Tell me how you met Thampy and maybe a little bit about Chester Bieson."*

Without hesitation he replies, "In all of those revivals we've been talking about there have been key people in our team. People one would never have picked out in the natural. In the selection of Thampy, if you were an institutional man looking for somebody of high class, you would have missed it altogether. Thampy was a bushy; a hard man from the rubber plantations. He didn't have the appearance of being anything special. If you were using only your five senses you would never have chosen Thampy for the ministry. But that wasn't the thing we were after. We were looking for signs of the calling of God. It was the strong anointing on his life that made Thampy stand out. You can have a very educated person with all the degrees in the world. You can get them out there and they can quote verses of scripture till the cows come home but they can't bring deliverance to the sick. They don't have the faith element. That was the thing about Thampy. He had creative faith. If nothing was there he could birth it. He was able to call the things that are not into being. He carried that enormous authority. All that you see here now and all that we have talked about would have been impossible if it were not for this man and his kind of faith. I am talking about thirty years ago in India when there was absolutely nothing here. Things were as tough as tough could be.

"The key people God chose to bless this ministry were the nobodies in our group. I'd finished preaching in the States at a Full Gospel Business Men's meeting when an old man came up and asked me to have lunch with him. This was Chester Bieson. Dear old Chester. Did you know him? He was seventy-four at the time. He said, 'I heard you talk at the meeting yesterday about all those people that have given their hearts to Christ in India.' I'd mentioned in my message that we'd win more people to Christ in one day in India than we would in the rest of our lives in America. He said, 'I've always wanted to win somebody to Christ. It has been my dream to win somebody to Jesus. When you were talking about India like that, I was wondering if I could come with you there on your next missionary trip?'

"I looked at this dear old man. I said, 'Chester, if you think you can make the journey you are more than welcome.' 'Oh, thank you, thank you,' he said. So he packed up and traveled with us on our next mission. I'll never forget our first morning in India. I always say to our team, 'Stay together.

Never separate. If one of you goes off on your own the rest of us have to worry about you. We don't know where you are. Everybody becomes anxious having to search for you. So tell somebody, even if you are only going to the toilet. We need to know where everyone is at all times.'

"We had arranged to meet next morning in the downstairs restaurant for breakfast. Before we gave thanks for the food we made a head count. Chester was missing. 'Is he dead?' some clown asked. 'No. I saw him earlier,' someone answered, 'but where has he gone to now?' I went out to the street to look for him and saw this huge crowd of people at a corner. Chester was standing tall in the midst of them. His arms turning like a great big windmill. He'd managed to find a local person who could translate for him. He was preaching Jesus on the street. That was his first real taste of soul winning and he loved it. He was really fired up. We couldn't stop the man after that. He'd found new purpose in life.

"At a time when other men his age were sitting in front of the fire in their slippers Chester started hang gliding with the Lord. When he went back to America, his wife and he sold a piece of land. With the proceeds they came back to India and had a mass crusade. They bought bicycles for the pastors and built a Bible School and a woman's refuge. He returned to the States and talked to his friends about selling their block of land. He returned once again to India for another mass crusade where thousands were saved. Unable to find any one else willing to sell their land he got a part time job. Every day he traveled from Seattle to Bellingham. He saved up every cent and used it for the work in India.

" I lost track of Chester after that. I met him briefly in the last year of his life. We were in Australia at a big conference. This old man came up to us. He said to my wife, 'Helen, you remember me?' 'You're not Chester Bieson?' she said. 'Yes, Helen,' he chuckled 'and I'm going back to India.' He pulled back his coat and showed this great wad of money he'd strapped to his body. He was now in his eighties but he was full of life and joy. People like that, the most unlikely people to the natural mind, have become key figures in this work. God still takes the foolish things to confound the wise." Cliff half closed his eyes. "Dear Old Chester," he whispered. There was silence at the table.

He continued, "There is a story of Thampy in the United States. One day we noticed he was very quiet. He didn't look well. Eventually we found out he had an ear problem. He had a germ in both ears that'd almost eaten through to his brain. If that germ had eaten through another fraction of an inch he'd have died. At that time a lady came up, loved him, put him in the hospital and paid all his expenses."

"You met Thampy at a crucial time in his life?" I prompted.

Cliff said, "I'd been to India a couple of times before I met him. He came to my hotel room, knocked on my door and said, 'God sent me to you.' I was busy and about to dismiss him with, 'That's nice but come back another time,' when suddenly the Holy Ghost moved upon me. He told me Thampy was an apostle and that I was to bless him. I took him into my room. His heart was just pouring out. He was weeping for India; a man with great passion. But he had absolutely no way in the world of ever fulfilling his dream of seeing India come to Jesus. He didn't have a cent. The only things he owned were the clothes on his back. As we prayed God began to move upon us. I told him, 'This might be a surprise to you, but the Lord has just shown me that I have to take you to Canada and the United States.'

"He burst into tears. I remember him saying, 'Why has the most high God dealt with me like this?' He was weeping and of course I was too by then. We arranged for him to come to Canada. He flew into Montreal. When he arrived they put him in immigration prison. All our efforts to get him through immigration were to no avail. They decided to deport him. I knew enough of Indian Christian culture to realize if he was deported back to India then that'd be the end of Thampy's ministry. No one would trust him after that. They would say he was an evil man and there was something wrong with him. It was a make or break time. He had to get out of that prison.

"One morning, during this, I was preaching in a church in Ogden, Utah. I felt led we should all join hands and pray the 'prayer of faith' for Thampy's release. God did a miracle in response to that prayer. I went back to my room, called immigration and was immediately put straight through to the top man on the tribunal. He began to ask me questions, 'Do you know this man? Where does he come from? Where are his children? Does he have a church? Have you been to his church?' They wanted to know if I belonged to a religious group that was illegally importing Indians into Canada. Then he said Thampy was not going to be any good to me anyway. I asked him why? He replied, 'Because he doesn't speak good English. Nobody will understand him.' I told him that was the very point. I said, 'You've just hit

216

the nail on the head. We want an original Indian and not some Westernized Indian that speaks good English. We want an authentic Indian for our meetings in the States and Canada.' That answer really stumped him. He said, 'Okay, I'll go back and ask him the same questions. If he verifies your answers, then we'll probably let him come.'

"'Praise the Lord.' They released him. He arrived next day at nine o'clock in the morning at Vancouver airport. We were overjoyed. We took him through Full Gospel Business Men and church meetings right across Canada and the United States. Every time before I preached he'd share and testify about the call of God on his life for India. His heart was always out front when he'd witness. The people could feel the man's anointing and his heart. He didn't need perfect English. We just let him talk. Folk would gravitate toward him after the meetings because they could sense the depth of his commitment to the Lord. That's when some people started to rally around him and support him.

"Shortly after he came back to India we began to bring teams from the West in order to conduct mass crusades. Initially we were disappointed. Only about five thousand people made decisions for Christ at our first crusade. The next time there was more. We brought another team and there was more still. What really brought the spiritual breakthrough was that time in the hotel when I said, 'Lord we have come a long way and we are spending a lot of people's money. We want to be good stewards. We want to succeed in our mission so please show us how to win a Hindu to you.' That's when the Holy Ghost said to me, 'By My presence.' 'But how do I get Your presence out of me and on to the people?' I asked. 'Through praise and worship and the gifts of the Holy Spirit,' He said. I turned to our team and told them the Lord had spoken to me about how to witness to and win a Hindu to Jesus. I said, 'Through praise and worship and the gifts of the Holy Spirit for when Jesus turns up even atheists have to believe in Him.'

"When I said this, the power of God hit the team and several of them went down under the Spirit. Three of them came up with demons screaming out of them. Jesus set them free. Then we danced and sang and worshipped the Lord for hours on end. The anointing of God was all over us. On the last day the Lord said to me, 'Everything you have done in this room in these days, I want you to do on the platform in front of the Hindus.'

"This was the first time we ever worshipped, danced and praised

217

God on a platform in India. While we were doing this there'd be a message in tongues. Someone would interpret into Malayalam. Someone else would interpret it into English. We just let it all hang out. That's when you could hear a pin drop. The people were just staring in silence. They kept looking at us with open mouths because of the anointing of God and the gifts of the Holy Spirit. When we prayed for salvation approximately two thirds of the congregation stood to their feet. We had ten thousand decision cards with us. We had only two thousand after the first night. The sick were being healed. Cripples were walking. Cancers were disappearing. It was marvelous. When we brought people up for testimonies there was a big long line. Some were crying and some were nearly hysterical as they testified about what they'd been healed from. The blind were healed. There was a great manifestation of Jesus at that meeting. We were soon completely out of decision cards. I believe many churches were established out of that crusade and are still going today."

Mariamma said, "Now the work has grown to over eighty churches in that area. That time was a great breakthrough in our lives, in the church and for everything. That was in 1979."

Cliff said, "We first came in 1972. Chester came in 1975. We didn't rush into these crusades with our eyes closed. It took me one year to raise enough money and to get team people enthused enough to come. It took Thampy the same amount of time to train the Bible students. There was a lot of preparation on both sides. Then came a tough year when we had sixty-seven Australians and seven Americans on the team. When, on the first night, Thampy told us the Catholics wanted to co-operate I was over the moon. I reckoned it must be God when the Catholics and Pentecostals came together to praise and worship Jesus. We finished up with about one hundred and ten thousand decisions for Christ in four nights.

"During this crusade the newspapers were giving a running commentary on how many were being saved each night. It was front-page headlines. They wrote when Helen Beard gave her healing testimony a group of twenty thousand people stood up to indicate they wanted Jesus in their hearts. The next night thirty thousand people stood up to receive Jesus. When this happened we thought that they didn't understand what was being said. We made them all sit down. We explained in detail what salvation really meant. Again the whole thirty thousand stood up. About that time some groups started to try and destroy the crusade but their efforts were to no avail. On the last night the stadium that held more than seventy five thousand people was over two thirds full. The newspaper reported that over fifty thousand people had given their lives to Christ that night.

"I remember two cripples running through the crowd up on to the platform shouting, '*Sthothram! Sthothram! Sthothram!*' They were leaping about wildly, throwing their arms in the air and jumping on and off the platform. The whole place was just electric. Throughout the crowd big disturbances would happen here and there. We lost charge of the meeting. God had taken over and was moving as He saw fit. We found out later, it was the cripples that were getting healed who were causing most of the disturbance. The whole attention of the people was focused on these things. There was no point in us trying to do anything further in that meeting. This was the first time I had the revelation of that verse in Ephesians 3 that says God can do exceedingly abundantly above all that we ask or think. So when you can't think anymore, just shut up and watch what God is doing. This was a big breakthrough in Thampy and Mariamma's ministry. They haven't looked back since."

I said, *"You mentioned earlier about them being quality people?"*

"Oh Yes! I have preached the gospel in forty-seven nations of the world; in some of them eighteen times. I've worked with nationals in all of these countries. I mean I've worked with them, alongside them and supported them. Like in Uganda where we maintain our orphanage to the tune of $150,000 per year. We've had disappointments in every other nation working with nationals. But we have never had one disappointment with Thampy or Mariamma in their ministry. Not one.

"They are the most upright, most ethical, most wonderful people. They have been steadfast from the very beginning. They have gone straight ahead, never turning from the right to the left. They have left no room for doubt in our minds about their financial integrity. They put the money into the work of God. They are the people most worthy of support that we know of out of our forty-seven years of ministry amongst nationals. They have the credentials. I would like to see someone give them a million dollars tomorrow and turn them loose to do what's in their hearts. It doesn't mean dollars to them. They did it before they had dollars. It's not been money, money, money; it's been faith, faith, faith. They did it when they had no money.

They have never turned their hearts to money. They have gone straight ahead with a passion to see souls saved and lives changed for the Kingdom of God. They are great pioneers. They are doing a big work here in India. I highly commend them for their faithfulness to the gospel and to the call of God upon their lives."

Thampy came back to the table. He and Cliff began to talk about friends they had in common. I excused myself. The insect bites were hurting again. I needed some emollient for my itchy ankles. When I returned John and Cliff wanted to video the ladies refuge. They asked me to join them. By Western standards the refuge is very basic. Our prisons would be places of luxury compared to this refuge, but then that's the situation in much of the third world. The refuge ladies realize something is afoot and come out to investigate. They are all smiles and warm welcomes. They join our procession as we intrude into their privacy. The rooms are small with four beds, at least, to a room. One hard wooden cot just about fills the length of one small wall. Beside each bed a few possessions are stacked. Some of the beds are bunks. One woman eagerly identifies her bed. I think of my own mother and tears sting my eyes. I am reminded of prisoner of war camps in old black and white movies. We go into one room and someone shows us a large old mildewed photograph of an aged couple. The photo has slipped slightly to one side. Mariamma is bubbling. Her enthusiasm is infectious.

"This is a photograph of Vivianna and Chester Bieson," she says. "This refuge was their vision. When they came here many ladies were living with us because of all the persecutions they were having. Vivianna was a person who believed in the equality of men and women. When she saw all these ladies beaten so badly she said, 'Mariamma, you must have a place for these ladies. They must have their own building and their own toilet.'

"She asked Thampy what would such a thing cost. He reckoned about $50.000. Vivianna and Chester were pensioners. They didn't have that kind of money. Thampy said, 'No worries. God will provide.' Next year, when Chester came he said, 'One of my relatives has just died and left me $50,000 dollars in her will. We can have the refuge.' We called it *The Vivianna Life Centre*.

"Some of our refuge ladies are Bible workers who have never married. They dedicated their lives to witnessing to others about Jesus. When they grow old they have nowhere to go. There are also Muslim and Hindu women who have been kicked out of their homes for following Jesus. One of the girls is a Hindu priest's daughter."

So many people, so many stories. During my stay with Mariamma and Thampy I noticed a beautiful young woman and her two little daughters. Occasionally they'd come in and out the house. Days later the mother and her children were separated. She and another girl took them on the bus to Goa to leave them in the orphanage there. Then they made the return eighteen-hour journey back to Chingavanam where the mum would study in the Bible School. Unfortunately there are no facilities here for children. Mariamma's problem is never an open heart. It's always financial.

She said, "For over fifteen years, we've been looking after lots of ladies with very little outside help. They are only the tip of the iceberg. If I had the finances we could help so many more poor and homeless believers."

When one talks to Mariamma, one realizes she is an Aladdin's Cave of stories and memories. She is a wisdom keeper. Talking to her is like surfing the Internet. You never know what you'll find. We are standing outside the refuge surrounded by old and young women. John Beard is videoing. Mariamma has her hand on a small lady.

"She says, 'For sixty years Miss Thomas here, has worked in North India for the Lord. But when she became old there was nowhere for her to go. That's why we have this refuge. Her people were very rich people. They had two or three houses. She has forsaken everything for the sake of the gospel. She has nothing now in this world though the Lord had shown her she has a mansion in heaven." Miss Thomas, who understands some English, shouts *"Sthothram!"* at this point.

Mariamma continues, "Miss Thomas worked mostly in Delhi. Her duties were to visit and pray for people. Witness for Jesus. To evangelize people. Her job was to talk to ladies about the love of God. She had a very effective ministry."

Mariamma moves to another lady. They embrace. Mariamma says, "This is Sosamma. She has been a Christian for over twenty-five years. I remember because I'd just given birth to Binu when she came to Christ. After her conversion she was persecuted by her family and put out of their house. She had been married at eleven years old to a man who was a eunuch. Thampy had been beaten up in her village many years back. Later we started a church there. It was through that ministry she got saved. After her baptism she was beaten up very badly. She managed to escape by hiding and running through the sugar cane fields. She has been working as a Bible outreach lady these past seventeen years. She is now over 70 years old. She is not able to do too much nowadays. She is still living with us and helping whenever she can. She is a great prayer warrior."

Mariamma moves on to another lady. She says, "This is Kunjamma. She is 80 years old. She came to us, in January, with a heart breaking story."

I walked away at this point. Mariamma continued with her thumbnail sketches for the video camera. So many stories behind each smiling face. I decided to wait until heaven until I'd see the full-length features. I always liked the big picture. I also realized that most of the refuge ladies would be in the better mansions and higher places in heaven. *Maybe they'll come down and visit me once in a while,* I thought. Then I'd get the full story.

21

In An Eastern Bowl

Binu, the youngest of Mariamma's children, had just arrived home from Australia where he'd been at Bible School for three years. He and Thampy were staying together in Goa. I'd moved in with Biju and Secu who were temporarily living in the converted gangsters home. I'd no idea of what was going on. I'd a great sense of it being something like the early days of the church when all things were held in common. I only hoped the gangster's enemies knew he wasn't at home at present. I didn't mind enjoying the hospitality of the early church; I just didn't want the sufferings that usually went with it. Leaving the planet in a hail of bullets, meant for India's answer to Al Capone, wasn't my first choice for an exit scene.

I'd met Binu on previous trips. He is energetic and friendly with a sense of fun that regularly accompanies youngest children. He showed me a portable CD player his friends Jinu and Marlo had given him as a going away present. He couldn't get it to work. He feared it had broken in his luggage. I looked at it, clicked the CD into place and it played perfectly. As I watched his large relieved smile I realized he'd never used a CD player before.

Binu's challenge after having tasted the freedom of Western Christianity will be to settle back into the role ascribed for him in conservative Kerala. In India everything is sacrificed for the family and the ministry. Personal choice is not high on the agenda. Binu is now a man of two cultures. His task will be to balance the claims and expectations of the church whilst remaining true to the recognition of his emerging self. It is a struggle that will equip him for his leadership role in the future. He must learn to make the contradictions dance. After we all came back to Kerala I spent two days on a backwater boat with Binu, John Beard and a new Indian Christian called David that Binu had met on the flight from Goa. David supplied the boat.

As we chugged along the backwaters we could hear rhythmic

chanting from small Hindu temples that dotted the riverbank. An occasional canoe crossed our path. Wonderful new birds passed overhead. Large kingfishers caught fire before our very eyes. Smiling women, washing colorful clothes at the rivers edge, would momentarily lookup from their backbreaking work. One man vigorously washed a herd of buffalo that wallowed and bellowed in the cool water. They sounded like a group of larger louts messing about in the river.

Binu and I were chatting. Our talk turned to cross-cultural issues. He said, "A lot of things we've accepted from the British are now hindering us in reaching out to our own people. Often the reason we don't do something is because the Hindus do it. We get defined by what we don't do, rather than by what we do. This is negative. For example, in the West you wear wedding rings. Here we are not allowed to wear jewelry. We don't wear necklaces at our weddings because the Hindus wear necklaces at their weddings. We don't give Indian names to our children because they'd be written off as Hindus. These are all small barriers that isolate us from our own community. I believe it's time to look at some of these things.

"There are many barriers that are cultural and historical rather than spiritual and theological. Colonialism forced a lot of things upon the Indian people. Recently I talked to one guy who said he hated Christianity because it was something the Westerners had imposed upon us. He thought it was a white man's religion. That attitude has to change. The packaging isn't the important thing. It's what's in the package that counts. For example, if you go to the untouchables and teach them about the enormous acceptance of God they will all respond. Because they have been so rejected the truth that God loves them is great news. If you go to a Brahman and preach about acceptance he is not so moved. He already feels accepted and very much a part of India's life and history. There are different issues for different classes of people. We need to realize this. We need to begin to identify with and understand Hindus. We cannot take the easy option and say that everything they do is bad. We cannot demonize everything they do.

"Their children's names are about their Gods and we say that is bad. Our children's names are about our God. Is that bad? Are we always right and they always wrong? To say what I am saying may sound radical to an Indian Pentecostal Christian. Some would not listen to me. They might think I was confused or demon possessed. I think the gospel is a very liberating

224

thing. It's free for everybody. There are circumstances in every culture that the gospel can speak to. Christianity is not just a set of rules of dos and don'ts. It is about a relationship with Jesus, 'Abide in me and I will abide in you.' It says in John:17, eternal life is about knowing God and His Son Jesus Christ. It's not a code of behavior for living. It's all about knowing. It's relationship, not rules. We must be careful we don't put barriers in front of people coming to Jesus. We mustn't become like the Pharisees keeping people from Jesus by our laws and rules. Have you heard of Sadhu Sundar Singh?"

"Yes, he was an Indian Christian mystic that lived at the turn of the last century. In those days in India, converts to Christianity imitated the Western missionary's customs; they learned English, ate in western ways, dressed in western clothes and sang translations of western hymns. They held services that were adoptions of those used in Britain or America. Their intention was to show the Hindus and Muslims they'd forsaken their old gods but they only ended up looking like a carbon copy of the church in the West.

"As your friend said this gave the impression to indigenous people that Christianity was an imposed 'white man's religion.' They had become merely an echo and not an authentic voice. Sundar Singh realized in order to reach the Indian people with the gospel he must present it in Indian terms. Hence he wore the turban and saffron robe of the holy sadhu. He understood what Paul meant when he said he had become all things to all men so that by all possible means he might save some."

"Right", said Binu. "Have you heard his Brass Bowl Story?"

"A good story is like having children. Once or twice is never enough. Let me hear it again."

He smiled, "One day Sadhu Sundar Singh was traveling in a packed third-class carriage of the Frontier Mail train. A Brahmin priest and his companion were also in the carriage. A big fuss happened when the train pulled into a wayside station. The priest collapsed due to the heat and crush of the crowded compartment. He was carried onto the platform where the Anglo-Indian stationmaster offered him a cup of water from the refreshment room.

"The fainting Brahmin was horror struck. He refused this offer of water. He would not pollute his lips with a common cup even to save his life. Fortunately his friend saw what was happening. He brought some water in the Brahmin's own brass bowl which, was quickly gulped down by the fainting

225

man. Soon afterwards he was able to rejoin the train refreshed and revived.

"As the train pulled out of the station, Sundar Singh said, 'This is what I have been telling my Western Christian friends. In India we are offering Christianity in a western cup and India rejects it. I believe when we offer the *water of life* in an Eastern bowl then our people will understand it and receive it with joy.'"

Binu looked very serious. He said, "Sadhu Sundar Singh understood Christianity must become an indigenous faith expressed in Indian terms. Otherwise it will fall far short of what God had intended for it. Unlike some others he realized the foolishness of cutting oneself off from one's birthright. He appreciated and valued his cultural heritage. He realized it was a bridge and not a barrier to the spread of the gospel. India is made up of so many people's groups, languages, dialects and cultures. The only way for the good news to spread is for the people to have it in their own bowl. It is not the bowl itself that is important. It is the water of life that it carries. Jesus is the water of life."

I said, *"The same thing happens in Ireland. Many people who come to a living relationship with Jesus are initially very annoyed with the apathy and insignificance of a traditional church that seems to have lost the plot. Often they are influenced by non-Irish Christians who teach, 'Come out from among them and join us.'*

"Unfortunately, very quickly they get isolated from their own people just like the Christians in Sadhu Sundar Singh's India. Strong bridges that could have been used for the spread of the gospel are needlessly burned. They usually end up offering the water of life in an unacceptable bowl across an unnecessary wall. Like the kindly stationmaster in your story their intentions are good. It's just that they lack wisdom and understanding as regards how to do it. This is an awful waste."

I changed the subject by asking, *"How do you cope with the assumptions and expectations put upon you as a preacher's kid?"*

Binu said, "Even nowadays a lot of things are coming to the surface that are deep within me. In the past I was more a sports person than anything else. I was good at sports. My life was sport. Because of the ministry all that was very much restricted. I used to play a lot of badminton but some people started seeing visions. I don't know if they were true or not. People would see things like me breaking my leg and being taken off the badminton court.

I got recognition from the people of my community for my sports but not from the people in the church. I feel the church never appreciated my sporting abilities. When we'd be playing cricket or football on the campus we'd occasionally break a window. They'd say, 'What are you doing? This is holy ground. This is a place for conventions and prayer. It's not a place for soccer.'

"As one grows up one thinks, *Am I being limited by my circumstances?* Even now I'm still battling with these same issues of being given space to develop. I really appreciate what Mum and Dad have done. I respect and honor my father for what he has achieved and from where he has come from. He is a man of little education so he doesn't highly prize learning. He is very much a man of faith and action. He expects us to overcome problems the way he did but we are brought up in a different situation. I love my Dad.

"I often feel I'm battling with all the pressures and expectations of others. I don't want to become noted as a guy who is causing problems just because I've been to Australia. Always I've felt I had to be myself and develop into what God created me to be. This was even before I went to Australia. People might think I'm talking like this because I've been overseas. They might say I'm not relating well to people. I need to come to a balance. I know I haven't reached it yet. When one is under pressure the temptation is to rebel. I don't like being pressurized. When I was abroad there were fewer demands. It was much easier to think. Now I feel squeezed from every angle. They want me here and there. All the plans and thoughts I had in my mind now seem under attack and of little use."

I said, *"Paul's admonition to be all things to all men cuts two ways. We need to be acceptable to those inside the church as well as those outside the church. Conservative Christians also need an acceptable bowl in which to receive fresh water. The story in Acts chapters fifteen and sixteen when Paul circumcises Timothy is a case in point. Paul and Timothy were going to Jewish believers with a decree from The Council at Jerusalem. It said Gentiles turning to God should not be hindered from coming to faith by having to keep the Jewish laws.*

"It was enough they abstain from food sacrificed to idols, from blood, from the meat of strangled animals and from sexual immorality. It also said believers didn't require circumcision in order to be a Christian. Nevertheless Paul circumcised Timothy so he'd be acceptable amongst the Jewish believers.

In effect, he got circumcised in order to tell others one don't need to be circumcised to be a Christian. He became all things to all men. This was painful for Timothy. But it was very necessary if he was to be a vessel for carrying fresh water to a more traditional people."

"That's what happened to my beard," said Binu.

"It's a bit less painful having your beard removed."

Binu had returned from Australia sporting a dainty goatee beard. Within a few days of his arrival it had been shaved off. We talked about how his mother functions in India, in a society where women's roles in the main are fairly restricted. She teaches, preaches, prays, prophecies, casts out demons and so on and gets away with it by calling it sharing. One can be killed challenging some things head on rather than finding a way to make the contradictions dance. I believe we must become all things to all men that women may be released.

It seems to me Binu, like his father, is a pioneer. He will lead the way into new things in the future. He will forge forward in the area of cross-cultural communication. This will enable the gospel to expand into new unreached areas. He will be like the Braham's friend who brings the water of life in an acceptable bowl. As a pioneer he'll need some people to understand and support him.

I'd once heard a leader from *Youth With A Mission* talk about the roles of pioneers, settlers and aristocrats within the church. Pioneers are the innovative, adventurous, risk takers who move the Church into new areas both physically and spiritually.

Settlers are those who follow in their trails and then settle down to protect and nurture the present truth they'd received. Aristocrats on the other hand want to glorify the past and create an elite way of life from it. They became the chosen few. Binu is a pioneer. His main opposition and misunderstanding will come from settlers and aristocrats. Binu said, "Not only do the poor need to be reached with the gospel. The Brahmans need to be reached as well. The gospel is not just for one section of society. If a Brahman comes to the Lord he can preach to the whole town. If a poor man comes to the Lord he can only reach his own community. If we are going to take this nation for Christ we need to breakthrough into the whole area of Hinduism. When you reach the untouchables the untouchables can reach their own people but they will not be accepted by the higher castes.

"The call upon us in *New India Church of God* is to reach the unreached. High caste Hindus are also the unreached. There are opportunities to go into their culture and relate the gospel to that culture. We don't have to rubbish their culture. We can make the gospel a stream running through it. My heart aches to reach out to these people with the gospel but for this to happen I can't just impose my views upon them. I want to reach out to guys like our friend David here, who are high caste. Those fellows will be very effective in reaching out to their own people and also lower down the social and economic ladder. We have tried it the other way around and it has been good but we haven't been successful in reaching the higher castes. If a Braham comes to the lord it would be a hundred times easier for him to reach out to the lower castes than the other way around. So if the present results are a hundred times less now, in the future they will be a thousand times more."

"The scriptures say the gospel is good news to the poor. It also says as regards the early Christians that not many were wise, not many were rich and so on."

"Not many were wise," said Binu, "but some were wise. Paul was wise and clever. Peter found some of Paul's writings hard to understand. The gospel is for all classes. Everyone needs salvation. India is such a big country. I believe we need to have strategies for different areas, peoples and peoples groups. Whatever happens we need to have Indians reaching Indians. I have been reading books that have said that.

"When the Portuguese came to Goa they evangelized the lowest classes of the people. You go to a tribe and get the leader saved. Then the whole tribe gets saved. These are the easiest people to reach. When you look in terms of results you tend to go to the poor people. It's like high and low-pressure areas. There is low pressure with the poor and high pressure with the higher castes. People from the West need to understand this. Many Westerners are not really accepted into India with the gospel. Indians love Westerners. They love all sorts of people but when they come with the gospel it is a different scenario.

"Indigenous Indians have to do the work and they have to start at both ends. There are hundreds of organizations reaching out to people in India. Most of them are among the poor. I believe we also have to reach out to the higher castes. We need to create city churches as a resource center to reach out to the villages. I want to see funds being generated in the cities.

This can be used for village outreach and for breaking down the caste system. If the caste system is broken down amongst the higher levels then it is easier at the lower levels. It is easier to come down the ladder than to go up.

"I don't want to be slotted into some position and told, 'Stay there for the rest of your life.' I want to make things happen. I believe in every generation God does something new; kind of like breaking out of a shell. My Dad broke out of the shell in his day. I think that is wonderful. He was radical in his time. He made a big impact in his day but I think over the last forty years that which was radical has now become the norm."

"Everything begins with a prophet and ends with a policeman. You get the man, the movement and then the monument. Its hard to keep the vision going."

He said, "The vision is alive and well in *New India Church of God,* but innovative things also have to happen. For us to go ahead with our missionary enterprises we have to have a renewed passion; something fresh for the next generation. I want something new from the Lord so as to really penetrate the darkness in this nation. Whether God knows or not I am fully committed to Him. I guess he understands that. When the time comes he will take me through. But I don't want to settle for the status quo."

I kicked into a teaching mode. I said, *"Things are difficult in all cultures. Take the whole area of repression of women in the Church that has resulted in so many women not reaching their full potential because of male prejudice. One way I deal with this is by telling stories about Angela and myself in which Angela ends up as the wise one and I become the fool. I also must put my money where my mouth is and do all within my power to help Angela achieve her potential.*

"But what I'm really doing in my storytelling is sabotaging the whole male dominance system of power, privilege and position. I'm doing it in a humorous way and at my own expense but everybody knows what's going on. Often the only way we have of dealing with divisive and sensitive issues is through humor. I've learned this in contentious Northern Ireland where for most of my lifetime Catholics and Protestants have been killing each other. God forbid we should lose our sense of humor. It's one safe way of dealing with prickly issues rather than hitting them head on. There's more than one way to skin a cat.

"We need to find images, pictures and stories to help facilitate

change. Again it's not just an either/or issue. It's a both/and issue. You don't have to reject the old so as to embrace the new. A good teacher from the scripture brings forth things old and new. Even when we're struggling with our own concerns we need to realize we are serving God's people. We need to be sensitive to them, their issues and the place where they are at present. The vision has to grow bigger and more understanding must come. We have to incorporate and accommodate previous models as well as moving on to new levels; new wineskins for new wine. At the same time we mustn't merely fall back into old outmoded patterns."

"Falling back into the pattern," said Binu. "That's my biggest fear. If I fall back then I merely become part of the system."

"I can see you and Biju liaising much more with the West. I can see you becoming a bridge of communication over which finances and resources can come to the work in India."

"There are lots of people in the West ready and willing to help. They have a good heart for God and they have the resources but many are unsure as to what is really happening in India. Today what we need is partnership and mutual accountability in the gospel. Financial help given to indigenous evangelists, equips, frees and enables them to respond to the call of God upon their lives. This is not just theory. Today it is harvest time in India. Right now as we sit on this boat thousands of people who never ever heard the name of Jesus before in their lives are coming to faith in Christ. Now is the day of salvation. Now is the time we need support. We are like the disciples in the boat with the large catch of fish. We need help to land the catch.

"In the past Western missionaries have given their lives to light the fire of the gospel in India. Now is the day for native workers to take that fire forward. It's starting to burn so brightly. There is still a great role to be played by our brothers and sisters in the West. I believe many new roles will open up in the future but financial support for the workers in the harvest is of paramount importance at the moment.

"It's as if we have huge tanks at the forefront of the battle but many are out of fuel. Prayer and money is the fuel we need to move these tanks forward. In India we have much prayer and many willing workers but as you know Brother Brendan, we have very little money. We truly do need financial support for the gospel to go forward. But fear not God will provide. I believe he will touch the right hearts at the right time so that his kingdom will be established in India, so that the name of Jesus will be lifted up and glorified."

We sat for a time in silence. Faint rhythmic chanting from a temple on the further bank was our background music. Suddenly a sparkling kingfisher flashed only yards away. It dived into the river. Seconds later it emerged with a fish nearly as big as itself. *Phew,* I thought. *The kingfishers are big in India.*

22

Gangsters and Murderers

In the darkness Thampy and I picked our way through the garden to his office. We sat outside on two chairs under a light bulb that mesmerized a batch of circling moths. Across in the auditorium a young preacher was practicing his art through a microphone. In the background rhythmic clapping and praise ascended from the prayer tower. Mosquitoes sat in on our conversation and munched on my warm Irish blood.

"What's the most important thing in the ministry?" I asked Thampy. The answer to a question like this usually pinpoints a minister's area of gifting. A prophet will say something along the lines of, "To hear the voice of God," while a teacher might answer, "To know the word of God." Thampy is an evangelist-apostle.

He said, "Jesus was very particular in His mission. The one and the only purpose of His mission is in His words in Luke 4:43. He said, 'I must preach the gospel in the neighboring towns and villages. For this purpose I have been sent.' His one and the only purpose was to preach the gospel. No one could stop Him. In John: 4 He said, 'I must go through Samaria.' Samaria is a neglected place to a Jew or a Jewish rabbi. They were cursed. They were despised. They were set apart from Jewish settlements. No rabbi was allowed to talk with Samaritan women. But Jesus told His disciples He must go through Samaria. They didn't understand the meaning of His *must*.

"He went to the well of Jacob in the city of Sychar. He told them He was weary and weak. The disciples realized He was tired and hungry. He sat down by the well while they went to get some food. Everybody knows the story of the woman at the well. He talked to her. He convicted her. He led her to salvation. Then she went back to Samaria and challenged the people to come and see the man who had revealed the mysteries of her heart. The whole Samaritan village was won for the Kingdom of God.

"In John 9:4 Jesus said, 'I must work the works of Him who sent Me. I must work while it is day. Night is coming when no-one can work.' Look at the *musts* of Jesus. The Father sent Him for one purpose. That's what Isaiah says, 'The Spirit of the Lord is upon me to preach the good news to the poor, and to open the blind eyes, to heal the broken hearted and to set the captives free.' That was the prophecy concerning Jesus and His ministry here on earth. Jesus was very sure, 'I must work the works of Him who sent Me.'

"While it is day He knows the darkness is coming; the darkness that covers the earth. Grim darkness. Jesus said in Mark 13:10, 'This gospel first must be preached in all the world to all nations.' What a *must*. The *first* and the *must* of Jesus is preaching the gospel. In the gospel of Luke, Jesus said that He *must* be about His Father's business. The *must* in the life of Jesus is preaching the gospel. The gospel is the only answer to the problems of the people of the world today.

"Here in India a lot of Christian organizations are involved in social activities. They feed the poor. They house the homeless. They care for widows and orphans. That is all good work. I appreciate that. But none of these things can solve the problem. A leper can be healed but unless he is saved he cannot go to heaven. A leper can be forgiven and go to heaven. The gospel is the only answer.

"I have seen destitute people living in slums and in poor huts in small villages. They were starving and suffering and sick. When I went there they said, 'Give us something to eat. Give us some clothes.' I said, 'I understand your problem. If I give you money for food it lasts only a day or two. If I give you clothes they will last only a year or two. But if I give you the gospel, the bread of life, it will last for all eternity.' I preach the gospel. I have seen people crying receiving Jesus. The deep desire in their hearts to follow Jesus after they have become Christians is marvelous. After that tremendous changes take place."

At this point the electricity failed and snuffed out the background noise of the young preacher at the microphone. My recorder stopped. In the darkness above us the stars sparkled like lights on a Christmas tree. All the while the rhythmic sound of intercession and clapping from the prayer tower grew stronger and stronger. Here in Chingavanam that particular dynamo never stops. A torch beam picked its way closer to us. Thampy's name was called. Some pastors had come from a long distance. He was wanted at once.

"Excuse me," he said, "I must go."

I sat alone for a while in the darkness, looking at the stars and listening to the comforting sounds of prayer. Coming back into the house I noticed Thampy and five or six pastors in the vestibule, laughing and praising the Lord by lamplight. One of them, a large man in stripped shirt and fancy braces stood out. He looked like a poker player. Inside Mariamma was reading her Bible at the kitchen table. One of the girls was noisily washing and putting away the crockery. I asked Mariamma about the man who looked like a gambler. She giggled, "His name is Appukkuttan. He used to be bad notorious man. He came to us through our radio program."

"Radio program?"

"We had a weekly radio program around 1985/86. We called it *Shanthimargam*, which means 'the way of peace'. It ran for about a year. Both Thampy and I used to speak on it. It was very expensive. In the end we had to stop it. One day as I was closing the program I said, 'If you don't have any peace there is a way for you. Jesus is calling you. He can give you peace and rest. Come to Jesus.' I then gave the address of our church telling the listeners to come there on Sunday if they wanted to find peace.

"Two friends were sitting talking that day. They just switched on the radio and caught the end of that program. One was a bank manager and one a communist. The communist man was forty-one years old and unmarried. He had devoted his life to the party. All his family were Christians but he was an atheist. They were both called Kunjumon. They only heard the closing part of my message about peace but they were both strangely interested. They decided to come to our service and find out more.

"The next Sunday they came to our church in Changanacherry and sat at the back. Whoever came to these meetings would always be touched. There was such an anointing on the prayer and preaching. They came for a few weeks, sat at the back and disappeared quickly at the end of each service. On the third week Thampy was preaching. When he spied the two men at the back he pointed to them. He told them not to leave the meeting without first speaking to him. When they came up to the front Thampy led them to the Lord. Afterwards a big revival began in that area. All the bank manager's family got saved along with many people from their neighborhood. Every week a big busload of people from that district came along to church.

"During this time, the man you are asking about, Appukkuttan was a friend of this communist man. He was a gangster. When he'd walk through the streets people would shut their shops and the ladies would go into their houses. He was like a wild animal. The police were always after him. He was married but his wife couldn't cope with him. Within two years she had two children. Then she left him. She was an only daughter. Her family told her to come back home. They said she shouldn't live with this bad fellow."

"What sort of things did he do?"

"He'd drink and fight and go with other women - everything bad. Soon afterwards he married another woman. She was a Hindu. He was working in the Gulf for some time. He made good money and built a big house. But he didn't have any peace for all the time people were trying to kill him. At one time there was sixty police cases against him. One day he started drinking. He decided, as no one loved him he would kill somebody. He'd then be put into to the central prison. He thought he'd be happier in prison with people like himself than outside with people who didn't want him. He went into the town with a knife looking for someone to kill but he didn't have the heart to kill innocent people he didn't know.

"Then he thought of a solution. He'd go to his friend Kunjumon the communist who had many foes. He'd get the name of Kunjumon's worst enemy and kill him. That way he'd be doing them both a favor. He didn't know that Kunjumon had become a believer. Appukkuttan came drunk with two knives in his pockets. 'Tell me, Kunjumon my friend,' he said, 'who is your biggest enemy?'

"Kunjumon invited him inside. He told him to take a shower and get cleaned up. In order to appease him, Kunjumon agreed he'd take him to the person whom he wanted killed. He took him straight to our house in Changanacherry. It was about 7 o'clock in the evening. Thampy was not here. I came onto the veranda to meet them. Appukkuttan had a big handlebar moustache, red eyes and sticky-out hair; very scary. He just kept staring at me as we sat on the veranda.

"When I realized he was not a believer I began to talk to him about Jesus. The Holy Spirit was speaking to his heart. For one and a half hours I talked non-stop. During this time he never spoke once. He just kept staring. Then large tears came to his eyes. He began to cry like a baby. I asked him if he was ready to give his heart to the Lord. We prayed the prayer of salvation together and now he is my brother. I then invited him inside my house - this

236

man no one would dare have in their homes - to give him food.

"An article in the *India Today* magazine featured the change in Appukkuttan's life. The whole community came to know about his transformation. After that we had to keep him in our house because of all the police cases. We began to pray and fast for him. Can you believe it, Brendan? All of those cases got sorted out. Then one after another his gang came to the Lord. He kept bringing people like himself to church and they all accepted Jesus. In the end we had this large group of gangsters. God really broke through to this bad notorious man. The Lord knows if you get the ringleader saved then the whole group will come along."

"Any more stories like that?"

"Have you heard of Reny George?"

"Reny George?"

"Reny George was the son of the national director of a Christian organization called 'Every Home Crusade'. He was at university in Madras. He got involved with a group of students that were taking drugs. They were all well-to-do boys. One of them was a Muslim from Mauritius, one a Hindu from Malaysia and the other the son of a priest from Kenya. Reny was the son of an Indian Pentecostal pastor. They were all in their early twenties. Because of their drug habits they needed huge amounts of money. They started stealing cars and air-conditioning units from hotels.

"One day, Reny told his friends he had a rich and childless aunt and uncle in Kerala. They decided to rob them. They drove all the way from Madras in a stolen car. The aunt had a servant lady who went home at night. She was about to leave when she saw the car coming. She asked Reny's aunt if she should stay to cook for the visitors. The aunt told her to go on home. She herself would cook. Excitedly she said, 'My mon from Madras has come.' In India *mon* is like a pet name for a child. I might say Biju-mon or Binu-mon to my own sons. Reny was called 'Madras-le-mon' by his aunt. While she was cooking for the boys they threatened the uncle and demanded money. In the end using a kitchen knife they killed the poor aunt and uncle. During the scuffle Reny gashed himself badly with the knife. Afterwards he went to a hospital in Cochin where he got the wound stitched.

"This whole thing became front-page news all over India. It stirred the interest of the people: the son of a pastor and the son of a priest on drugs murdering a favorite auntie. This all happened over twenty years ago. Within two days of the murders the boys were caught doing drugs in some hotel. They were discovered because the servant remembered the auntie saying, 'My *mon* from Madras has come.' The lawsuit became known as the 'Madras-le-mon' case. Even today if you mention 'Madras-le-mon' everyone in Kerala remembers all the details. The young boys were all found guilty and given life sentences. This was a great shame to the whole Pentecostal community in India. After eight years they were allowed out on parole. A man called Roy witnessed to Reny in prison. Even though he knew the gospel message from childhood, only then did he give his life to the Lord. He got saved during his first parole session but no Pentecostal church would have anything to do with him. Even his own family would not accept him. That's when we got involved. He came to live with us and became like one of our own children. Any time he got parole he caught the train and came straight here. We gave him the key to our house. We believed him when he said he'd become a Christian. There was such a change in his life. Tears would run down his cheeks when he testified.

"He went everywhere with Thampy witnessing for Jesus. When the people heard the name 'Reny George' the whole town would come out to listen. There was a movie made about him called *Madras-le-mon*. For five years he was one of our boys. He then married a girl, called Tina, from Bangalore. She'd been saved through his father's ministry. She herself had been delivered from drugs. She married him during a parole session without telling her family he was a murderer. She stayed with us until his final release. He was in prison in Trivandrum where he was the pastor to sixty inmates who'd become believers.

"We used to visit; Thampy would preach, Biju would sing and I'd pray for the people. I also visited the ladies jail. We were very involved. When the believers were released Reny sent them straight here where we baptized and cared for them. Many of them are still involved in prison ministries full time. Tina is a very capable girl. They have a prison ministry based in Bangalore. She is the coordinator of the whole Karnataka State. They have an orphanage for the prisoner's children. They are doing a great job. Over the years so many prisoners have come to know the Lord. The change in their lives has been wonderful. As these prisoners came out one by one we kept them in our home. Some of them have become great friends. Many went through our Bible School and now they are pastors. Appukkuttan, whom you saw outside just now, is also one of our area pastors. One man, when he saw the change in Appukkuttan's life, offered 10 lakhs of Rupees to build a house for him. Upstairs in that house there is a large open hallway where the church meets. It's amazing what God can do."

"Did Appukkuttan stay with his second wife?"

"His second wife had gone by the time he became a believer. Eight years ago he got married again to a believer from a Hindu background. She was thirty-nine at the time. Now they have two children aged six and four. They are very happy. That is the story of Appukkuttan. The Lord saves all sorts of people. The gospel is good news to the poor.

"He saves murderers and all the notorious gangsters. Reny went on with the Lord because of the love shown him. We really loved and accepted him. He was like one of our own children. He was always grateful for that. Whenever he needed anything we were always there for him. One day the top man of the Indian Pentecostal Church and his wife came to visit. They were an elderly couple. I was sitting talking to the wife when Reny came downstairs. He was a smart looking boy. She asked me who he was. I told her it was Reny George. She was terribly shocked. She whispered, 'Mariamma, are you not scared to have guys like this in your home?'

"I thought, *Lord, these people don't even know Your saving grace.* Reny was a blessing and a great friend. It was a privilege to know him and to see God's grace in his life. We don't see him and Tina as much as we would like too nowadays. We are all very busy in the ministry."

"Time passes, the big sky moves and the rivers roll but Mariamma remembers the stories."

"I can't forget the stories of all that God has done."

"Tonight you mentioned the word love a lot."

"We must never forget that God is love. Our God is a God of love. Appukkuttan is the story of a notorious wild man tamed by love.

"One day a drunken friend of his came to our house. I hadn't the heart to turn him away. Somebody once told me if you gave a drunk a whole lime with plenty of salt, it'll help the alcohol subside. That's what I did, all the time praying *Lord, have mercy on this boy.* If some Christians had seen me doing this they might not have been happy. But with these tough fellows you must be tolerant and patient. Love is the most powerful weapon any Christian has. People must understand we love and accept them when nobody else does. When we treat them like human beings and call them *'mony, mony'* they will respond. It was not easy at the time to get these guys on the right track. But now we can see what a blessing they are."

"Appukkuttan certainly looks happy tonight, laughing and praying on the veranda."

"He tells everybody I'm his mum. 'Mariamma is my mum,' he says."

"Mum's the word."

23

The Scatterer

In the cool of the morning, Mariamma and I are sitting on the veranda, watching butterflies. Waves of prayer and hand clapping flutter from the prayer tower. A memory of an unfinished conversation with Biju flashed through my mind. I said, *"Mariamma, Biju mentioned a dream you had about a wolf and a lamb? Do you remember it?"*

"Yes. That was many years back. Thampy and I had gone to minister in Sydney, Australia. The day before we returned I had a dream about an animal. It looked like a huge wolf with fire flaming from its eyes. It was standing with its claws extended. Underneath it was a lamb. For a long time I watched the anger of this animal. All the while the little lamb walked slowly out from under this raging beast, totally ignoring its threats. I knew if the lamb looked back and acknowledged the wolf's presence, the wolf would pounce and tear it to pieces. As long as the lamb ignored the wolf it was safe.

"When I received this dream I knew something bad was going to greet us back in India. I had an ominous feeling. I told Thampy, 'Soon after we get home, we are to pray and fast for one week.' When we landed in Madras, Thampy's eldest brother met us with the news; there was disquiet and disunity amongst the leadership. Some were hinting we'd secretly bought property in Nagercoil or elsewhere. Others were insinuating we'd lots of money hidden in off shore bank accounts. When the leadership is divided the people will be scattered. If the leaders believe a lie then so will the people. Attacks from within are more difficult to deal with than attacks from without.

"Thankfully the Lord had forewarned us. We knew we were not fighting flesh and blood but a power that had come against us. It's a big grace of God to alert us to the enemy's tactics. We fasted for seven days. We didn't speak to anybody. We didn't go to see anybody. By the time we had finished the fast, every one of those who were speaking bad against us came and apologized for their behavior. If we had reacted to the rumors and threats we would have been destroyed.

"Last year, Brendan, you spoke at our Sunday service. You prophesied, that a demonic strongman named *The Scatterer* was coming to attack us. You prophesied the attack would come from without and within the church. You quoted from Psalm 133 where it says, 'How good and pleasant it is when brothers live together in unity . . . For there the Lord bestows His blessing, even life for evermore.' You said the attack from within would be the most serious one. We were prepared. Shortly afterwards some of our key people became bitter against Thampy and I. The enemy was trying to cause disunity. Because we were forewarned we prayed and fasted against *The Scatterer* and broke its power. Now we are in unity again, the place where the Lord can bestow His blessings.

"Unless the Lord shows us the root cause we can't deal successfully with these attacks. We are never fighting against flesh and blood. Our enemies are powers and principalities in heavenly places. Their whole purpose is to stop the advance of the Kingdom of God on the earth. If we ask, God will always show us the source of the attack. He will also show us how to deal with it. Leadership and key people will always be attacked so as to cause division. If the shepherds are in disunity the sheep will be scattered. They will become easy prey for the enemy. Unity is vital if the work of the Kingdom is to go forward."

"*It was through a dream the Lord revealed to me that a strongman called The Scatterer was going to come against your ministry. In that dream a voice said, 'He that scattereth is coming.' I find your dream about the wolf very interesting. In John 10:12 Jesus talks about a wolf that attacks and scatters the flock. You must have seen that particular strongman in the Spirit.*"

Mariamma said, "By 1987 we had about two hundred churches. Our place in Changanacherry had become too small for us. Then the Lord showed us this place. It was nearly four acres of land. They were asking a big sum for the property. We were negotiating and praying and fasting. A prophecy was given. It said we were to fast and pray for twenty-one days. It said before the fast was over the owners would call and offer the property to us. The prophecy also said that twenty-one days were necessary because the Lord was sending fire to this place to burn out the demons. Otherwise we

242

wouldn't be able to handle it.

"We were praying, *Lord, make it as a power house. Let people come and get deliverance.* By mid afternoon of the twenty-first day of the fast nothing has happened. That night, a few hours before the fast was to finish, the owner rang and said he was prepared to sell the property. He asked for twenty-five lakhs of rupees. We could only raise eleven lakhs."

"You lacked a lot of lakhs."

Mariamma's look made me wish I'd kept my mouth shut. She continued, "The owner gave it to us for the eleven lakhs. In reality we got the house for nothing. There was so much warfare over us coming here. Discord arose amongst the leadership. Some folk were unhappy we were moving to a larger property. They organized meetings. Many prophets came to these meetings and prophesied against our move to this property. They said things like, 'It's all going to be taken away. All the churches are going to be broken and scattered.' Some said if we moved we'd lose our children. All sorts of disasters were prophesied against us."

"Isn't that interesting, the strongman whose job it was to scatter was able to influence the prophets to prophecy on his behalf. Sounds a bit like what happened in Mark 8 when Jesus rebuked Peter by saying, 'Get behind Me Satan!' One minute Peter was speaking under the influence of the Holy Spirit recognizing Jesus as the Christ and the next moment he is the mouthpiece for Satan. We need to be able to discern prophecy properly."

Mariamma said, "One day I was praying at home when a man of God came to one of these meetings. From reputation I knew he was a real prophet of God. I prayed earnestly, *Lord, if it is not Your perfect will we should move to Chingavanam, then please speak it publicly now and we will give it up.* This prophet had never seen me before. He prophesied, that spiritual things had happened in my life from the time I was nine years old. He then prophesied about past events. Everything he said was spot on.

"Then he said, 'Within two years, the Lord says, I am going to give you a home of your own. When you are living there you will begin to travel all over the world but you will always have a home to come back to.' Then I wasn't traveling much. This was news to me. I felt his prophecy confirmed it was God's will we should move. His words brought peace to my heart.

"My sister Usha and her husband Pastor Lincoln had just decided to fast for twenty-one days. We had purchased but not yet moved into our new

243

property. I asked them, 'Why don't you do your fast at our new home? Some of us will join you.' I knew if they conducted their fast here that any remaining demons would have to leave. On the thirteenth day of the fast Usha and I were in the kitchen boiling water. A man rushed in. He said, 'Please come now. God is about to do something.' We hurried back to the room. The worship was so anointed. We forgot all about ourselves in the midst of the glory. The presence of the Lord was so strong.

"Usha saw a vision. She was facing the door. She saw Jesus walking towards it. He had golden hair. He was wearing a fine, pure white, cotton material. She saw the scars and blood so fresh on His body. He stood on the first step. He bent down, touched the second step with His hand and said, 'It is sealed.' Jesus Himself had come and sealed this property for His work.

"Later that afternoon a prophet wandered into our meeting. Without any knowledge of what had happened earlier he prophesied, 'The Lord says, *My dear children, today I have came to this place and I have purified all the rooms of this house.*' Usha's vision and this prophecy broke the power of the other words that had caused so much anxiety. The spirit of fear left and joy came into our hearts. Before we finally moved here another prophet said to me, 'You are shifting to a place that is going to be like the tabernacle of Moses. There will be people living around it like the Israelites. That means they will all be believers. All those who don't get saved will move. They will sell their houses to believers.' After we settled in it was exactly as the prophecy said. Now all the houses around belong to believers. Three houses were sold to believers; the rest were all saved. It really blesses me to see how faithful God's promises are.

"The wife of a key-worker, caught up in this conflict died of cancer. She was a very good friend of mine. He is ministering elsewhere now. We feel very sad. He was a tremendous support to us during the early difficult days. Now the ministry has expanded he is no longer here. His wife and I used to see each other every day but after the discord we didn't meet for over a year. Things were very bad. One day I felt inspired to go to their house. I took another lady with me. I didn't tell Thampy.

"When my friend saw me she couldn't believe her eyes. She was sitting, with her daughter, in the porch of her home, when we arrived. I climbed the steps and hugged her. Both of us broke into tears. I said we'd come to visit because three times in the previous week God had given me dreams about her. She told me she had cancer and had been in the hospital in Madras. She showed me the effects of the radiation. Before she'd gone to Madras she'd wanted to see me. She feared she might not come back alive from the hospital. We sat and cried and prayed. I ate some food she cooked for me. Then I went home.

"Another day she sent word, 'Mariamma please come and pray for me.' Her leg was very sore. The cancer had gone into her bone. They took her back into hospital. She believed it was the bitterness of disunity that allowed the cancer to thrive. She hoped our forgiveness and reconciliation would open the doors for healing. Oh, how much pain she went through. If someone touched the bed she would scream in pain. I arranged for two of our intercessors to remain beside her at all times. Every day I'd also pray with her. I even prayed in the radiation room. For six months she was in hospital. All during this time her husband wouldn't talk to me. If he was in the room when I entered he'd turn his face and walk out.

"I remember one day she lay on my shoulder for a long time. It got very sore, but as long as it gave her some comfort I was happy. Once the nurse asked in my hearing, 'Who is this lady who helps you?' My friend replied, 'She is everything to me.'

"Until the time of her death I was there for her. It was very hard. I was very upset. Even at the end we were still not reconciled to her husband. He was so hurt. After her death his mother also died. His mother had been like our own mother. We'd all been so close. When my friend died we were there praying until the very last moment but still the rift remained.

"Then one day two years later he came to our home. It took that much time for us to be reconciled. He'd just retired from his full-time job. He came here with his son who was going to the United States. He took Thampy's right hand and said, 'Thampy, this is the hand that blessed me first and separated me for the ministry. Now I am going into full-time ministry. I want you to lay your hand upon my head and pray for me. I also want you to bless my son before he goes off to America.'

"Later he built a new church and asked Thampy to go along and dedicate it. It took time but healing eventually came. It was all so painful for everyone involved. It's always the enemy's way to cause division and death and bitterness. So much better when the brothers are humble and wise enough to dwell together in unity. Unity and love are the two weapons that will

245

always destroy the power of *The Scatterer*."

24

Mariamma's Children

This morning I stood alone on the veranda watching six dragonflies hovering above a dark red rose. I couldn't figure out what they were doing. Suddenly the largest butterfly I've ever seen in my life fluttered within inches of my face. It made me catch my breath. It was shades and patterns of blue and about the size of a woman's hand. I watched entranced as it kept circling the garden. It was so beautiful, so new to me. Then suddenly it turned a corner and disappeared forever.

One of the great things about life is that one never knows when something marvelous is about to happen. Nor can you hold onto it when it does. From inside the house, the clatter of crockery called me to breakfast. I didn't know it but this was to be the last meal and conversation with Mariamma I'd have before I returned to Ireland. The Thampy household is permanently busy with people and phone calls. Overseeing so many churches doesn't leave a lot of time to smell the roses. Phone calls and people have regularly interrupted my talks with Mariamma. Circumstances were to take over and finish my quest for the present but as in watching the butterfly I enjoyed it while it lasted. Mariamma's children were on her mind today.

She said, "In 1989 we were back in Chingavanam, the town we'd been kicked out of for not being able to afford twenty-two rupees rent for one small room. The denominational leader who was behind our eviction was not happy when after twenty years we returned as leaders of two hundred churches and a big army of Christians. Thampy was viewed as a big threat. In March 1990, most of the people we baptized were from this leader's people. He'd been mad at his clergy, 'Why are you allowing your people to follow this Blackbeard's religion?' Now his mouth was stopped for people from his own congregation were coming to new life in Christ.

"When the move of the Lord began, this leader was so stirred up. A rumor war was started against us. They said things like, 'Thampy is locked up in the jail. They've discovered he had millions of rupees and so many biscuits of gold. He is kidnapping people, stealing their kidneys and selling them for four lakhs of rupees each. He also has many foreign wives.' All sorts of crazy rumors were told about us. They spread like wildfire. When they saw us building the auditorium and realized that we expected hundreds of people to come, the rumors got worse. Brendan, you wouldn't believe what we went through.

"At the same time, there was a revival in the backwater villages. Two to three hundred people were getting saved every night. We were very busy with that. People who love us were phoning and calling to ask us about the rumors. Thampy's relatives were coming to visit and find out the truth; so much confusion.

"The Word of God says when people speak evil things about us then our reward is great in heaven. We were preaching and getting people saved, so we'd get rewarded for that. Plus somebody was working for us by spreading rumors about us. We'd also get rewarded for that. I used to tell this to our people to encourage them but privately I was so broken hearted. I couldn't even look at the face of Thampy, wondering what he was going through.

"The children were the ones who'd to face the brunt of it. The four of them were still at college. When they'd reach the bus stop the whole conversation would be about this, 'Have you heard? A preacher man called Thampy is kidnapping people and stealing their kidneys.' These rumors were in all the colleges. Despite what our children had to put up with I never heard them say one negative word.

"The only person who complained was me. In the end I couldn't tolerate it. It got to a stage where I couldn't even pray. Every day the sun would rise with a new story. I can't even think about it. Beena might have told you about the vision she had of Jesus on the Cross? In that dream, all during His persecution Jesus didn't say one word. This was a big consolation for me. The Lord was telling us we had to react like Jesus. Some of our pastors asked me, 'Why are you keeping silent like this? How can you keep quiet? They are saying all these nasty things against you and you haven't answered. When they put the black oil, you must take a bottle of the good oil and wipe it away.' I said, 'But that's not what the word of God says. It says we win over evil by doing good. We cannot fight fire with fire. That's why we keep quiet.'

"Once our pastors took Thampy to Ranni. They said, 'You must come and show yourself to the people. Everybody believes you are in the jail.' They made announcements by a mobile loudspeaker that Thampy would be preaching that night. They took him from the revival in the backwaters and rushed him to Ranni. He slept on the way. When he awoke in Ranni he got a big shock. Thousands of people had gathered for the meeting. His vehicle was stuck in the middle of them. Dozens of eyes were staring through his car windows. He asked, 'Is there something happening here?' They replied, 'You're happening here. The people think you are in jail. You must speak so they can see this is not true.' People were everywhere; clustered up trees and on the tops of buildings. Thampy didn't even mention the rumors. He just used the opportunity to preach the gospel. Wherever there's a crowd he'll always preach.

"One day I was so mad, I said, 'Oh God, what judgment is going to come upon these people?' Little Binu overheard me. He looked up and said, 'Mama, are you not praying for these people?' I was stunned. 'Are you praying for them?' I shouted. 'Yes, Mama, I'm praying.' The children saw my anxiety. Once at dinner Biju warned me, 'Mama, I'm afraid you have lost all your rewards in heaven because you are talking like this.' I shrieked, 'I don't want any rewards in this matter. You and your father can keep all the rewards you like. Leave me out of it.'"

Mariamma goes into kinks of laughter at this memory. Eyes closed, head thrown back, face to one side and tears rolling down her cheeks. She said, "I was the one who was most upset. My children were more mature than I'd realized. They were the ones daily facing the outside world, yet they never said a word. They handled it so well. They never complained once. They were a real strength to me. One of them said, 'Mama, do you think that politicians and film stars don't get annoyed when lies are told about them in the newspapers? They are not getting any reward in heaven. So you think about it. We are serving the Lord. We will receive our reward in the end.' By words like this they tried to comfort me.

"Many of our believers children suffered ridicule at school. Their teachers would ask a question and say, 'Hi, *kidney*, you give the answer.' They shamed the children by calling them *kidney*. But that year, despite all these rumors and taunts, thirty-eight new churches were started. It was a year of persecution but also a year of breakthrough. Before every growth the Lord tests us to see if we are worthy to go ahead. God allows us to go through trials so as to test the foundations.

"Now that denominational leader's mouth is shut. He has nothing more to say. I was telling, 'Oh how foolish they are. They should have kept some rumors for later. They said all they could and now they have nothing left to throw at us.' But God is good. He has brought us back to the town we were kicked out of. He is the God who restores the years the locusts have eaten."

Mariamma's thoughts turned to her eldest son. She said, "Biju's three years in Bible School in England was the time for him to really learn to live by faith. He had no money. He had to believe for everything, from a razor blade to his school fees."

"Already he has gone beyond his father in matters of faith?"

"In what way?"

"Thampy never had to believe for razor blades," I said, alluding to his famous black beard.

Wry weak smile. She continued, "Biju would pray, *Lord, I have heard all these faith stories from my parents. Now I want to live that way myself.* His second year Bible School fees came about in this way. He went to America for a month to visit some friends. While there he met a man called Leo Little. They spent a few hours together. Biju was then going to spend his vacation working in the ministry back in India. Before he'd left Bible School they asked how he was going to pay his second year fees. In India he needed a letter from the school so as to get a visa to return to England. Before the letter could be released the fees had to be paid.

"During these two months holidays we traveled as a family and had missions in Bangalore, Belgaum, Goa and Poona. The time was nearing for Biju's return to England. He was growing restless. He prayed, *Lord, You must do a miracle for me. You must provide my fees.* It was only a couple of weeks before he was to return. Thampy was keeping quiet. I didn't know what to do. Biju went to spend a few days at our headquarters in Delhi. One day he rang me. He was very excited, 'Mama, God did a miracle for me. Uncle Abraham is in America ministering. He rang and told me that Leo Little has given $8,000 towards my fees and upkeep in Mattersey Hall.' The

Lord had spoken to Leo. He'd told him to pay the fees, which were $6,000, but Leo, knowing the Lord loves a cheerful giver, gave an extra $2,000.

"That year Bini finished her BSc. We really wanted to send her for a course at Mattersey Hall. After we found out about the $8,000, Biju rang the college and said his sister would like to come for one year. Biju was well liked in the college. He was one of the eight student leaders. The Principal said they'd give Bini one of the three semesters free. Leo's extra $2,000 meant that only one semester's fees had to be believed for. They also, of course, had to believe for normal every day needs, but God was so good. Biju also had to believe for the tickets to and from India and for all his traveling. At the right time the Lord would put the money into his hands. Many of the boys from England didn't have this kind of faith. They'd ask, 'Biju, who pays for all these things? Who pays for your flights to America and India?' Biju answered, 'My Dad.' 'Your dad must be very rich,' they said. ' 'Yes,' he replied. 'My Dad in heaven is a big rich person.'

"Eventually Bini needed the $2,000 for the third semester. Thampy was visiting in England that year. I thought he might be able to supply the money, but he hadn't anything to give. With the fee deadline looming Bini started three days of prayer and fasting. On the third day, just before she broke the fast, she was called to the office. The college had decided to waive the fees for that term also. Her prayers were answered. No one had mentioned this need to the college. Bini had just gone into her room and prayed in secret and God who sees what is done in secret rewarded her openly.

"So like that, God was giving our children opportunities to believe and receive from him. When Biju came back to India his faith was much increased. Before he returned the Lord gave him a vision to start a work in Goa that would spread out over all the states of India. We were able to buy a six-acre property in Goa for $44,000 Australian. It's a miracle. You have seen the property, how beautiful it is. Based in Goa but going out to the different states of India. That's coming to pass now, with new works started in Maharashtra, Karnataka, Goa, Madhya Pradesh and many other places.

"When Bini was at Mattersey Hall, a marriage proposal came from Shibu's family. Shibu was studying chemical engineering in the USA. Over the years his family has been so close to us. They have played a big role in the ministry of *New India Church of God*. They have always been there for us. Shibu is a boy of great potential. We know one day God will call him for his work in the ministry. When the proposal came, we could never have thought of anyone better for Bini than Shibu. They've known each other from childhood but hadn't seen one another for six years. It was arranged they'd meet again before the wedding so he flew from America to England.

"Biju had to play the part of the matchmaker. It was his job to make sure the proper customs of Indian matchmaking were adhered to. There is a family from Kerala that lives near Mattersey. The father is a doctor. He is the nephew of Mary Koover, the lady who looked after Thampy when he'd been hit by the bus. She was also the woman who washed the blood from Thampy when he and Fr. Thengelil were attacked on the church steps. The matchmaking meeting was arranged in that house under Indian tradition. After a communal cup of tea, they were given a short time to talk. Bini was laughing all the time. She told Shibu, 'My heart is for an orphanage in India. That is what I want to do.' Shibu said, 'I am not against that but I won't do it only if you tell me. But if God tells me, then I will do it. My desire now is to work as a chemical engineer. I have studied so much for this. But if God speaks to me now, nothing bothers me. Then I am ready to go, even now.' This is how they talked. Next day he returned to America.

"In 1996 a proposal came for Beena also. She wanted to marry a full-time minister. Martin's family came forward. After his degree, Martin spent five and a half years ministering in Papua, New Guinea, with pastor Barry Silverback. It was a very tough training. Both Shibu and Martin had been away from Kerala for around six years. One thing I'd like to tell you about is the role of the dowry in India.

"From the time girls are born the parents will save little by little so as to have a dowry for her marriage. Otherwise, many times they have to sell their property and home. If, for example, you wanted a doctor, or a similar professional to marry your daughter you might have to pay ten lakhs of rupees. Nowadays it might even cost a crore of rupees. (One crore is ten million, written 1,00,00,000.) So much money you have to pay to get a good boy but it didn't cost us a penny. None of our children even had a bank account. In our case, everything goes into the church account. The money goes for the Kingdom. That's where our heart is.

"My parents used to say, 'Mariamma these girls are growing up and you have no dowry for them. Who will marry them?' Thampy had married me without any dowry. He'd say, 'Look, I married you without a dowry.

Don't worry. God will provide when the time comes.' Thankfully when the time came the Lord provided two families who know our circumstances. Many others wouldn't believe us. Some people imagine Thampy has a lot of money to give for dowries but these families knew the real situation. They both came forward to marry our girls without any dowry. This is a total miracle in India. When there is an opportunity to get some money everybody wants it so as to start a family. Dowry is the only chance most of them have to get any money.

"When Shibu was in America there was a girl from Kerala who was interested in him. Her father is a very wealthy man who said he'd pay Shibu fifty lakhs as a dowry. Another father who owns five Burger Kings said he'd give two Burger Kings and any amount of money that Shibu asked for if he'd marry his daughter. So like that, offers came but he refused them all. He married our daughter Bini without a dowry."

I asked, *"What amount of dowry do you think I'd have been worth?"*

Mariamma said, "In your case, Brother Brendan, you would have been the one giving the dowry to Angela for her having to give birth to all those fourteen children. She is worth more than many Burger Kings. I don't think you could have afforded her." Now it was my turn for the wry weak smile.

Mariamma said, "It was all God's justice. God is a debtor to no one. Because we invested our money into the Kingdom of God rather than save it for dowries God gave us boys that are worthy for fifty lakhs and two Burger Kings. God gave us these great boys at no cost. Even if we'd saved up for dowries, we could never have saved enough to get these two men. This is a good lesson for the people to learn. If we have faith and are obedient the Lord will look after our needs.

"Martin is such a nice boy. He is completely sold out for the Lord. We could never have got anybody better than Martin for Beena. He understands her very well. She was a very shy person. He very tactfully was able to bring her out of her shell and help her reach her potential. All the credit goes to Martin. God gave us two great boys as husbands for our daughters.

"Bini and Beena's marriages took place in July 1996. Within one week we had four big functions. Bini's engagement was on the eleventh and her wedding on the fifteenth. Beena's engagement was on the twelfth and her marriage on the sixteenth. There were three thousand people at Bini's wedding and around two and a half thousand at Beena's. Thampy and I were responsible for the weddings. The boy's families were responsible for the engagement functions. It was a wonderfully hectic time. My four sisters and my brother and their families stayed with us for the whole week. We arranged it like this to make the best use of time and money. Ours was the marriage house. This means we must provide chicken and fish and all that stuff. We have to feed them all very good. I don't know how we did it. Everything went so well.

"One thing really blessed us. All the churches had a collection without our knowledge. About three lakhs of rupees were given to us. Nowhere else that we know of has any church ever done this for their leaders. This was a very good thing. It covered all the expenses of the wedding food; chicken biryani, fried rice and some dessert. It was like feeding the five thousand. We made a huge *pandhal* of banana leaves. Everything went so smoothly. It was a talk in the city. Everywhere people were saying, 'What a blessed wedding it was.'

"New brides from India accompanying their husband to America find it very hard to get a visa. They usually have to wait two or three years before they can join their husbands. Praise God, Bini immediately managed to get a visa. Shibu and her were able to go back together. People told Bini, they were the first newly married couple from India that'd arrived together for fifteen years. This meant they had a year of feasts in Oklahoma. People were continually inviting them for dinner because of the novelty of entertaining newlyweds from India. Bini also got a job very easily. I always remind her of the time she heard the voice that told her, 'This is My right hand. I will lead you by this hand.' God's hand is leading her every day.

"Binu first came to Australia for a visit with me in 1997 when Beena and Martin were studying at the Hillsong Church Bible School. We stayed with Bob and Jane Uden in Wagga Wagga. Binu had hoped to go to Mattersey Hall Bible School. The college had kindly offered half fees. One day we were talking to Bob about this. Next morning when Binu and I were leaving, Bob and his wife said the Lord had told them to give Binu $6,000 Australian towards his studies. That was a big thing.

"This was half the money needed for England but as it turned out his visa application for England was rejected. It was all in God's plan. I then heard about Southern Cross College in Sydney, which is accredited. Martin and I had a talk with the authorities. They said they'd give places to Binu and his friend Marlow but they'd only provide a letter of acceptance if we'd deposit a lump sum. We needed that letter for the visa applications. Bob and Jane's money was truly a Godsend. It enabled us to start the ball rolling. Marlow has studied with Binu from the fifth grade. After the death of his dad, Dr. Phillips, we felt a responsibility towards that family. We thought, *Whatever we do for Binu, we'll also do for Marlow. If we send Binu to Australia, we'll also send Marlow.*

"Recently Binu was sharing about how God was teaching him faith in Australia. When he first arrived he'd no money. He couldn't even buy detergent to wash his stuff. His dirty clothes were piling up but he wouldn't complain to anyone. He prayed, *Lord, You'll have to help me. I have nothing to wear now. Everything's dirty.* Next morning outside his door, he found a new bucket with soap powder and clothes pegs. He still doesn't know who put them there for he'd never told anybody about his need.

"Eventually he and Marlow got jobs weighing and carrying 25kg sacks of seed. They were able to pay their fees and accommodation from this. When Binu told me of his job I felt sorry for him. He said, 'Mama, why are you sorry for me. Now I know the true value of a dollar.' He came twice to India during that time; once for my sister Valsala's funeral and once for Biju's wedding. He paid the fares himself.

"Our children must learn to look to the Lord for themselves. I used to worry when I saw My children without money or support. I'd say to Thampy, 'Have you no mercy? Our children are really suffering.' He'd say, 'I'm so happy to hear that. They have to learn in a hard way. They must learn faith. We had to learn it. Now they also must learn it.' They all love and want to serve the Lord. That's what makes me happy. Now that Binu is back it's my constant prayer that Bini and Shibu will also return to the harvest fields of India. I hope they'll get their orphanage. Looking after widows and orphans is pure religion. I hope they will come soon. There is no point in wasting our time. It is so precious. Why should we waste time and effort on things that don't count in the light of eternity?

"It's a lie of the enemy that says, 'If you get caught up too much in the ministry, your children will go astray and won't follow the Lord.' God says, 'If you'll do My business, I'll look after yours.' If you are careful. If you are faithful to Him then He will look after your children. They will never go away from the Lord. They will serve the Lord. Now everybody says, 'Oh, look at Thampy and Mariamma's children. They are such good children.' Everyone says that now, even people who discouraged us in the past. But those women who looked after their husbands and children, locked up in the kitchen. They are still there cooking curries but as we went on for the work of God we have seen thousands of souls come into his Kingdom.

"Over the years the Lord used me in many areas. My main ministry started when I went door knocking. That's the ministry I love best of all. I love speaking with individuals and getting them saved. Every day I'd normally lead five or six people to Jesus. There is a special anointing upon me to speak to people and bring them to faith in Christ. Whoever I talk to, I will never leave them unless I get them saved. I love that. That's the ministry I like best. Through this ministry many churches have been started. First I go and get some people saved. Then their neighbors will come along. Once a week, they'll bring half a dozen people along to a meeting in their home. I'll get these people saved. After a few months it will turn into a church. Then we'll put a pastor in. That's how so many of our churches have started. When we began the Bible School for ladies this ministry multiplied. After one year's training, we sent them out two by two and they do the same thing.

"In Kodungallur, where the apostle St. Thomas arrived in India, there was no believer's church at all. The whole city is built around a huge temple dedicated to Kali. There is only an old Christian church in the tradition of St. Thomas. They have one bone covered with red velvet. They say it is a bone of St. Thomas. Unfortunately the faith of the people is as dead and as powerless as that old bone. Over the years so many people have tried to start a believers' church there but they could never break through.

"We had a church in nearby Paravoor. From there we went to conduct an open-air meeting in Kodungallur. We began to pray, *Lord, please open a door so we can go and work there.* After a couple of years Thampy felt led to try and arrange a meeting. First we'd to get permission from the local police force to hold a gathering and to use a microphone. When Thampy went to the police station, to his surprise, the Police Inspector turned out to be one of his cousins who'd just been transferred to Kodungallur that very week. He said, 'Thampy, come on, you can hold your meeting in the police parade ground in the middle of the city. We'll even give you police protection.' We had a mini crusade. On the last day, three hundred people gave their lives to the Lord. This was in 1985/86.

"As a follow up, I took two of our best girls from the Bible School, Leelamma and Sally. I rented a little house, in a remote area, six kilometers from the city. It was near a toddy shop where people got drunk. After midnight I took the girls there. Some scared fellows asked me, 'How can you allow these girls to stay in such a bad place?' I said, 'The angels of God will look after them.' After two months Leelamma and Sally came with seven new believers who wanted to be baptized. I told them they might well have been the first real converts since the days of the apostle Thomas.

"Leelamma and Sally knew how to pray and fast. The powers of darkness in that city were being broken. They received poison pen letters saying things like, 'We are going to rape you and kill you.' They were not put off from their work by these letters. They knew God would protect them. Eventually we started a church there. The pastor is always fasting and praying. Even now, after sixteen years, our church is the only believers' church in that whole city. That's the kind of work our ladies are doing. I used to be so much involved in this ministry for my heart's desire is to reach the unreached. I loved that work so much."

Mariamma said, "Since 1990 there have been Indian Pentecostal conferences in which all the churches come together. One of the days is always earmarked for a ladies' meeting. Over these years the Lord has put me in leadership as the convener of this Women's day. I've been given the opportunity to work with all the ladies of the Indian Pentecostal churches and many other Christian groups. Everybody knows me now. When Paul Yonggi Cho was in Kerala at the all India Pentecostal conference I was the ladies' convener. We'd over five thousand women at that meeting.

"I used to say Ruth picked the wheat heads from the ground, one after the other. Then she lifted the clusters that were placed in front of her. Finally through faith and obedience she became the owner of the whole field. I tell the ladies, 'We don't become big overnight. First we must start from little, faithfully doing one thing after another. First we go door knocking and speak to people one after the other. Then if we remain faithful, the Lord will put us in clusters, in little groups. If we continue to be faithful, the Lord will put us in front of thousands of people.' Over the years this is the way the Lord has been working with me, little by little, one thing after another, helping my faith to grow. He has been so faithful."

"Earlier you mentioned the death of Martin and Marlow's dad, Dr. Phillips. You said you and Thampy felt some sort of responsibility towards that family. Could you explain?"

Mariamma said, "Dr. Phillips was from the same village as Thampy. He and his wife Rajamma, had seven children; Marshall, Martin, Merlin, Merin, Mercy, Marlow and Marvel. They were a very popular family. From an outsider's perspective he was a very successful man with a good home and family. One day, in 1977, I was traveling by train to Trivandrum. On the journey I fell asleep. I'd a dream about Dr. Phillips. Although I'd known of him I'd never actually met him. In my dream the Lord told me to go and share the gospel with him.

"Shortly afterwards I went to his home. He was on his lunch break when I arrived. There was a canal beside his home. The house was on one side of this canal and his clinic on the other. I knocked at the door. When his wife opened it I said, 'I don't know what is happening in your family but the Lord has told me to come and share the gospel with your husband. The Lord loves you. He wants to do something good in your lives.' She invited me in. She went into the next room to speak to Dr. Phillips. Through the door, I could see them talking. He was holding onto the bars of a window. He was looking outside and smoking. He was wearing the exact same lungi, dark green with little dots, I'd seen in the dream. He said, 'I don't have time to talk to her.'

"Although he wouldn't see me I was still encouraged because he was wearing the same clothes I'd seen in the dream. I told Rajamma, 'Even if he doesn't want to talk, I'll come again on Friday and we'll have some prayer.' She agreed to this. My brother Abraham and a few others came with me for that Friday prayer meeting. Afterwards Thampy's brother, who was a close friend of Doctor Phillips, was standing outside. He said, 'Don't you have any thing better to do? If you go to a poor person's house and share the gospel, he will at least hear you. Do you know what was happening in the next room when you were praying? Doctor Phillips was drinking alcohol.'

"I was very upset to hear this. I said, *Lord, that's it, You told me to come here. I obeyed, but I'm not going to come back any more.* A few days later I had another dream. In this dream, I was at a prayer meeting. I saw Dr. Phillips jumping up and down and singing in the Spirit. Then he began testifying and preaching to the people. I thought, *Lord, what is this? Why are You telling me this again?* God was showing me not to be offended with Dr. Phillips. He was going to save him in the end, no matter what was going on at present.

"Again I went to his home to try and share the gospel. I thought to myself, *This is the last time I'll go and visit this man.* As I came near his house, I again saw Thampy's brother. I said, 'Please go and tell Dr. Phillips the Lord has given me a message for him. Ask him to come to his house where I'll be waiting.' I walked across the canal bridge. Rajamma opened the door. She was not a believer at this time. She was wondering what was going on. I sat down and prayed, *Lord, You have sent me here to share Your gospel just like You sent Peter down to Cornelius's house. You talked to Peter but You also talked to Cornelius. You have spoken to me. Please also speak to Dr. Phillips? Tell him he must come now.* Within a few minutes Dr. Phillips came walking over the bridge. He came into the house and sat down near me. I was so full to talk to him.

"I said, 'I don't know what you are going through but I do know its decision time for you. You are like a drowning man going down for the third time. If someone throws him a rope he can catch it and be saved. This is where you are right now. This is the rope of salvation that the Lord is throwing to you. You'd better catch it and be saved. It is the only way you can escape from whatever bad situation you are in.'

"Although I knew nothing whatsoever about his state of affairs I was confident in sharing these words I knew God was putting into my mouth. All I said spoke directly to his heart. He was really in a big mess. Things were so difficult he and his wife had discussed suicide. They'd many problems. He told me, 'I don't think there is a sinner like me in the whole world.' I said, 'You are enjoying all the pleasures of this world, but do you have any peace?' 'No, I don't have any peace,' he said. 'Okay, I will pray for you,' I said. He stood up and I started worshipping in the Spirit. He was chewing tobacco. He went, spat it out, and came back. He was only forty years old then. A very handsome young man, he was. I prayed for him. Then he prayed. From that moment the Lord began to work in his life.

"I had been reading a book called, *From Witchcraft to Christ* by Doreen Irvine. That was a very powerful book. I gave it to Dr. Phillips. After a few days I went to visit. I couldn't believe it. His face and eyes were red from weeping. His wife said, 'I don't know what's going on. He is crying the whole time, saying, 'How can God love a sinner like me?' He was only eating one small meal a day. I took him to a prophet who encouraged and strengthened him by revealing things that'd happened in the past and by speaking of things to come. Little by little the Lord was bringing him along. Their seventh child, Marvel, was in Rajamma's womb at that time.

"When Dr. Phillips came to the Lord there was a big commotion in the whole locality. The entire community was in an uproar. I used to visit in our van. Some people threatened, 'We will beat Mariamma and we will burn the van.' Then the whole faith life. After a few months the Lord spoke to Dr. Phillips. He said, 'Give up your job and come full-time into the ministry.' This was a big step for him. He had six children and a seventh on the way. Dr. Phillip's mother was only nineteen and pregnant with Dr. Phillips when her husband died. She never remarried but devoted her life to caring for her only child. So his mother, wife and children were all depending on him. They had a very good standard of living.

"Like Elisha, who broke up his plough and killed his oxen before following Elijah, Dr. Phillips sold all the equipment connected with his profession. He determined that nothing would lure him from his life of faith. He knew if his children would cry for lack of food, he might be tempted to go back to his medical work. That's the way he was. There was no double-mindedness in Dr. Phillips. He suffered so much because of his decision to follow the Lord. Many in the community who'd benefited from his medicine now turned against him. Everyone was against these Pentecostal people; his family, her family, all were against them. They came to beat him up; so much trouble, so much persecution. Even the children suffered."

Just then a young woman came into the kitchen and whispered quietly in Mariamma's ear. Mariamma nodded and turned to me, "Sorry, Brendan, we'll have to stop there for the moment. Something urgent has just happened. We'll finish this story later."

We never did finish the story. Life went on and like the big blue butterfly turned a corner. My time in India was over for the present. Other voices were calling. In 1 Corinthians 13, Paul says our prophecy is incomplete and imperfect. He compares it to seeing a poor reflection in a mirror. Only Jesus is perfect. When He returns we will see things as they really are.

For my part, I am only too aware of all the stories I never heard, or that I wasn't listening for. Stories of the thousands upon thousands of our brothers and sisters in the *New India Church of God*. Stories of their dreams and their sacrifices in a land where the best is yet to be. When He that is perfect returns then all our stories will be well and truly told and like the front side of a master craftsman's tapestry they will make amazing sense. He who created the beautiful blue butterfly and the little prophetic bird that daily proclaims, *"Sthothram, Sthothram, Sthothram,"* amongst the rubber trees of Kerala is the greatest storyteller of all. Make sure you read His book - often!

Exciting Investment Opportunity

Jesus gives us a tremendous piece of investment advice in Matthew 6:19-21. In fact this information is so good it would probably break the London Stock Exchange's rules on *insider trading*. The owner of the company knows something no one else suspects and he tips off his friends.

This advice is:

> "Do not store up for yourselves treasures on earth, where moth and rust destroy, and where thieves break in and steal. But store up for yourselves treasures in heaven, where moth and rust do not destroy, and where thieves do not break in and steal. For where your treasure is, there your heart will be also."

This is wonderful counsel for those wise and farsighted enough to *invest in eternity*. I also have some inside information for Jesus' friends – all those in the Body of Christ. This is perhaps one of the greatest pieces of *eternity investment* advice of the twenty-first century. **Invest in the harvest fields of India.** Let me show you why using dollars as an example,

1. Currently 96.8 cents of each dollar the Christian Church spends is invested in the 2 billion folk who already call themselves Christians.
2. A further 2.9 cents of each dollar spent is invested in the 2.6 billion people who have already heard the gospel and have rejected it.
3. Only *one third of a cent* is invested in the 1.6 billion people who have never ever heard the gospel of Jesus Christ even once.
4. Only one *tenth of a cent* is invested in India where 412 million unreached people - **one quarter** of the world's entire unreached population live.[1]

Think of it! *Only 1 cent in every 10 dollars* the church spends is being invested in reaching *one quarter* of the unreached peoples of the world. Only one *thousandth* of what the Church spends goes towards reaching *one quarter* of all the people alive who've never ever heard tell of Jesus. What a wonderful investment opportunity for the Body of Christ. Hardly anyone has heard of or is investing in this amazing opportunity. You can be one of the first to take advantage of this. Tell all your friends. Be like the four lepers, outside the camp of the Arameans in 2 Kings 7:9, who when they discovered God had wrought a great deliverance for Israel said to one another, "We're not doing right. This is a day of good news and we are keeping it to ourselves."

Please don't keep an opportunity like this a secret. If you are anything like me you have probably invested in all kinds of disappointing scams in the past. If so, India is a unique chance to get your *eternity investment portfolio* back in profit. How much should you invest? My advice is, invest as much as you can possibly afford. To paraphrase Mother Teresa, *invest* until it hurts because the people of India are extremely open and responsive to the gospel message. Jesus shall see the travail of his soul and be satisfied.

There are vast amounts of *treasure in heaven* to be gained by those who properly invest in India and the other unreached peoples of the earth. So lets get our acts together and get on with the Lord's last command in Matthew 28:18-20, which is also excellent *eternity investment* advice,

> Then Jesus came to them and said, "All authority in heaven and on earth has been given to me. Therefore go and make disciples of all nations, baptizing them in the name of the Father and of the Son and of the Holy Spirit, and teaching them to obey everything I have commanded you. And surely I am with you always, to the very end of the age."

Please partner with the indigenous Christian leaders of India and other nations in the world where the gospel has never been preached. Please support and pray for these brothers and sisters as they bring the healing light of the gospel to a lost and dying world.

If you catch hold of this eternal perspective you'll spend a long time thanking me for it in the future. A very long time. Guess where my money's going?

[1] From *World Christian Encyclopaedia: A Comparative Survey of Churches and Religions in the Modern World*, edited by David B Barrett, George T Kurian, & Todd M Johnson. (Oxford University Press - 2nd edition – 2 volumes - 2001)

Contacting the Author

Finance and gifts for India can be channelled through *One Act Of Kindness Trust*, which Brendan Mc Cauley has agreed to manage. This vehicle is especially suitable for residents of the United Kingdom who wish to take advantage of the government's present generous tax incentives concerning donations and covenants to charities. Cheques etc should be made out to *One Act Of Kindness/India* and posted to the address below.

One Act Of Kindness Trust has charitable status and operates on a non-profit making basis. All donations will be acknowledged and receipted.

If you would like to contact Brendan or Angela Mc Cauley or would like any information on their ministries or the *One Act Of Kindness Trust*, please use one of the following methods.

1. Brendan McCauley
    PO Box 38
    Downpatrick
    Northern Ireland
    BT30 6YH

2. Email: irishprophet@hotmail.com

3. View their website at http: www.irishprophet.net

4. View their website at http: www.oneactofkindness.net

God Bless You.

**New India Church of God Ministries
Contact Information**

In India
New India Church of God
Bethesda Nagar
Chingavanam P.O.
Kottayam, Kerala, India
Tel. (11 91) 481 243 1637
Fax. (11 91) 481 243 2860
Email: office@nicog.org

In the USA and elsewhere:
Christ for India
P.O. Box 271272
Oklahoma City, OK 73137
www.christforall.org
Email: office@christforall.org
Tel: Toll Free: 1-(877)-265-0811
Fax: 1-(405)-265-0811